# LIVING
## IN THE
# HOPE
## OF MY
# IMAGINATION

A Compelling Story that Proves the Bible to be
A Living Revelation of God

## WRITTEN BY
## WILLIAM D. SIMPSON

Interior design and layout by Velin Saramov

Published by Thorncrown
A division of Yorkshire Publishing
9731 E. 54th Tulsa, OK 7146
www.yorkshirepublishing.com

International Standard Book Number: 978-0-88144-488-9
Written by William D. Simpson
Copyright 2010 by William D. Simpson

# TABLE OF CONTENTS

# INTRODUCTION

Child of the Living God,

Through the pages of this book, I describe events that happened to me from my earliest memories and the impact they had on shaping the life I chose to live. As the pages are read, I honestly believe you will see yourself and many of the people you care about reliving the horrors kept under lock and key. These subjects are never discussed, but what people really think of themselves is written on their faces for everyone to see.

Life is hard and I make no apologies for my writing style because people need to hear the truth even if it is uncomfortable. Education, media and entertainment influenced by corporate elites and this nation's bipartisan government have deceived the masses.

Most Americans have no clue what is happening, for all attention has been intentionally diverted to their perceived intellectual advancement, and issues promoting a person's right to cultural diversity. Sporting events, television and the weekend's indulgence of self-gratification have become the precedence to escape the pressures of everyday life, with no hope in sight. Everyone is being affected and it seems as though no one really cares as long as they are left alone to do whatever might bring temporary pleasure.

We have become a nation of people divided and confused by an agenda so evil its true motive has been hidden in the subtle dumbing-down of our moral conscience. These events are currently unfolding right in front of your face, and you have done nothing to prepare yourself for what is about to happen. Whole societies happy in their blissful ignorance!

I was just like you—angry at life and doing everything I could to try to feel better about me. I was totally ignorant of what has been done to methodically rewrite our constitutional rights in favor of special interest agendas. Numerous events happening over my lifetime eventually brought me to the place where I was sick and tired of life as I'd always known it—a place where I opened the Bible to try and find meaning in it all. What I learned liberated me. Now I want to take the truths I've learned and challenge the way you think, the same way God challenged me. This book is intended by God to be your wake up call.

Should your life be transformed by the application of what I encourage each person to do and someone comes to mind who you think could benefit from our example, do the right thing and give them this book. I don't know where this book will go or the impact it could have on those who might read it. I'm just in a position where I have no choice but to tell you what God has done for me. The life-transforming power of the Gospel of Jesus Christ is free to those who believe, but your soul's transformation will cost you everything... I hope you answer the call.

Sincerely,
William Simpson

This book is dedicated to my wife, Shannon. When I needed encouragement the most, you entered my life. Our days together have been a whirlwind of emotions revealing two wounded souls divinely brought together. A flower bruised but not broken, you have bent to the winds of this life only to stand tall in the radiant beauty of a woman in love. How rare is your willingness to give with no other motivation than wanting the same in return, as your kindness stripped my defenses and proved the good in each of us. Thank you for allowing me time to discover a future in writing about the struggle of submitting to something I didn't understand, to then realize the answer to a question we have all asked: "Why did this happen to me?" Always and forever I am yours.

# FOREWORD

W hat does it really mean to be a Christian, a disciple of Jesus Christ? Reading the New Testament reveals that when a person accepts Jesus as their Savior, there is a price to be paid. This lifestyle will be painful at times. It will require that you die to the life you've hoped for, and this sacrifice is what God requires of you.

> *And calling the crowd to him with his disciples, he said to them, "If anyone would come after me, let him deny himself and take up his cross and follow me. For whoever would save his life will lose it, but whoever loses his life for my sake and the gospel's will save it. For what does it profit a man to gain the whole world and forfeit his soul?"*
>
> Mark 8:34-36

Being a Christian is hard especially in the culture we now live in. Our choices are few and this lifestyle will lead to persecution for those who desire to live their lives to honor the Lord Jesus Christ. The choice we make to separate ourselves from the worldly mentality becomes a sign to the unsaved humanity of our love for Jesus Christ. Those of us in America who call ourselves Christians want to receive from God, but few ever give themselves wholly to Him. The seeker-friendly crowd wants to enjoy all of God's blessings, but they won't dare suffer for Him! This spirit of anti-Christ has permeated today's postmodern church movements.

We come to church to rejoice and gladly receive the perceived blessings of an easy gospel, but we're not willing to lay down our lives as a living sacrifice. When it's time to stand up for the faith we proclaim, when the situation is uncomfortable and maybe even being threatened, we cower. We don't want to bleed, so we succumb to the personalities around us. We're ashamed of the Gospel of Jesus Christ! Our denial of Jesus is not only in word but more evident in the lifestyles we live, for this is how most people perceive the message of the Gospel. And for those who claim to be Christian to then have their lifestyle prove different, is to reject the message of the cross.

> *So everyone who acknowledges me before men, I also will acknowledge before my Father who is in heaven, but whoever denies me before men, I also will deny before my Father who is in heaven.*
>
> Matthew 10:32-33

What is the real benefit in achieving what you think is material success when in reality all it does is stroke your ego? Unless the wealth earned is used to enrich the lives of other people through a community outreach, charitable giving or just to be a blessing to someone who might need encouragement. If helping others is not the motivation for achievement, then the flaunting of your success is a vain attempt to justify the shallowness of your character. The end result is a life wasted in the pursuit of vanity and the loss of your eternal destiny. Compared to the eternal life the Bible says we will live, if we by faith in God's finished work of salvation through Jesus Christ win the race of this natural life, what here has any real value? This is the reason why it is so dangerous for the church to compromise the true Gospel of Jesus Christ for the lie of living your best life now.

In this day and time of political and cultural correctness, God is calling the body of Christ to stand up against the flow of humanity even if it means suffering for the faith we proclaim. Will you answer the call?

To be effective in the Great Commission and have your life's witness prove the Bible is a living revelation of God, you will have to give your life. What you want is not important; Jesus is the one who saves. What God will do in you is for the purpose of people seeing Jesus Christ being glorified and honored by the lifestyle you live. No matter the cost.

Being a disciple of Jesus Christ means that everything we do reflects the hope of what we proclaim. No one can come to the saving knowledge of Jesus Christ unless God has first drawn that person and revealed to them the truth of who Jesus really is. And once you have been truly transformed, that is when you can confidently tell other people what God has done for you.

The hope we have is the knowledge of what God did by the sacrifice of the person of Jesus Christ. Jesus is God in the flesh, who came among us to experience human weaknesses and the atrocities we face, yet living in a way that proved we can overcome. The only person to ever live a sinless life was then crucified and paid the ultimate price so you and I would not have to.

Beaten and stripped naked, bleeding and humiliated, Jesus was nailed to a wooden cross as a living sacrifice to suffer the punishment of separation from the presence of God. There God's wrath was poured out upon Jesus. He became sin, sickness and dis-ease and all of the depravity within each of us. By taking in His body the penalty we are deserving of, Jesus became the atonement for your and my sin. Jesus willingly sacrificed His deity to redeem a lost humanity, and once again enjoy unbroken fellowship with those who would give their lives for Him. And when the purpose of His death was fulfilled, Jesus raised Himself from the dead to be a living witness to the testament of His deity.

> And Jesus came up and spoke to them, saying, "All authority has been given to Me in heaven and on earth. Go therefore and make disciples of all the nations, baptizing them in the name of the Father and the Son and the Holy Spirit, teaching them to observe all that I command you; and lo, I am with you always, even unto the end of the age.
>
> Matthew 28:18-20

By this, Jesus proved to be the only true and living God! There is no other name or false religion known to mankind that can save, transform and make us righteous before God other than Jesus Christ.

Child of God, there are grave consequences for you if you do not take the time to understand what being a Christian is all about. For if you live your life in a way that you enjoy the temporary pleasures of this world then one day as your body lays down in death with no atonement for your sins, there will be a reality you do not want to face!

This message should be the very foundation of every Christian's life, but sadly it has been far removed from what people actually see. There has been too much compromise of the validity of God's Word by pastors and ministers of every Christian denomination and independent movement as they try to attract numbers and not offend.

If you are ever to be an effective disciple of Jesus Christ, the life transforming power of the Gospel must be evident in your life. You have to know the hope you proclaim is real! The only way it becomes reality is by giving yourself wholly to your mind's renewing study of the Bible, soul searching prayer and a lifestyle of worship to God. When you sincerely make the time to learn about Jesus Christ, God will meet you in any circumstance to prove His reality and show you the way out of a life controlled by the dictates of a sinful nature. As you witness this change in how you think, the words you speak and what you do, the Bible then comes to life as its words transform your soul.

Jesus becomes so real to you that at the thought of what He endured, you weep, knowing He did this in your place. This then becomes the compassion people will see in you, in your testimony and in the work of ministry God has called you to do. It becomes the motivation to reach out to other people no matter who they are or where they come from, because you know what God has done for you. The Gospel of Jesus Christ is the life-transforming power of God to those who will dare to believe.

The good news is that a person's life can really be changed and you, child of God, are a living epistle that takes everyone's excuse away. The Holy Spirit of God, who indwells our recreated spirit, and a renewed mind will help us and those who know us believe by a life forever changed; it's not something we can do in our own ability. Everybody needs a Divine Savior! For the day is coming when we will all stand before the Judgment Seat of God to give an account for what we have done. Will you allow Jesus Christ the opportunity to transform your life?

> *For we will all stand before the judgment seat of God; for it is written, "As I live, says the Lord, every knee shall bow to me, and every tongue shall confess to God." So then each of us will give an account of himself to God.*
> Romans 14:10b-12

This book is my testimony. I want my life to be an example for those of you who don't know how to change, and a voice to challenge what you believe. Overcoming what I believed to be a life that had no purpose, it is now my responsibility to tell other people how a relationship with Jesus Christ transformed my life. And it just might be the example you need, should you choose to do what I have done...

# INFLUENCE BY DESIGN

*Even before he made the world, God loved us and chose us
in Christ to be holy and without fault in his eyes.*

Ephesians 1:4

God has an expectation of the man He intends for me to
become...

If this statement is true, why did so many bad things happen
to me? My childhood was supposed to be a time of learning how
to trust and having each youthful imagination become reality, but
what really happened created emotional scars on a boy abused. The
price I had to pay for the many wrong decisions I made was the loss
of my innocence and youth.

I don't have any memories as a child when I wasn't angry, and
knowing the damage that was done by people I learned to hate
created an expectation of what I believed to be all I would ever
know. This is why so many people today are of the opinion: "What
right do you have to try to tell me what some obscure book says is
the way I should live?"

I know you, who have had a beginning like mine. You're mad and
have built walls so high in defense of pain that not only can no one
get in, you cannot get out. It hurts! You live with this shame, always
having to justify how you respond to the circumstances your mind
creates. On the surface you look normal just like everyone else, but

deep down inside lays a wounded imagination lost in the memories of physical abuse and words that crushed your confidence.

To never feel the touch of another person's affection, hear their words of approval or experience the warmth of a smile has made you believe you have no value as a person. Nothing in life is what your innocence imagined it would be and every day has become survival.

You try to hope for change only to get knocked down time and time again, always reaching for what is just beyond your grasp in an attempt to not feel ashamed, while using alcohol and drugs to help deal with the pain. Despising the image you see in a mirror, having become like those who influenced what you now think of yourself. The people who know you, do not understand the demons you fight and they stay away.

To those of you who've had the privilege of being born to good parents and given the opportunity to grow up in an environment that created an awareness of self-worth, and knowing how other people should be treated, what is your excuse for the person you have become? If this is you, what I'm trying to do is help you understand the world people like me live in, and why you and I think and act the way we do. I don't envy you anymore because our worlds are really not that far apart.

You avoid the places, the people and the things you are not familiar with, and you're quick to judge another person not like you. You're educated and the income you earn is above average. You have a house, cars and all the toys. Your social clubs cater to an ego that's inflated and filled with conversations about what another person didn't do to try and feel better about yourself. Your world has become vain, and nothing and no one is what it seems. You live at an income level your bank account cannot afford and the pursuit of what you think is material happiness has cost you everything.

Yet you did everything you were told was right. You earned a Bachelor's Degree and PhD's from people as clueless as you, and then poured your life into a career that has left you broken as a person and void of having done anything of lasting value for your family or the people you thought really cared about you. And what do you do to fill that void? The same things I did.

You drink alcohol and use drugs, and pursue every other means of escape to not have to deal with the pain. So you see, there is really not that much difference between you and me. You may have been born a different color or maybe you're from the up-side of suburban America, but you want the same things I do. Like me, you've searched for it in all the wrong places. What goes around comes around and it hurts, doesn't it?

Misery attracts its own and you don't know who to talk to because everyone in your circle of influence struggles with their own issues and are in no position to challenge you and give the support that is needed to overcome what is in your past. So you go through life never realizing the choices you make imprison what could be to an inner image of insignificance.

> *My people are destroyed for lack of knowledge.*
>
> Hosea 4:6a

Most people today, regardless of the environment they grew up in, live their life only thinking of themselves. "It's all about me, my, and mine and what can I do to satisfy me." Mad at the pain of yesterday, people reach out to everything that passes by, with a faint hope of, "Maybe this will make me feel better." The person, the situation, or the inebriating substance might be different, but its result will always be the same. No peace, no happiness and no fulfillment, nothing but another empty day. And this is not the will of God.

> *You must not have any other god but me. You must not make for yourself an idol of any kind or an image of anything in the heavens or on the earth or in the sea. You must not bow down to them or worship them, for I, the Lord your God, am a jealous God who will not tolerate your affection for any other gods.*
>
> Exodus 20:3-5a

What I could do to overcome this feeling of insignificance was a question left unanswered because I never had an opportunity to learn the truth as a child. As a result of my ignorance, my potential was never realized.

I lived a miserable life. It was not until I came to the end of me did I discover that the answers to all of life's questions are hidden, waiting for those who will make an effort to search them out.

> *The secret things belong to the LORD our God, but the things revealed belong to us and to our sons forever, that we may observe all the words of this law.*
>
> Deuteronomy 29:29

It was a study of the Bible that brought correction to what I thought of myself and taught me how to become the man I had always hoped to be, free from the influence of my past. Now is the time for you to stand up and say: "No More!" What is more important than realizing the peace of mind God has made available to those who will make an effort to look past life as they know it to experience what could be?

> *I am leaving you with a gift—peace of mind and heart. And the peace I give is a gift the world cannot give. So don't be troubled or afraid.*
>
> John 14:27

What negative image do you have of yourself would you not be willing to overcome in order to enjoy a feeling of self-worth and the confidence of knowing your life has purpose? To one day look in a mirror and like the person you see.

This is a desire every person should have but sadly, most do not. My challenge to you is this: "*Will you dare believe, if shown a way, to become the person you have always hoped to be?*" You can! To do this, you must learn the truth about who you really are to no longer be influenced by what the enemies of God have intentionally misled all of the American people into believing. I go into great detail in the latter chapters of this book to explain what the deception is and its influence upon today's culture.

Through the conditioning of each new generation, our God-given freedoms and constitutional rights are being taken away, and we are not far from becoming a godless socialist society.

> *For as he thinks in his heart, so is he.*
>
> Proverbs 23:7a

> *Where there is no vision, the people perish.*
>
> Proverbs 29:18a

The majority of people today have no clue as to what is really happening. For those of us who have taken the time to become aware of this evil, educating others is the priority. We do this regardless of the consequences to our person or reputations. I don't want to tell everybody my personal business, but my life's witness is no longer my own.

Take a really good look at what the American culture has become and then ask yourself: "Does how we live really have any meaning or value?" If you cannot answer yes to this, then my next question is, *"Are you willing to do what is necessary to change?"* I really hope you are...

> *Humble yourselves, therefore, under the mighty hand of God so that at the proper time he may exalt you, casting all your anxieties on him, because he cares for you.*
>
> 1 Peter 5:6-7

For those of you who have had an experience in life similar to mine, have you ever wondered why you made it through and did not lose your mind? Could it be that just maybe what God wants you to do is use the experience you have learned from to give hope to someone else? It's not for you to understand or even question why life happened to you the way it has.

I believe God is leading you by an unseen hand to a conclusion of realizing you are not the one in control, and when a decision is made to surrender all of who you think you are life as you know it will forever be changed. What you choose to do with your experience reveals true character and this is what defines who you are!

If there is still, somewhere deep down inside of you, a child-like faith that wants to believe hope has not been lost, then allow God the opportunity to heal your pain. Through a process of overcoming the experience, God will reveal the purpose your calling is to influence.

I made all of the wrong decisions and wasted half my lifetime doing anything I could to try to feel better about myself. Not until writing this book did I realize that the same time given to a study of what God has to say in the Bible would have brought correction to what I thought of me much sooner than later.

It's my hope, as you read this, a decision will be made to do the one thing that will transform your life and give you the knowledge to find good in everything that has turned out for your wrong. Then you will be able to see clearly to help someone else.

> *And be constantly renewed in the spirit of your mind [having a fresh mental and spiritual attitude], And put on the new nature (the regenerate self) created in God's image, [God like] in true righteousness and holiness.*
>
> Ephesians 4:23-24

If you so choose, this time of study to learn what God has to say will answer questions you will never figure out on your own. God's greatest desire is to complete you as a person, and it is through your life being forever changed that the message of hope and eternal salvation through Jesus Christ can be revealed to a lost and hurting humanity.

For the people that know you and those who have had an experience in life similar to yours, there is no greater example to create hope than this. Your transformation can be a bridge for others to cross over through a discovery of their purpose in life. There are people who need to hear what you have to say, who can only relate to you.

The gift of what God has to offer in this life has been given to transform lives. Your life as a Christian is the example of what hope acted upon can do. There is a higher calling to answer.

*I once thought these things were valuable, but now consider them worthless because of what Christ has done. Yes, everything else is worthless when compared with the infinite value of knowing Christ Jesus my Lord. For his sake I have discarded everything else, counting it all as garbage, so that I could gain Christ and become one with him. I no longer count on my own righteousness through obeying the law; rather, I become righteous through faith in Christ. For God's way of making us right with himself depends on faith. I want to know Christ and experience the mighty power that raised him from the dead. I want to suffer with him, sharing with his death, so that one way or another I will experience the resurrection from the dead! I don't mean to say that I have already achieved these things or that I have already reached perfection. But I press on to possess that perfection for which Christ Jesus first possessed me. No, dear brothers and sisters, I have not achieved it, but I focus on this one thing: Forgetting the past and looking forward to what lies ahead, I press on to reach the end of the race and receive the heavenly prize for which God, through Christ Jesus, is calling us.*

Philippians 3:7-14

# ABUSED
ဆဝ ငြ

Child abuse is one of the great tragedies of American culture. Children from every race, social class and economic level are victims of verbal, physical and sexual abuse. An estimated 1,500 children die every year as the result of a moral breakdown in the parent who should be their protector and provider. Many of these parents were themselves victims of child abuse.

I don't know how agencies come up with statistics on child abuse, but the reality of what happens in a person's private life is witnessed in the lives of people every day. You don't have to be a behavioral professional to see signs in a person's mannerisms that would lead you to this assumption. And what are we doing about it? Nothing!

Every year the statistics increase and this is evidenced in the skyrocketing numbers of children who experiment with drugs, pregnancies, hospitalizations, crimes and incarceration and sadly, suicide. It's become an epidemic and rather than deal with the moral issues causing this harm, children are now drugged to numb their emotions as parents are allowed to continue the abuse.

Of all the federal and state-funded programs claiming to be child advocates and defenders of the helpless, none are capable. They are restricted by politics and cultural correctness. These agencies are themselves at fault for what happens to children. Those in charge of deciding what treatments are offered refuse to even consider the only textual manuscript that has within itself the ability to transform a life. Hence the culture we have become.

When did you last take the time to think about how good your childhood and teenage years really were? Many of you came home to a safe and comfortable environment, knowing you were welcome. You had parents who loved you and did what they knew to provide an example of how you are to care for your children. You had a social bond that developed by interacting with people you learned to trust, having experienced for yourself the goodness in people who value each other. That hope many of us have never known.

What I talk about in the next few chapters is sadly a very real description of what many children have experienced. These victims of indifference then grow up to become like what they hate most. I am not writing about this for a feeling of sympathy, so please don't feel sorry for me. I want to lay a foundation of events that brought me to the place where I made the decisions that have negatively affected my life.

From my youth up until the time when I began to write this book, I had no hope and no vision for a future. There were things done to me you don't do to a child. Being scarred emotionally robbed me of all sense of purpose and I grew up angry. I didn't know what it was like to be loved by my parents and happiness was something I couldn't relate to. Trust was an emotion I never learned.

I didn't know how to think about what life could have been like had my parents treated me differently and was given the opportunity to grow up in a healthy family environment, so alcohol and drugs became my escape. This dependence created an image of insignificance and from the time of my youth, I've hidden in shame behind a lifetime of substance abuse. And like so many people today, my potential was never realized.

Most of the people I know have a story to tell very similar to mine. Maybe not as graphic and violent, but to have had an experience anywhere close to mine, you know what its like to believe you have nothing of value to offer.

As a child I was quite, always watching what people did and I knew I didn't want to be like what I saw. But children have no say in what they are subjected to or the inevitable long-term effects unless someone who really cares intervenes. Sometimes love needs to be tough.

I was a child of rape. By age three I was taken from the woman who gave birth to me because of physical abuse. I have no memory of this and I did not learn about the details until much later in life. It was at that time I understood why I behaved the way I did as a child.

The married couple who adopted me had as many dysfunctional habits as my mother did and bad things happened. My earliest memories are at about three-and-a-half years of age, just as the adoption process was coming to its completion. At that age, I had no idea how mean and untrusting I had become. Trust was something I never had an opportunity to learn about so I wouldn't listen to my new parents.

It seemed as though being whipped or punished in some way was an everyday event. I remember times when my mother locked me outside with no clothes on as a means of punishment, and the children who saw this would laugh and make fun of me. I was often locked in my room or a closet and this really freaked me out. There were times when I had to go to the bathroom and I couldn't get out of my room, so I had to use a cup or whatever could be found. There were occasions when I was forced by my parents to either drink or eat what I had passed, and I would throw up.

I'm sure as a little boy there were things I did that frustrated my parents, but it does not warrant what was done to me. I vividly remember the day I was whipped and made to stand in a corner because my zipper was down and in spite of being punished, I unzipped it again.

When my mother saw this, I was laid backwards across her knees and my pants were pulled down. A knife was then put to my groin and I was told if I did not listen, she would cut it off and make a little girl of me. Events like this are never forgotten and from that day I was afraid of her.

Often I would be found hiding in bushes or under a bed. I was slapped in the face, and other times it was even worse. As I got older, I would try to fight back, only to have the whippings become beatings. I was too young to understand what my parents were going through or the events that shaped how they thought, but the long-term effect of their actions robbed me of my future. And so it continues with each new generation of American youth.

When school started, older kids would pick on me and I was often beaten up. I was kicked off the bus regularly because of all the trouble I was involved in, and my parents had to take me to school. It was quite evident they were resentful of this and on many occasions, for no other reason than just being there, I was slapped in my face.

The principal whipped me several times every week with a big wooded paddle because my father gave him permission to whip me, and when I came home, I would get beaten again. This was an environment I did not like and I was expelled from every school I went to due to my behavior.

I was bad and whatever was on my mind is what I said. My attitude kept me in trouble. I didn't know what it was at the time, but now I realize I had no respect for people who were unkind to me. And it wasn't just my parents; it seemed like everyone took their shots at me. I've lost count of how many times I was slapped or kicked by someone and then told to shut up and go somewhere else, and not be allowed back in the house until dinner time regardless of the weather.

The dirt road we lived on was all family from my mother's side. I had eleven cousins: two were girls and the others were boys who fought with me every day. On many occasions, I escaped to the tree tops to avoid a beating by a bully or someone who was drunk.

Violence is something I've experienced from my earliest memories, but nothing prepared me for an event I believe was meant to alter the course of my life and keep me from ever discovering the person I was created to be. It was during a holiday weekend when I was eight years old and my parents were visiting family. I remember there not being enough beds for everyone to sleep in, so a friend of one of my uncles took me to his home.

That night he touched me and did things that should never be done to a child. He had played with me on several occasions at my grandparent's house, but this was a game I did not like. I managed to pull away and curl up on a couch and that's when he left me alone. I never spoke of what happened to me that night, because it felt as though I had done something wrong. I was afraid of my parent's reaction. They never took the time to notice or even ask why my behavior changed.

Every time that man came around, I was scared. The memory of what he did has followed me through life. I go into more detail later to reveal how life-altering events like what happened to me really are, and just how vulnerable children can be who are members of an ever increasing dysfunctional family environment.

When a person who has committed this type of crime is caught, they are punished by the judicial system, but nothing is being done to keep these people from acting out this perversion upon another victim at some future time. Neither secular counseling nor education is capable of healing the lasting effects on a victim who has been violated. Read for yourself the statistics on child abuse and of children that have been sexually molested. Hurt people hurt people!

This is why there is such an epidemic of sexual perversion in the lifestyles of people today. Straight or gay, these confused people who commit pedophilia are acting out in anger to what happened to them. They were violated children who have become predators and are being driven by an endless urge to regain the innocence of what was taken from them. When children are robbed of their confidence, they have been robbed of the ability to understand who they are. The mistake made with me and the masses of child victims today, is trying to correct an emotional condition without the influence of a spiritual transformation.

Around the time of the incident with my uncle's friend my parents separated. I was then told about being adopted and that they were not my real parents. I became untouchable and no one could tell me what to do. Their separation was verbally vulgar and cruel things were said. I remember being told I was the reason for their trouble. The cruelty of what parents actually do and say to a child is appalling!

During arguments between my parents, things were thrown, but I have no memory of physical violence between them. Many nights when my parents were out on a date with the person they were having an affair with, I was left in a car or the living room by myself and could hear them having sex. By this time I had a strong dislike for my parents, and not wanting to have any interaction with them when I was at home, I would stay mostly to myself.

I would intentionally stay away from home all evening after leaving school and when I came home around dark my parents would whip me for not answering their calls. The environment at home was what made me want to stay away because I knew the whippings were waiting for me. It got to a point that I wouldn't eat the food my mother fixed, and when eating something I had made and someone came in the house, I would take my plate and go to another room.

There were many times when I was lying in bed or sitting on the couch watching TV, minding my own business, and for no reason I was grabbed by my hair and slapped around or told to go outside and not return until I was called. My parents told me I was no good, a mistake and I'd never amount to anything, and I did my best to live up to their expectations. I really don't know how my behavior affected what they thought of me, but those actions proved our feelings were mutual.

The only solitude I could find is when I went to the woods by myself. The farm land where we lived seemed endless. It was adjacent to the water front, and this is where I found peace. The sound of wind blowing through the trees and hearing water running over rocks was music to me. The crops growing and the forest of trees with all the sights and sounds of its wildlife was amazing. I explored and discovered and I often wondered how all of it came to be.

I watched with the change of each season how everything seemed to die, and to my surprise, by the warmth of the spring sun, everything came back to life again. I fished and hunted occasionally with my father, but I never enjoyed taking a life because it was all too surreal. I found in nature what I never experienced at home and I didn't want it to end. It was in this environment where I felt safe.

I didn't realize until much later in life just how close God is in the display of His creation.

*For since the creation of the world His invisible attributes, His eternal power and divine nature, have been clearly seen, being understood through what has been made, so that they are without excuse.*

Romans 1:20

I remember the night my father gave me a cigarette to smoke and I drank my first beer at age four. By age ten, I was smoking in front of my parents. They tried every way imaginable to make me stop but it didn't work, and that was when I was introduced to marijuana. One of my uncles was a dope head and he would often let me get high with him. I enjoyed the feeling of being able to escape, and I was hooked. To this day he walks the roads homeless, his mind is gone, and I've often thought how easily that could have been me.

My father remarried and so did my mother, and with this came their shoving match. Child custody was shared and I would never be at one location more than a few days. The people my parents were having affairs with were a married couple and they ended up swapping husband and wife. The other couple had a son who was a few grades higher than me and we had a history at school. This set a constant uneasy tone of frustration at home. I didn't like him and he didn't like me. My mother's home was always in an uproar with alcoholism and physical violence, and many nights I witnessed things a child should never see.

I was with my stepfather one evening at a crab cookout and just about everybody there was drinking, including me. He asked me if I wanted to go with him to get some more beer and when driving to the store he took out a row of at least thirty mailboxes. And we thought it was funny! Environments like what I grew up around is why children become just like their parents and then do what they believe is normal.

We lived in a rural area called "White Oak." An area like this is what you would classify as the country ghetto. Families here were middle-to low-income and a reputation followed the community. It was known for its violence and there was a heavy white supremacy influence in the lives of these people. I remember what was said about people being different and I witnessed several really cruel events. The name-calling, windows shot out of homes, the beatings and crosses burned in front yards caused the few black families that moved into the area to never stay more than a few weeks.

All of my family members were prejudice, as was the community. My parents told me to never speak to black people and my mother said, *"If you ever marry a nigger we will disown you."* So as I grew up there was a dislike for people, not for what they had done, but for who they were. Even at my age, I knew this wasn't right. I do not believe idiocy is inbred—it's passed down.

There was a still on the property and I would watch how the alcohol was made. Drinking the moonshine or corn whisky became a daily event once I found a way to sneak in the building to steal it. I would trade the alcohol for drugs with teenagers hanging out in the woods around my house or at school.

It was in the late seventies, and many of the men I grew up around had served in Vietnam. Drugs were readily available, and because I was the youngest person at these tailgate parties, I was often an object of their amusement. Alcohol and drugs were given to me just to see how I would react and wanting something to make me feel better, the drugs got harder. I did all the drugs that were predominant in that era.

I was twelve when I did cocaine for the first time. In the woods around my house marijuana was grown to smoke, or I would sell it to buy narcotics. I'd experiment with drugs. Each one having a different effect on how my body responded would leave me stoned for days at a time.

This is how I went to school, and I would come home having no memory of what I had done. On more than one occasion after arriving at school, I was escorted off the property or my parents were called to come and pick me up because of being suspended the day before. My ruin was the day someone shot me up with a cocaine and heroin mixture called speedballing. The drug use abused my body and twisted my perception of everything, and this is when the real trouble began.

At age thirteen I overdosed on a bag of speed sold to me at school. I had no idea what was in my hands, popping at least six or seven pills in the first hour. By the time the bus dropped me off, a tripping sensation had begun. I remember walking into my house and going to the bathroom looking at myself in a mirror.

What looked back at me was repulsive. The only thing I can describe it as being like was the manifestation of a demonic spirit, something you would see in a sci-fi horror flick. I had no idea what it was, but the memory of what that thing looked like is still with me to this day. It had a menacing expression and I will never forget the smell. It didn't make a sound; its presence was loud enough.

We stared at each other for what seemed a long time and then it leaned into me. I remember falling and heard myself hit the floor, but I didn't feel anything. When my stepmother came home, she found me laying in vomit on the floor, passed out. She put me in bed and when I woke up, there was no memory of what she had done. I was sick for several days.

After that experience I became extremely violent. One morning at home room another student hit me and we fought. The assistant principal had to be notified and when he questioned me, I ignored him. He had a reputation for being rough with students, and after several questions I didn't respond to, he grabbed me and slammed my face into a wall.

It was hard enough to knock me down, and as I was getting up my nose started to bleed. When I turned to face him, I started swinging. I landed several punches to his face and had to be pulled off by two gym teachers. The principal's eyeglasses were broken and he was bleeding from the nose, and a couple of days later both of his eyes turned black. He was reprimanded for his behavior and no action was taken against me. I remember thinking how funny that whole situation was. "Who gets to beat up a principal and gets away with it?"

I already had a reputation, but that incident elevated me to instant celebrity status with the girls at school. I was then introduced to all of the drama that came along with a confused and undisciplined teenage youth.

My teachers became very strict and gave me no room for error. I was in and out of the court system and I could never stay in school for any length of time due to fighting or just being bad. I had already been held back a school year and was made to attend a special education class with students who had attention disorders. I hated this. I would skip school to hang out in the woods to get high or go fishing. In one year, I was expelled from three different middle schools.

The situation at home was too much to deal with, so I started running the streets. Truancy officers and police were always after me and I'd play a game of hide and seek to make them angry.

The road my mother's family lived on was one-way in and one-way out. When I saw someone looking for me I would hide in the woods and tattoo their vehicle with rocks. On several occasions they chased after me unsuccessfully. My mother's house was located on thousands of acres of woods, and I knew the trails and several tree houses to stay in. I never got caught in my backyard.

I was a teenager before the first time I went to church and heard people talk about God. My stepmother was a member at this little country church and as a family we were all baptized. It was summer time and the church was just a few miles from my father's house, so we were there several times a week. In addition to the regular meetings, I was taken to fundraising events, fairs and Sunday school classes. I really don't know why. Other than the big family Bible under the coffee table in the living room, there was never any talk of God at home.

I can't say that I ever learned anything when I was at the church because there were no classes for children. I had to listen to what the preacher said to the adults. How I grew up and the environment I was familiar with was so far away from what I heard some man in a suit and tie talk about. None of it made any sense to me. And what he said about how people are to treat each other was definitely not what I saw at home.

One Sunday service several people were arguing loudly and as they were leaving the building, a fight broke out in the front yard.

The preacher was beaten up and when my father and several other men got involved to try and break it up, the fight got even bigger. The police arrived and people were arrested.

Standing there watching the behavior of these people as a child, this is what I remembered about church. Because of what happened that day and to the best of my knowledge, my father to the time of his death never stepped foot in a church building again.

Whatever hopes my parents had for me at that time were lost. Many nights I would lay in bed and smoke marijuana to help me sleep or to just escape. One late night my mother came upstairs and was yelling because of the smoke. She thought I was smoking a cigarette in bed. The door was locked and she opened it with a knife. As she came in, I tried to close the door and she reached around and cut my hand. Throwing the door open in anger, my reaction was to hit her in the face. I then got dressed and left home to run the streets until I was arrested.

By this time the judge had no sympathy for me and ignoring my mother's withdraw, I was charged with assault and battery and committed to a year of incarceration at a detention camp. The judge said I was a menace to society and he had seen enough of me. The way the counselors used their authority to be corrective did not help my opinion of people and I became even more distant.

Every day there were in-your-face group sessions that usually ended in me being thrown to the ground and having some ego maniac screaming and spitting in my face. I had had enough of people putting their hands on me and being made to do what I didn't want to. No one ever took the time to sit down with me and ask why I was so angry. It was always, "Do what I say or else." The punishments often left me in tears, but deep down inside I was standing up in defiance.

All of this is what I grew up around and I do not believe I had what people today want to call a chemical imbalance. It was the result of how my parents and other people treated me and what my environment subjected me to.

I never had the opportunity to be a child or learn how to believe in myself. Each day was basic survival and so it has been every day of my life. This is the mental conditioning we have all been subjected to and no one can make me believe anything different. Here is a prime example as to why I think the way I do...

Just after my release from the detention camp, the new school year had begun. I was still being required to attend the special ed class. My father spoke to me one evening about my behavior, a very rare occurrence. I remember him asking me what I would like. I told him all of my cousins had motorcycles and three wheelers, and I was still riding a bicycle. They made fun of me and I was never given the opportunity to ride with them, and this was something I really wanted to do. So as we talked, my father said if I were to make the honor roll at school he would buy me the motorcycle I wanted. I took him up on it.

Before that I was a C-D student and I always got an F in science. I did just enough to get by. School bored me because most of what was taught did not challenge me, nor did I believe I came from a monkey.

After the conversation with my father, I started bringing home my homework and actually doing it. And looking back, I realize how smart I was as a child, but my environment clouded my potential. At that time I also joined the football team. Everybody took notice! I did so well that I was moved from the special ed class and placed with the regular students.

When it came time for report cards, and to everybody's shock, I made all A's and one B. *I made Honor Roll!* And you know what my father did? He didn't buy the motorcycle, and it crushed me. I think I understand now why he didn't, but at that time it was my only goal. I had put all of my efforts into achieving what I wanted and he robbed me of my hope. That's when I gave up. This is not the behavior of a child with a chemical imbalance.

I believe this is the reason why people today have no hope. Every day we are told by the government, media and the educational institutions what to believe and who to believe in, to only accept as truth what makes you feel good and if you do what everyone else is doing, everything is going to be okay. As we grow up to realize it was all a lie, where do we turn? Who do we trust?

This is why everyone is so skeptical of not only other people, but also the one institution that should be able to win the confidence of people. But sadly, the church in America has lied to and abused the trust of these same people. This is why, in the day and time we live, faith in the Christian message of hope and eternal salvation through Jesus Christ is mocked. Again, who can be trusted?

Shortly after that incident with my father there was a heated argument with my mother. After she slapped me in the face, I was told to leave the house. We lived in the country, so if someone wanted you they would holler your name. I heard mine, and walked up to the house. I saw my father's truck and knew it meant trouble, because it was not his time to keep me. My mind raced, trying to figure out what to do, and I had no clue as to what was about to happen.

I was met at the front door by my mother and told to go to my room and pack the clothes I wanted to take with me. Upon entering my room, I heard the door shut and as I turned to look is when my father hit me in the face. I was knocked to the floor. The only thing I could see was stars, but I stood up and yelled, "Hit me again!" He did; again and again and again. I tried to fight back but was never given a chance.

I was bleeding from the nose and mouth and my right eye turned black. He had whipped me and hit me on several occasions but never like that before, and I hated him for what he did. My father took me to his house and then left to go to work. I then got into an argument with my stepmother who slapped me in the face. So I left home and ran the streets. I didn't care anymore.

For weeks my parents, school officials and police looked for me, but I would not be caught. On several occasions I had to outrun the police after being identified. I was a wild child. I had to steal from stores or break into homes to find money and food.

One night, a group I was running with got into a fight with a rival gang and people were hurt. When the police showed up, we scattered. A police officer chased me through the city's park and when I came to a river bank I never missed a beat and dove in. I swam across the river and sat on a log to watch the glow of flashlights as the police looked for us. The other side of the river was a different county, so I got away and found the situation amusing.

At this time I had just turned fifteen and I did any drug combination I could get my hands on, hoping I would die. It was during a weekend park event, after doing drugs all day and drinking beer and most of a half gallon of Old Forester whiskey, when it all caught up to me.

This was my second overdose in less than two years. The combination of alcohol and drugs left me passed out and when I was found, I didn't respond. I had been in a fight and was cut in the face by a beer bottle broken over my head and left where I fell. I don't know how, but someone told my father where I was and it was late that night when he found me in the woods.

When I woke up, I was laying on a hospital bed, not in a room, but in the hallway right in front of the nurses' station. There were wires all over my body and I was told if my father had not found me when he did and taken me to an emergency room to be treated, I would not have lived through the night. The alcohol level in my blood stream had poisoned me and that didn't even include any of the drugs I had taken. There were several stitches in my face from the cut and I looked like I felt.

My stay at the hospital was about a week and upon release the juvenile authorities took custody of me. I was then incarcerated at a high security lock-down facility to be held in isolation for a year. I was often restrained or put in a straight jacket when I didn't cooperate with the guards. I was charged with assaults and a list of felonies. The court then sentenced me to juvenile life, and I was moved to an adult jail. Because of my age I was kept in isolation for another year and a half awaiting my eighteenth birthday. Just a few days after turning eighteen, they transferred me to the state penitentiary. Problem solved…

And you wonder why the American culture is so screwed up! How else can a child act when all they have ever known is similar to an upbringing like mine? With no parental or moral guideline to set a standard to live by, children now murder other children and babies give birth to babies at an unprecedented rate.

This nation's governmental control over education is the catalyst for all of the atrocities witnessed in the lives of everyone you know. Yet we're taught that no one is really to blame, because it's all a part of the natural process.

Darwin's evolution theory of natural selection which is being taught in schools and universities as irrefutable truth, refutes its own claim of a species advancement, by the decline of our societies. Yet parents still allow this filth to indoctrinate their children. And now the government wants even more control over the education of children with programs like Early Childhood Development. Parents, for the sanity of your children do not allow this!

What I experienced, and the methods being used to brainwash children today, have removed from a person's conscience all though of accountability. Each day is met with the basic instinct of survival at any cost to everyone else. What we are witnessing is humanity at its worst, and not much separates America's future from Europe's not-so-distant past.

# FORSAKEN BUT NOT FORGOTTEN

## ℬ ℭ

There are currently 2.5 million adults incarcerated in both federal and state prisons and local jails in the United States. These are the statistics as of 2009. For every 100,000 men in the population, the black male has the highest number of incarcerations with an estimated 3,200, Hispanic is second with 1,300 and Caucasian is third with 500 people incarcerated according to the Bureau of Justice Statistics. There is a reason for this.

The example of my childhood, lack of proper education and what environment a child is familiar with are unquestionably the reasons why there's so many people incarcerated today. Think back to when Bill Cosby, in the early years of his show, was doing stand up comedy, and children were featured. He would ask these children to quote their favorite verses from the Bible and many were able recite the verse word for word. But as the seventies, eighties and nineties passed, children became more and more ignorant of the Bible and the evidence of this is today's culture.

Neither Hollywood nor the documentaries on TV will ever leave you with an accurate impression of life in prison. It is a world of its own! From alcohol and drug use, to sex and prostitution, violence and corruption of every kind imagined can be found inside the walls of this nation's penal system.

The goal is not to reeducate those who have committed crimes, but to use the system as a place to profit from. There is no sincere attempt to help a person think differently about themselves. This is why over eighty percent of male inmates do consecutive prison terms. Probably the most abused system of all is the death penalty appeals process. The yearly cost to house an inmate is $30,000. The cost of an appeal process can exceed $3 million dollars and years of litigation. Do the research. Just like everything else in today's culture, it's all about the money and who benefits most, regardless of the cost to human lives.

Trouble started for me the moment I stepped off the prison bus. Comments that were made, the looks, and people testing me to see what they could get away with was an hourly event.

The second night I was in a fight because an inmate who bunked with me came off of the top bed and put himself in my face, telling me I was going to give him oral copulation. I snapped and we tore that cell apart. When he realized I was not going to back down, he backed off and said he was just testing me. I responded, "I bet you were!" The next day the guards could tell we had been in a fight and I was moved to another cell.

I stayed to myself but youth was against me. Homosexuality is a way of life in prison and the majority of long-term inmates are active sexually in some way. I was the young boy everybody wanted to own. I had to be careful of where and what time I went to a toilet or shower room, and I paid close attention to who followed me. No one spoke directly to me but I could hear what everyone was saying, and as their courage progressed, the comments became more vocal. I had come to the resolve of what my prison stay would be like, so I was ready to fight.

On one occasion there were at least ten black inmates making comments and gestures about me being the new punk, and with no warning, someone hit me in the head with a prison issue boot and then I was yanked into a cell by several men. When I hit the floor, these men were trying to pull my pants down, and my reaction was to kick, hit and bite until they let go.

The fight then went to the open floor with three black inmates against me. Dozens of other inmates circled the fight, hollering at me or laughing about what was going down. Every ethnic group wanted to see what I would do. I was hit from every direction. The fight lasted for several minutes and I was bleeding from a cut to my face, but I would not back down.

As guards entered and took control of the situation, the building was then locked down. I was shackled and taken to isolation and held there until an investigation proved I did not instigate the fight. I am so thankful I grew up the way I did and learned how to fight. Had I not, I would have become one of the many statistics raped and then made to be a prostitute in the penal system.

After being released and moved to another building, I was approached by white inmates who asked me what I wanted as far as drugs or alcohol, and just about anything I could want, trying to get me in debt to someone. That's when I said I didn't want anything they had to offer. I knew what they were after and I said as much.

Recess would find me walking around the compound by myself and the only time I ever spoke was to tell someone to get out of my face and leave me alone. This was not liked and I was told by the white society they would not help me if I were to get into another fight. In that environment you really didn't know a person until their real motivation was made known, and for the next three years I kept everyone at a distance.

Prison has its own rules. To be safe you stay with your own, and if you do not follow the order of its societies you are fair game. Whether it was the Cripps, Aryan Nation, Mexicans or whomever, not a day passed when inmates did not approach me in some way. And more times than not, it ended in a fight.

I watched as young men, who were tattooed tough guys on the outside cowered to the pressures of prison life and were raped several times a day, sometimes by groups of men. I had no sympathy for a person who wouldn't even try to fight. I was young, but fortunately my youth bred meanness into me and I refused to be taken advantage of.

What happened to snitches was very real and I knew better, and this forced me to fight so as not to be raped or have people take what belonged to me. The hole became a place where the majority of my time was served and when I was moved out of a cell, my hands were cuffed to waist restraints and my legs were shackled.

Even after being transferred to several medium-security compounds, my reputation still followed. There always seemed to be a fool who wanted to be the one to beat me. Fights were with men much bigger than me and there was no such thing as fair. I used a bar of soap in a sock, a shank, a 2x4, or a pool stick—anything to give me an advantage. Many of these fights were never witnessed by guards. A person would say something that angered me, and at a later time that day I would choose a location away from supervision, approach this person and lay into him. There was no talking, I went after him!

Several fights I was involved in were bloody and this is what landed me in the hole. I got a shower once a week. Every morning the guards would enter the cell and remove a thin mattress and blanket, leaving me to sit on a cold sheet of metal until that evening with nothing but my underwear on. I was served food by gang members of a person who had been in a fight with me, so I went hungry.

At night I'd wake up to cock roaches on the bed, in my ears or up my nose. It was disgusting. The smell of feces and urine thrown at a guard by another inmate in the lockdown unit was sickening. When my time was served, I would then be released to population only to get into another fight. Sometimes I'd get away with it and other times it was back to the hole.

Isolation is a place where you discover things that no one else, not even yourself knows about you. More than half of my time served was in lockdown. There were weeks and sometimes months I didn't see daylight. I had no interaction with people at all. In that environment you're alone and when you realize no one cares, all hope is abandoned. You then respond to everyone in the same way life has treated you. I was hateful and quick to say what I thought about someone. I didn't care whether it was an inmate or a guard. I was on my own and I had become the monster my environment created.

There is no man-made rehabilitation in this nation's penal system. Until there is a change in how people think of themselves, what is in their past will always repeat itself. The system has proven itself to be a failure because the majority of men released from prison return, having been convicted of a similar or greater crime usually within a short period of time.

I have seen this happen. It's because the system cannot change a person when its focus is to punish what was done in an environment of negative influence designed to beat a person down. There is no reeducation nor has there ever been. It's a money market for state taxes and federal grants, and jobs for a lot of people not really qualified to work anywhere else.

Here is just one example. I was taken to a prison's dentist office to have my impacted wisdom teeth removed and the doctor proved to be a quack. This man made an incision in my gum and then took a poker of some kind and jabbed it into my tooth. He then pushed down really hard and broke my tooth in several pieces and began to dig it out. The pain all but knocked me out and this idiot proceeded to try and cut me again. I hit him and he backed off as a couple of guards restrained me. Blood was everywhere and I wouldn't let him finish. This is the kind of care inmates are given, paid for with your tax dollars.

In prison you are caged with hundreds of people like you and just as it is in the animal world, the weak are preyed on. Guards do not run a prison system, the inmates do. The only thing guards do is keep some sense of order and when necessary, they use force to put down trouble. On a couple of occasions, I've had to stare down the barrel of a sawed-off shotgun... Not a very warm feeling!

You have a choice of three lifestyles in prison—either *you fight, snitch and then check into isolation for protection or you become someone's punk.* These were the only options and it was in this environment where I learned what hate really was. Your race did not matter—I hated you.

After half a dozen transfers due to fighting, they reclassified me as a violent inmate and I was then moved to a maximum-security prison. Upon entering the cellblock to see 130 violent men on three tiers verbalizing what vulgar acts they were going to do, I made a decision to never become a victim. Even if it meant spending the rest of my life in prison, nobody would rape me or get away with being disrespectful.

Whatever I could find to make a weapon with was then hidden close to my cell. This was an everyday thought process. I had no peace! Even here, my reputation followed me and word spread. It took about a week for the societies to do their probing before they made their first move.

The fights came and each fight was more severe than the one before. The societies tested me to see how far they could go. Here these men had a purpose for what they intended me to be, so I did whatever I had to. There were days several fights would go down. I would be in a shower room naked and have someone walk up behind me and put his hand between my legs, it was on. I'd be in my cell and another inmate would walk in without asking, and it would go down. I had only one response to anybody that disrespected me.

This lasted about a month before I was confronted by a life-timer who told me I was going to be his punk. He stood there with a shank in his hand. I had no weapon and a choice to make. He was big, about 250lbs, and I knew who he was and the reputation he had for cutting up a few people. I told him that's what he'd better do, and then I dove into him!

During the altercation, I was stabbed five times. He knocked me down and as I looked up at him, he said, *"The next time I see you, you will be my punk or I will kill you."* He then turned and walked away. I lay there in a pool of my own blood with both pectoral muscles severed. I could see my sternum and ribcage vibrate with each heart beat.

I bled heavily while being taken to a hospital, and I laid there for about two hours before anyone even took a look at me. It seemed there was no real concern for me because I was nothing more than a convict who had probably gotten what he deserved.

I remember a doctor pulling the gauze bandages off of my chest wound and the searing pain that took my breath away. Blood splattered his face as he was prepping the wound for staples and he removed a blood clot about the size of a tennis ball. He showed it to me and said that's what kept me from bleeding to death. There were eighty-five staples in my chest, back and left arm and numerous stitches to sew up muscle and artery.

After my return to prison they kept me in isolation. I was given no treatment except for heavy doses of pain killers to keep me knocked out. It took several months to heal completely due to the severity of the stab wounds.

Snitching was not an option. In a maximum security prison, and to be labeled a snitch is to sign your death warrant. Or permanent placement in isolation under protective custody. This is why snitching was not an option with me. The prison officials had no regard for my physical or emotional well-being because I did not cooperate with their attempts to press charges against the inmate who stabbed me. I told the warden I had fallen down. My hope was that I would cross paths with this inmate again; I would have killed him or died trying. The guards called me all kinds of names, and threatened to label me a snitch and place me back in population. I had no respect for these people, and called them what they were. I was then transferred to another prison where the system began again.

There were several fights at this location and one went down that put me in the infirmary because of my injuries. Having had words with another inmate earlier that day, I was walking down a flight of stairs, going to the library, when he hit me with a lock tied to a shoe string. I didn't see it coming. Twice the lock split my head open and left me sprawled out on the floor.

After coming to my senses and going upstairs, a guard took one look at me and sounded an alarm to lock the building down. I was put into shackles and escorted to the prison's clinic to be treated. I was in this room alone for several days and remember thinking if I didn't change, I would be dead in six months.

I hated life and I will never forget that day. I had every right to be angry because life was never kind to my youth. And this was the first time I cried in regret over the many wrong choices I had made.

I didn't know what to do and in that environment there was no one for me to talk to. In six-and-a-half years my father came to see me once and my mother came twice. I was left with no option but to accept the fact that nobody cared. I was alone, I had no hope of change and I was mad. Then God penetrated the darkness.

I did not grow up in a healthy family environment and do anything a parent would be proud of. It was just the opposite. I was everything a parent didn't want and they were unable to give me an example of how to trust someone or know what it was to love. I could not relate to these emotions or express them in any way. And when I was at my worst, God reached out to prove He is real and was willing to meet me in my sin.

> *Although my father and my mother have forsaken me, yet the Lord will take me up [adopt me as His child].*
>
> Psalms 27:10

I do believe there is a time in everyone's life when God reaches out. God's invitation to show up is when you realize change is not something you can accomplish by your own ability. I was finally ready to listen.

> *No one is able to come to Me unless the Father Who sent Me attracts and draws him and gives him the desire to come to Me.*
>
> John 6:44a

This was the day of my visitation, a day God ordained to be the beginning of my healing. I remember thinking, "I don't know how to change," and that's when I heard a voice say, *"Pick up my Bible and read it."* Sitting up and looking around, there was no one else in the room. I didn't know what to think about this so I ignored it.

The next day that voice said again, *"Pick up my Bible and read it."* This time I got out of bed and walked to the door and looked out into an empty hallway. My mind was racing and I sat there thinking about what this might mean.

The following morning I heard a stern voice, *"I said pick up my Bible and read it!"* Just at that moment the door opened and another inmate walked in. He put his belongings on a bed beside mine, introduced himself and asked if I believed in God. I said, "No, but you do have my attention." And until the next morning when he was released to population, we talked about God, Jesus and eternal salvation. He said salvation was God's free gift to me if I were to accept Jesus as my Savior.

Why God chose to introduce Himself to me in this way is hard to understand. It was probably because life had scarred me so badly only God could have revealed Himself. I would not have been receptive to a person who said anything to me about God. I thought about the church where I was baptized and how those people acted. That was my only knowledge of God.

Life dealt me a hard hand. I had no memories of ever being hugged by my parents or feeling protected. It was difficult for me to believe that a God who loved me would allow what I had experienced in my young lifetime. I had a lot of questions, but the reality of hearing a voice speaking to me could not be denied.

What that inmate said to me didn't make a lot of sense but when I heard God's love is unconditional and He accepted me for who I was, it captured my emotions. The man handed me his Bible and said, *"This is God's gift to you."*

I used to wonder why some people became Christians while other people hearing the same message, chose not to believe. Why is it that two people can hear the same thing and both come to completely different conclusions? It would not be until years later that I realized what a person has been exposed to has the greatest influence in the choice they make.

This is the reason why it is so difficult to reach people with just a verbal message of the Gospel of Jesus Christ. Telling a person it is their choice to live either right or wrong is a biblical mandate, but what has been neglected by Christian leaders today and reflected in the lives of those they lead, is meeting people at their need. This is something Jesus did in the gospels and to this day, He still continues to do.

After my release from the infirmary, I was taken to a lockdown unit. For the next three months I had an opportunity to read the Bible several times through. I had a lot of questions that went unanswered. But as I read the Bible I saw so many examples of how a person's life was transformed, and this gave me hope that I could change.

I asked God if He could help me change to be a better person then I would accept Jesus as my Savior. I had been angry all of my life and for the first time, I wasn't mad. The realization of this was overwhelming. It was an emotion I had never experienced before and kneeling down on the concrete floor, I asked God to forgive me for how I had lived.

God spoke to me again and this time there was no question as to who it was. His voice came from everywhere and He said to me, *"Repentance is turning away from that which you are doing."* God knew who I was and yet He cared enough about me to reveal Himself in this way. It was a life changing experience.

There was nothing different about me physically, but upon release to general population, my actions were different and people took notice. They wanted to know if the change was real, and my witness was having nothing to do with everything that had given me the reputation I had.

I stopped using drugs, I didn't cuss anymore and I walked away from several fights. My change was radical. What had actually happened was beyond my understanding and I couldn't explain it. The memories of my past had been wiped clean and it seemed as though I had been given a new start.

When an opportunity to meet with the warden was given and I asked about attending school to take the GED, my request was granted. Everybody was watching because I went from being a bad boy to someone who went to church and didn't get into anymore trouble.

As the teacher was gathering study material, I asked him to let me take the test. He said I needed to study first, but I explained that while in isolation all I did was read and had even read a dictionary, and he agreed. After grading the test he was shocked.

The score was so high he offered to have my work orders transferred to the school so I could be his assistant. He wanted me to help him prepare the other men for their tests but I declined his offer. I did not like having to interact with people. I saw them for who they thought they were. This teacher was a homosexual and blatantly open about his attraction to me. Was he really there to help inmates or use the system for his sexual preference? Again, these are the kind of people employed by the penal system.

There's not much you can get away with in a small environment where everybody makes it their business to know everyone else's. The majority of inmates involved with church events were trying to hide from the realities of prison life. I saw it every day and it was a turnoff to me.

I often said to these men, "If you are going to talk it, then live it." Most of them never did. Some were released and either violated their parole or were convicted of another crime and returned to prison before I made it out. Had these men really changed or was it just for show? Once again, I knew that I didn't want to be like them.

A minister who came to the prison every week asked me if I wanted to be baptized, and I told him I did. He made arrangements with prison officials and the day came when I was told to report to the guard's office and suit up. They gave me an orange jump suit with PRISONER painted across the shoulders and my inmate number below it. My classification was still that of a violent inmate and I was handcuffed and shackled.

The minister and two guards walked with me across the complex field to a creek. It was February and the minister had to break ice. I was baptized in freezing water with two shotguns pointed at me. A "shotgun baptism".....go figure?

For the next seven months all of my time was given to reading the Bible and I attended every church service until the day of my release. God cleaned me up and for the first time in my life, I had hope.

Several inmates approached me just before I was released and asked if I could tell them how my life had changed. They said I was different than the other men who went to church. Some even apologized for the things they had either said or done and asked me to forgive them. They said to have seen me the way I was before and stay consistent in my walk with God made them want to experience God in the same way.

I told them what happened while in the infirmary and in isolation, and that God had spoken to me face-to-face. I told them I had accepted Jesus as my Savior and when reading the Bible, I'd realized I needed to quit doing what I had always done to have my life's witness be effective. I prayed with these men and led them in prayer by asking God for forgiveness.

All of these men were life-timers and would never see the streets again. They were forever confined to their physical environment, but eternally they had been set free.

Twelve days after turning twenty-one, I was told to report to administration. Upon arriving, I was notified of a pending release order. The necessary paperwork was signed and I walked out of prison with $90 to my name and no place to go. I was a free man….. so I thought!

For the six-and-a-half years of my incarceration, I did whatever I had to in order to survive, and I was in the hole for close to five of those years. It was near the end of my sentence when I realized change was needed, but I knew it wouldn't happen without someone's help. What amazes me is during this time I had no consciousness of God, and yet He revealed Himself in a way that I could no longer deny His existence. What will it take for you to allow God into your world of isolation, so you can experience for yourself what only He can do?

Prison is an environment much like the life many people live in the confines of their own minds. The only difference is that inmates are confined to an actual location, while everyone else can come and go as they choose. They're oblivious to the bars of confinement restricting the freedoms of an imagination condemned to a lifetime of ignorance.

This is the mindset that plagues American culture today. The worst of society in all of their unrestrained behavior, having no moral conscience or thought of accountability. Free to commit crimes of injustice against the sanctity of human life and the knowledge of our true selves, and condoned by laws passed so the enemies of God may prosper. Few people today realize just how similar their self-perception is to a man or a woman confined to a cell. They have no hope for the future because all attention is focused on surviving today.

I can tell you this from my own personal experience. The confinement of a man's soul is a darkness that will never be penetrated until Jesus Christ illuminates the darkness with the light of His Gospel… What are you prepared to do?

# HOPE SHATTERED

ᛞ ᚳ

G rowing up where I did and being so close to the water, crabbing was a part of life. Something I remember watching as a child is when a lone crab was in a bushel basket and left unattended, it would always get out. But when there was more than one crab in the basket, none ever made it out.

This exemplifies today's culture. Like crabs in a bucket, people are so afraid someone else just might have the audacity to try to get out of the mess everyone else is in, peer pressure does everything possible to pull them back in. How dare you expose my weakness and compromise are the real issues at hand. This is why so few people ever make it out.

The masses are all moving in the same direction and there seem to be few who are willing to try to sway the tide. Because moral conviction and truth have been all but eradicated from this culture's postmodern conscience, everybody seems to just blend in. Should a person ever bring to light the wrongs being committed or an answer to one of today's social dilemmas, the powers that be do everything possible to discredit them. This goes to prove the meanness in those who have been and are now in positions of leadership and what they have done to suppress the truth.

*The [basis of the] judgment (indictment, the test by which men are judged, the ground for the sentence) lies in this: the Light has come into the world, and people have loved the darkness rather than and more than the Light, for their works (deeds)*

*were evil. For every wrongdoer hates (loathes, detests) the*
*Light, and will not come out into the Light but shrinks from*
*it, lest his works (his deeds, his activities, his conduct) be*
*exposed and reproved.*

John 3:19-20

Until this mindset is confronted with the truths of Scripture to wake people up to what is really happening, those responsible for the substandard of living affecting every class and culture of people today will never answer for what they have done. I really hope you are honest in seeing yourself and the people you know in these vivid examples of everyday American life...

The minister who baptized me had given me his phone number and I made a call to tell him I'd been released. When he heard I had no place to go he came and picked me up. That same day someone at his church provided me an apartment free of rent for six months and I was given money, stuff for the apartment and a job the next day.

Being out of prison was nothing like I hoped it would be and I quickly learned about the realities of life on the outside and how similar people are. I lived for the experience of each day with no consideration of tomorrow. I was on my own with no skills, no training of any kind and I didn't even know how to drive a car. I was nervous. I had always been alone but never on my own, and it took me a couple of weeks to get somewhat comfortable with the people I was around.

After getting settled in and making enough money to buy a ticket, I took a bus home. I was greeted with reserve by my parents. During the weekend I made a visit to both of their homes and they gave me some money. My father gave me a S10 pickup truck that was a five speed and I had no clue how to drive it.

That Sunday afternoon he drove us to the beginning of a long hill, put the truck in park and turned the engine off. He then said I was not welcome and he did not want me around. Because of that conversation, I would have nothing to do with my family for several years. He told me what I needed to do to get out of first gear. He then got out of the truck and left me by myself to figure it out. It took several attempts to get off the hill and I then drove four hours to my apartment, and by that time I could drive a stick shift.

The next day I went to the DMV to get a driver's license, registration and tags. I was told by the preacher to open a checking account and start saving money, but I knew nothing of money management, nor did I have sense enough to ask. And to this day, everyday has been an experience of learning what not to do.

I was really motivated about the changes in my life and I'd start a conversation anywhere I went. I tried to be as diplomatic as I could to open the door for me to tell other people about what God did and how it changed my life. I was bold in my witness, but on many occasions I did not have the spiritual maturity I needed to stand up against the verbal attacks of people whose ego had been challenged. On many occasions I was left with my head hung in shame at having nothing convincing to say.

The minister was a pastor for young college students and they would have nothing to do with me. During service times at church they were polite, but after the service they avoided me like I was the plague. There was no one for me to talk to on my level of excitement.

I thought being honest with people was the right thing to do, but it turned out to be quite the opposite. People did not like hearing the truth, especially when it challenged their beliefs or the lack of. All I heard was, "You can't say this and you don't ever imply that, miracles only happened in Jesus' time and God will make you sick to teach you a lesson." I was told weak people used religion as a crutch and to get anywhere in life you needed to be educated. People said I was crazy to think God would talk to me.

It came at me so hard and so fast my confidence was lost in defense of my sanity. I went to several churches and what I saw in the lives of these people and how they treated me really hurt the innocence of what I wanted to believe in. So I quit going. It's sad when people who claim to be a Christian rob you of hope.

I hate it when ignorance criticizes what another ministry or individual is doing to help someone believe they can live a better life just because it's being presented differently than how organized religion thinks it should.

What right do you have to judge what God is doing in and through another person when all you are doing is being legalistic and have become the true definition of what a hypocrite really is? Look around at how many people are following the example you are setting. If all you see is your own shadow, then shut up with your criticisms. What you need to do is repent and ask God to help you change.

It really frustrated me that people were so cynical. It seemed as though every person had an attitude about something and I cannot count how many times my response to someone's gripe was they had better learn how to appreciate life. I knew how easy they really had it.

By age twenty-one, I had experienced more anger and pain than most people will in a lifetime. I didn't know how to relate to these people and like I had always done, I said what was on my mind with no consideration to how it was taken—a definite way to not win friends and influence people. I wanted to do what was right and help people in any way I could so they would not have to experience pain and regret like I had, but that hope was shattered. The opposition that came against me was successful in silencing my witness because of my lack of knowledge and because I was alone.

I believe if a person is insecure they will do anything to avoid being challenged. This reaches across every culture and society today and no one is exempt. When a person can avoid being held accountable for what they say and do they feel comfortable. This is the mindset I want to challenge with the message of my book.

The apartment where I lived was near a university campus and I had never seen so many girls in my life. Bars became a place of refuge and these young women were intrigued with my background, but it put me in situations compromising to my new lifestyle.

I began to drink alcohol socially and I would spend all of my money on someone I met at a bar. It never lasted past the first night. I wanted to have friends and be liked but it never turned out that way. I made a mess of everything I put my hands to because no one would take the time to show me what I needed to do. So I became the prodigal son. It would take me another twenty years of hard living to finally come to my end and do what God told me to do in the first place. And it was not until then that I learned about the real me.

Driving a vehicle was a new experience and just like every dumb kid, I tested fate. In the first eight months of driving, I totaled three vehicles and walked away each time. Alcohol was involved in all three crashes.

I ended up quitting my first two jobs because both managers made me mad. I did not respond well to being told what to do in a tone of voice that was demeaning. Because I wasn't working, I couldn't pay rent. I had to move out of the apartment and took only what I could fit in a gym bag. This was my first experience at being homeless, and I would stay with whomever I met at a bar or I would walk the streets at night.

It was winter-time and it took me about two weeks of being in the elements and cold all day before I hitchhiked south until the highway ended. For the next year I lived under the boardwalks and in the alleyways, doing anything I could to survive. It was here I experienced just how cruel life can really be and I met people who were abused by life and forgotten. At night I would hang out around the fast food restaurants and as they discarded what wasn't sold that business day, I helped myself. Some night's food was plentiful and others it was very lean.

Eating out of a dumpster is not something I ever imagined I would do and when I hear someone talk about other people and what they think will never happen to them, I just smile. No one is ever more than a few wrong decisions, or a traumatic event, away from finding themselves trying to survive in an element once thought to be unimaginable.

It would surprise you to know the backgrounds of homeless people. Some have made wrong decisions while others are casualties of this nation's corrupt economic system. There are many corporations more concerned about profits and executive benefits than ensuring those who manufacture a product or provide a service have at least the basic of necessities. I've been homeless because of decisions I made, but no child should ever have to experience this in a nation with so many resources available and housing locations sitting vacant. Go to the tent cities or homeless shelters all across the country and ask these people how much money would it take to get off the street and into a place of their own. You would be shocked. And if you are so naïve to think America could not become a third world nation, you are fooling yourself.

Millions of people are no more than a paycheck or two away from being homeless. Many have limited or no healthcare and even more are addicted to some kind of substance abuse. This is the reason why there is so much domestic violence and child abuse in American culture. These are the results of hurt people trying to suppress the painful memories of their past. How many people suffer with mental illness or an emotional condition who really can't take care of themselves? There are those who have experienced a traumatic event or a serious illness that caused their handicap, but what I'm referring to is a person's mind void of any hope. All because of how we have been made to think and feel about ourselves, and not willing to do anything about it.

What is the government and all of the programs funded by our tax dollars doing to help these people? Nothing! They are giving billions of dollars to corporations through so-called stimulus packages without any regulation, yet people are still homeless and going hungry. There's something very wrong with this.

These people are motivated by only one thing. How it will benefit them. Either monetarily or their political careers advancement. They do not care about you. Those who are controlling banking and economics from within the ranks of government are guilty for what we're witnessing in the housing market and its impact upon every aspect of our lives today.

One example is Congressman Barney Frank who lied to the American people when he testified in front of a congressional hearing denying any knowledge of the crimes committed by those heading mortgage giants, Fannie Mae and Freddie Mac. This man committed perjury to conceal the financial rape of the American people, and he's never been held accountable for the damage inflicted upon so many lives. I have to question his qualifications to hold the positions of influence he has, based upon his private life. How can a man who is so utterly confused with his sexual identity ever make decisions to rightly lead a nation?

Why does government seem to employ only those who, in all honesty, are not ethically capable to lead by example? The reason the American people are so divided, is because of this image portrayed by what ignorance perceives to be the party of public choice. As long as people think someone else is the reason for their personal and social frustrations, the government will continue to rape people of the freedoms and rights bestowed upon us by the God who created us.

Demoralize the people long enough and eventually they will come with hat in hand, hoping big brother will offer some kind of assistance program with no concern for the consequence. It makes me sick to my stomach to watch what is happening and to know church leaders are doing very little to expose the truth.

These mega church pastors who make millions of dollars, drive exotic automobiles, and living in mansions have done more harm than good by flaunting their lavish lifestyles. So few in their congregations ever attain the success promised by prosperity messages. Church leaders spend a large portion of their budgets on personal and staff incomes and benefits, and devote very little of their resources to a community outreach.

It's at times like now when we realize just how invisible we really are. Each generation, from my birth until now, have their stories to tell about what government and man's religion has done to destroy the hope we want to believe is real.

Because you have nothing of sustenance to offer or a means to profit by, you're made to feel irrelevant. People walk by and never even take the time to look at you, avoiding what they do not want to have to deal with. What we are witnessing is a culture whose hope has been shattered.

People are starving for attention and wanting to know there's someone out there who cares. But sadly, the self-centered lifestyles of so many people today have proven just how rare of a commodity compassion really is.

One day I was lying on the beach and I remember watching a man walk towards me. I was still homeless at that time. His hair was white blond and his face was a beautiful tan complexion, and he had piercing ice blue eyes. He had on jeans with a light blue linen button down shirt and the sleeves rolled up to his forearms, and he was barefoot. I will never forget him.

He leaned over, putting his hands on his knees, and said to me, *"God sees you right where you are and He loves you."* Standing up straight, he then walked behind me. I sat up and turned to look at this guy, and he was gone. The moment before he was right beside me and then he disappeared. I stood up and looked around in every direction and he was nowhere to be seen. That really unnerved me. I don't know for sure and I probably never will know, but I believe he was an angel sent by God to get my attention.

It accomplished what was intended. Just a few days later I met someone and they took me to a homeless shelter. I stayed there for about six months and they helped me find a job. God did this for me, but when was the last time you reached out to help someone?

It was a struggle to try and find myself and figure out what I could do to create some feeling of fulfillment. I went through a number of jobs. Working in restaurants paid the most money and I learned how to be a waiter and a bartender. Within this industry also come its demons. Most of the people I worked with used drugs and at first my use was casual but, liking that escape, it soon became every day. The real party started after last call and this was my way of escaping that empty feeling of having no purpose in life.

The amount of money I made as a bartender allowed me to get away from the homeless shelter and rent a room on my own. But I was stuck in the lifestyle of alcohol and drug use and all the mess that came along with it. I didn't know what to do to change my circumstances. There was no answer to be found in the circle of influence I chose to be a part of. I wanted to be liked and have friends, but I was always kept at an arms distance. I was alone and I couldn't communicate with anyone who related to me and I withdrew into depression. I believed what I had experienced in life would be all I'd ever know.

Every so often I went back to church, and without fail, people made me feel unwelcome. I couldn't figure out what it was about me that turned people off so badly. I was very quiet and never spoke to anyone until I was spoken to. I did what I hoped would impress people, wanting them to like me. Maybe I was trying too hard or maybe people could actually see what I thought of me?

At this time, as the money allowed, I moved around and eventually returned to where I was after my release from prison. I met an older gentleman one evening and as we talked, he invited me to come and visit Valley Word Ministries, which was the church he attended. I was ashamed of the person I had become, but I went hoping to make things right. Curtis Gray was the pastor of this church and I remembered him from a musical he'd done at the prison.

There was an instant contact with Curtis. Something about him appealed to me and he seemed to have the relationship with God I longed to experience for myself. He was very open and honest, but most of the church members would have nothing to do with me. I stayed for about a year and I became very resentful towards these people because they lived a double standard of life.

It seemed like everybody was jockeying for position, and they were always trying to elevate themselves while undermining everyone else. It got really bad and these people proved to be as judging and unkind as those who didn't go to church, so once again I stayed away. As often as I went to church in an attempt to find meaning and try to better myself, all I was exposed to was nothing like what's taught in the Bible.

I would see many of these same people at a bar where I worked dancing or drunk and I'd think, "You hypocrite!" If they could not live what was taught in the Bible, then what right did I have to think I was any different? Depression hit me really hard, so I did my best to escape what I thought of me. I had never been close to anyone or knew what it was like to believe my life had purpose. Thinking it would always be like this made me try to commit suicide.

I had recently bought a used car and one evening as I was driving on a mountain road, and coming into a sharp curve I gunned the gas pedal and closed my eyes. The car came to an abrupt halt as it landed in a tree. It was at night and I could see nothing past the headlights as they faded into darkness. After coming to myself and sitting there for a few minutes trying to figure out what to do, I began to move around to see if the car would dislodge but it wouldn't.

The sunroof was open and I climbed through to pull myself up and stand on the bumper. After looking around, I saw my only option was jumping to the embankment. After reaching the roadside, I stood there looking at the car.....mad!

I couldn't even kill myself—nothing ever went my way. I started to walk away but I stopped and yelled, "God, send somebody up here to get me out of this!" and then I turned around walked back to where the car was and waited. Now, this was on top of a mountain at midnight in the middle of nowhere.

A few minutes had passed when a vehicle pulled up and the driver looked quite surprised when he saw my car in the tree. He said a friend of his owned a large wrecker and he left to get that person. It took about forty-five minutes for them to return and when they managed to get cable hooks into the frame of a bumper mount, my car was pulled out of that tree and up onto the road. I started the car and he then followed me to an ATM machine and said $65 would pay for his service. During the time I'd been waiting for them to return, not one other car passed by. God answered my arrogance and I have often wondered why.

The next day curiosity had me wanting to see what had happened the night before. What I saw was numbing. Where my car had left the road, it dropped off about the length of a football field at a really steep incline. There was only one tree on the side of that mountain big enough to stop the car; everything else was shrubbery and weeds. The tree had fallen and its branches had turned upwards making a net. This was what my car landed in. God spared my life again, but I was mad at Him because of the life I had to live. Life had robbed me of everything I'd ever hoped for and I wore that emotion on my face. I was an ugly person.

I don't know what made me say that to God! But knowing He allowed me to walk away from being knifed and those three car wrecks, trying to kill myself on two different occasions and every other negative life relentlessly threw at me, I was beginning to realize what God is capable of doing. I had never forgotten about the times when God spoke to me and the hope I once had was still there buried under a lifetime of anger and regret.

After my attempted suicide, I went back to the church where I'd been before. On several occasions when preaching, Curtis made statements either directly or indirectly to me that he could not have known anything about, so I would listen to him. He was gifted, but the fullness of his gift has yet to be realized.

I made the decision to become active in several outreaches and I hoped through doing this, happiness would somehow come to me. I even went to several prisons with a group of church leaders who asked me to give my testimony. I remember how it made me feel when what I said had no impact in the lives of these men because once again, I had nothing convincing to say. I was as lost and confused as they were.

For two years I immersed myself in the church environment. I kept the grounds, parking lot and building spotless and everywhere Curtis went, I was his driver. He became the closest relationship I ever had and was more of a father figure than a pastor. I was offered room and board in the basement of their home. They also had two teenage daughters. That trust had a profound impact on my behavior and it caused a deep respect for this couple. To this day I do not understand why they took me in, when knowing the kind of lifestyle I had lived. And they were black…

Growing up where I did and being exposed to racism from my earliest memories had altered my opinion of people and my experience of prison life was fuel to the fire. But I experienced something different with this family and I wanted to know what made them want to do things for me and never ask for anything in return. This was new and it intrigued me as to how my opinion could be corrected by a selfless act of kindness and being trusted.

One evening after service, Curtis invited me to dinner and as we were talking he said my future was something I had to look forward to. He said there were things I would have to go through first and when I asked him what they were, he wouldn't tell me.

He said if I knew what God would allow in order to prepare me for the ministry I was called to do, it would cause me to not serve Him. I didn't know how to respond to this and mentally I put it away. Little did I know how accurate his words would later become.

When we first met, neither Curtis nor his wife could do any wrong. They were the perfect couple in public but at home, it was quite a different story. I was very close to them both and the problems they were having played out right in front of me. The arguments, accusations and fights over money issues took its toll. I saw this every day and when it was game time, what Curtis said from behind a pulpit did not always mirror his lifestyle at home and it really confused me about Christianity.

By this time, I never talked about my past except when it was necessary. I was afraid to open myself up to people. All of my life people have been unkind to me and church proved to be no different. Change was something I longed for, but everyone there was just as confused as I was. From the pastor down, there was no example to demonstrate how a Christian lifestyle was to be lived.

The volunteer work I did at this church was an eye-opening experience. It was a soap opera. There were arguments and fights, affairs, leaving one to marry another and a whole lot of drama. The church's affiliation was non-denominational and seemed to attract all of the nuts, flakes and fruitcakes from surrounding counties. Certain days after leaving the church I would think, "What have I gotten myself into?" More animosity and division was expressed in church than at the restaurant where I worked. It reminded me of the country church I went to as a teenager, only this one was bigger and there were many more nationalities and personalities to try to figure out. I often thought there had to be more to being a Christian than this. I wanted to be different, but since I had no example to follow, nothing ever changed.

Curtis and his wife separated, and the news became public when he was accused of fathering a child with a woman who was a member of another church. I don't know if that really happened, but the rumors took their toll. And I watched as this church's membership began to decline. One Sunday morning service, with no warning, Curtis announced to a shocked congregation that he was resigning his pastorate effective immediately. He was not stepping down as a result of his actions, but had decided to return to his evangelistic roots as a traveling preacher. He had become my only friend and without even saying goodbye, he was gone. These are the kind of people in leadership positions where we are to learn how to live the Christian witness. They have no one to hold them accountable to the gospel they preach.

An attractive young woman had become a member shortly after I went back to the church and we started dating. It was apparent from day one her parents did not approve, even though they knew nothing of my past. They took her to dinner one evening and said she was forbidden to date me. She ignored their criticism as we continued to date and about a year-and-a-half later, we married.

We were both young and had no idea what we were doing. Jenelle was a registered nurse and the work I did was not a steady income. We were stressed. We argued every day and when not working, she would often go to her parents' home up in the mountains and wouldn't talk to me until she came home.

My intentions were good and from the beginning she knew about my past. She never spoke of it to her parents, and that really irritated me. Jenelle never said so, but I knew she was ashamed of me. I believe she married me just to spite her father. This affected our relationship and the stress we had because of what her parents thought of me did not help. She was the only child of a father who was well-off and very critical of other people, and he made it known I was not good enough for his daughter. I did my best to be nice to them, but eventually I refused to have any interaction with her parents. That was the beginning of the end to my marriage.

During this time, I was still doing a lot of volunteer work at church. I was looking for the acceptance I had always hoped for, but it was never realized. A new pastor was hired and after a time of getting settled in and bringing together his staff, Eddie Crabtree, offered me a position over grounds and maintenance and service set-up. I was now in the church environment everyday and what I witnessed really turned me off.

All of this church's outreach programs came to an end and service events were being run like a business. There was no genuine show of compassion for anyone and those who held the church together between the time when Curtis left and Eddie became pastor, were rudely kicked out of the church. People stopped coming and it was an ugly time. One afternoon I was driving Eddie and his assistant Richard Dent, back to the church office after lunch. When he was telling us what changes were being made that would affect how each service was conducted, he laughed and said, "I get paid to do this." I kept asking myself if this was something I really wanted to be a part of. I wanted to use my experience to help people, but not in an environment like this.

About a year passed when Eddie had his new office manager give me an ultimatum—choose between my position at his church or the job I had in the evenings. For the six-and-a-half years I'd spent in prison, I was told what to do in a demeaning tone of voice. What this person said did not agree with me at all. To this day my personality is not one of a soft push-around kind.

I told the office manager what I thought of Eddie and then I told the secretary to remove my name from the church register. I quit my job and walked out the door. I had no respect for a person that would hide behind his position and delegate to someone else a responsibility he lacked the intestinal fortitude to do himself.

There were three worship services and special events almost every week and Eddie wanted me to always be available to open up and lock down the building. This was my expected service to God. I kept my job in the evenings to better myself financially and no one had the right to tell me I couldn't just because it's not what they thought I should be doing. That's what turned me off so much about church. Because I didn't show up to every service and event the church hosted, I and everyone else were told on Sunday that our priorities were wrong. There was never a service I went to when tithe and offering wasn't taken. Yet I never witnessed a person's life being impacted in a relevant way. It was always about what God, through the church, requires of you. I have witnessed a lot of inappropriate behavior in this environment and yet these people think they are the authoritative voice of God. Where I come from this is what you would call ignorance gone to seed.

I believe the motivation for many of those in church leadership today is knowing there are people who have no direction spiritually and will submit everything to what they hope is real. And when you play with a person's emotions in an environment that's meant to be holy, you are walking on dangerous ground. I had had enough. It would be two years before I walked into a church building again and after experiencing what I did, it took another five years. What I had hoped to find in the evangelical church movement of today proved to be a false representation of the Gospel. And it was only by the divine intervention of God that I ever came back.

Soon after my wife and I left the church, I was offered a job in the area of my home town and we relocated. We continued to have our problems and were living together separately. Days would go by without speaking to each other.

When eating dinner at a restaurant or any time we were in a public place, Jenelle would openly flirt with other men. I watched her do this but I never said anything until one evening when we were at a restaurant talking, her countenance changed. She stared at a nicely dressed young man as he made his way across the room and her eyes never left him. I told the waiter to bring our check and asked my wife if she would be interested in going over to his table to introduce herself. Sarcastically she said that might just happen, so I got up and left the restaurant. Jenelle caught up to the car as I was leaving and we went home. I never accused her of having an affair, but I often wondered.

We were not intimate and hadn't been for quite some time. I wasted my evenings at home looking at pornography online. At that time I was willing to do just about anything and I would never have thought at age thirty my life could be so empty.

Jenelle told me she was going on a vacation to Cancun with her mother and while she was gone I found her diary. Nothing prepared me for what she had written. I was far from being perfect, but to know that my wife was repulsed by my mere presence, was more than I could take. I frequently read self-help books in an attempt to feel better about myself and learn how to interact with people. I did what these pages suggested but in reality, it didn't work.

My self-image was fragile and after reading my wife's thoughts, it crushed what little confidence I had. For six years we were together and I tried to do the right things, but it seemed as though my past was always held against me. I couldn't figure out how to escape it. That day we were mentally separated and it was a few weeks later when Jenelle asked me for a divorce. I gladly moved out. I had hoped my marriage could bring an end to rejection but it proved to be just the opposite, and that is what hurt most.

It was during this time, I was told how to contact my biological sister and we met. I never knew how close she really was. Immediate family members had adopted me and they'd agreed to never reveal their identities. On top of everything else, my childhood was a lie.

My sister was five when they took me away and she had the memory of a brother, but she didn't know what happened to me. There were times during holidays, weddings and funerals both she and my biological mother were in the same room with me, and no one would ever tell us who each other were. After we met, she introduced me to some of our relatives. They talked about my biological parents and events prior to the adoption.

My mother left her husband because he was an alcoholic and would abuse her. He showed up one evening drunk, beat her and raped her, and it was in this act of violence that I was conceived. I did not learn the whole story but they said I looked like my father and in frustration of what had happened to her, my mother would beat me.

Enough questions were asked to learn that every man on his side as far back as our family tree could be traced had been a drunk and a woman abuser. I have an aunt on my biological father's side of the family who wrote a book titled, Whisky's Song. It's a poetic account of how children are affected by alcoholic parents. We have never met but if you can find the book, it is a sad depiction of the typical American family I was born into.

I was shown a picture of my father, who at the time it was taken, was probably in his early fifties. I looked just like him. They were willing to give me his address but I didn't want it. You would think a son would want to know his father, but this was not so with me. I knew what would happen if he were to enter a room with me there. The only thing he had ever done was give seed, but the legacy he left me with and the environment I had to grow up in because of how he lived his life caused me to hate even the thought of this man. Praised among the "Who's Who in American Art" Bill Cross failed as a man, and a father.

My abuse continued for three years and it became severe enough that family got involved. They gave my mother a choice of adoption or they would have her other children taken, so she gave me up. I asked questions on both sides of my family to try to understand what happened and they told me about some of the things she'd done.

Apart from the beatings, she would pull chunks of my hair out and would lock me in a closet with no food or water while she was out on a drunken binge. After passing feces, I would wipe it on walls or myself and be in this for days at a time. An aunt who is on my adoptive mother's side of the family said the first time she saw me there were sores on my arms and different parts of my body that appeared to be cigarette burns. This was how my mother treated me during the first three years of my life.

This woman had messed me up. Now that I understand, it's no wonder why I behaved so badly as a child. I never had a desire to meet her and I did not stay in contact with my sister. It didn't feel as though she really wanted me to be around. She was too concerned about protecting her mother. I wanted nothing to do with that part of my life because the anger and pain were all too real. Since then, the only time we have seen each other was at the funeral of a cousin who was my age.

When I'd first gone home after being released from prison, my mother had everyone get together at her sister's house so we could eat. This cousin, who was still living at home, had a keg tapped on ice in the back yard and he poured me a beer. When I told him I didn't want it he looked at me really strange. He asked me why I didn't want to drink with him and that's when I told him I had become a Christian.

He cussed me out and said I was weak. He went out of his way to put me down every time I came around. It got to the point where I avoided him, but over the years I heard stories about how his life fell apart. At the young age of forty he suffered a drug-induced heart attack that killed him. The drug addicts who were there stood around and watched him as he died and did nothing about it. That's a hell of a way to die.

At his wake I saw someone I thought might be my sister, and when I walked over to ask her name, is when she recognized me. There was a heavy uneasiness in the air and as we talked a woman came over and asked my sister who I was. The look on this woman's face was priceless…..when my sister told her mother she should recognize me because I was her son. I knew who she was by name and had seen her walking around, but I had no desire to speak to her. The way she tucked her tail and ran was one of the greatest feelings I've ever experienced, and I didn't have to say a word. Carol, I hope one day you will read this book and make things right with God.

It was during the separation from my wife that I met my sister, and was exposed to the truth of my families past. Jenelle filed for a divorce and I didn't contest it, and in six months it was done. It's what my wife wanted, so she was made to pay for it. I wanted out with no ties so everything we had, as little as it was stayed with her in the apartment. I was mad but did what I thought the man should do and only my clothes left with me.

When our separation happened, she was driving her father's convertible, but she also wanted the car I was driving. I asked her to let me keep it because she made a lot more money than I did and could afford another car. She then got ugly about it and had her attorney serve me papers. What Jenelle did upset me and knowing I had left her everything, I made a phone call and told her where she could meet me that afternoon, saying I would then give her the car. When she asked why I wanted her to meet me at this particular location, I told her I was going to drive our car into the river and after fishing it out, the car would be all hers. She knew I wasn't kidding and said the papers would be withdrawn.

I got really bitter about what happened and did something I'm not proud of. There was a small loan amount still on the car and I never made another payment. Because both of our names were on the title and I couldn't be found, she had to finish paying it off. It was wrong for me to do that but it was my way of payback for all the frustration she and her parent's had given me. Between my wife and her parents, what went on behind the scenes at church and finding out the truth about my family, I shut down emotionally.

I was angry. Just as my life seemed to take on meaning it all came apart and I was again left with the feeling of being a failure. This was when I turned and went bad. I cursed at God saying, "I hate you!" My hopes were buried once again under a lifetime of anger and regret. The only way I knew how to deal with my anger was by using alcohol and drugs, and I did every day.

*As a dog returns to its vomit, so a fool repeats his foolishness.*
Proverbs 26:11

# CASUALTIES OF CHOICE

With a church building on virtually on every street corner and the false religions of this world claiming to be the way, why are people so intent on escaping to misery? Have you ever wondered why most of the people you see have a scowl on their face? What do people have to actually look forward to each day?

If you did not have the good fortune of being born with a silver spoon in your mouth or one of the pretty people being lured in by the entertainment industry and its promise of stardom, your life has been one of uncertainty.

People of my generation and younger have watched our hopes of a comparable lifestyle to that of the baby boomers slowly erode away. We want what they have worked for all of their lives, and we want it now. This is what government and businesses for profit have gambled on and won. And now that jobs are no longer fulfilling and personal debt is owed to everyone under the sun, stress is boiling over and the flow of liquid encouragement is at an all time high to try and escape despair.

The culture we live in today is cold; it is unkind and it can be cruel. You really don't know why people act the way they do until you have lived like they do. "It's called survival." Like people have done to me, I have walked by the down and outs and never once gave them another thought. No emotion, no hope and all alone.

Everybody is hurting because we have all had to wake up to that sickening realization of living in the same circumstance another day, mad at life. We've become so accustomed to this surrounding that no one gives any thought to what could be. Every day the masses escape to clouded justification, for this is a place of laughter with those who are just like you. Misery wants company and every discussion is inevitably about the question: "Why did this happen to me?"

If you have ever watched the entertainment channels, you know places like Miami and Washington, DC are must-see destinations for partygoers, where self-indulgence is nonstop. It's in places like these where you see just how twisted and confused people really are. If you only knew what your next door neighbor did to find satisfaction it would intrigue most you. The stories you hear about but no one wants to talk about because of its lewdness, and the pull it has on your dark side.

Anything that satisfies a demented imagination attracts the masses. I have seen thousands of people in clubs high on Ecstasy with a martini in their hand, while dancing to a rave beat with hardly a stitch of clothing on. These people do in public what the rest of you watch on a porno film, and they're not ashamed of their actions. All for the enjoyment of the moment. And should you have money or drugs, they will bare it for you...

Every night these clubs rock as people throw away millions of dollars in their attempt to feel good and be wanted. Environments like this are never at a loss for an audience hoping to live out twisted fantasies.

Just a few days after my divorce was final, I drove out of town. I headed south once again to bartend on the beach. Miami thrives on sensuality and how I presented myself physically greatly affected the work I was offered. My looks and physical build gave me this opportunity, and I took advantage of it. The scars on my body were eye-catching and women were intrigued.

Everyone asked how it happened, and when I said it was the result of a fight, it only made me more appealing. That lure of being a "bad boy" attracted all the women I wanted.

Men are not the only john's cruising the streets, night clubs and strip joints hunting for someone young and fresh to satisfy their sexual hunger. On days not at the bar, I would strip or be an escort for the women who paid my price. Sex was nothing more than a warm bed to sleep in and money in my pocket. I had a different person every night and there were few boundaries.

Sex for hire is impersonal and most tricks end without names being exchanged. The younger women are exploring the thrill and older women are usually either lonely or acting out in anger for what their significant other did to them. There is nothing glamorous about this lifestyle and the effect it has on a person's self-image is degrading. What you see and the physical acts you commit with another person will twist your imagination, and if it was something you enjoyed, nothing will stand in the way of satisfying that desire. This inward depravity is what makes prostitution one of the oldest professions known to mankind.

Every dollar I made went to self-gratification. Cocaine was my choice of stimulant and alcohol put me to sleep. There were days I didn't eat; my only goal was getting high or meeting the next trick. I lived in a blur of alcohol, drugs and sex to escape what I thought to be a life that had no purpose, as do many of the people you know.

I made money but I never had anything to show for it. I smoked it, snorted it and drank it away. I went to the gentlemen's club and met several strippers. They would come to the restaurant at night and drinks would flow all around, and after leaving work, we went to the after hours clubs.

These places were often someone's home or a private members club and you only knew about the time and location if you were invited. Once you're there everything was accepted as long as it was not forced. Doctors, business owners and attorneys, professionals from every class of people attended, and these parties never ended.

A lot of these people had money and this was their playground. I witnessed, and took part in things seen on HBO or read in smut novels. You hear about the rich and famous Playboy Mansion parties because of the popularity of those involved, but they are not the only ones to indulge in the pleasures of sin. These freak shows take place in every city and in every neighborhood, crossing economics, education and both genders. Alcohol and drugs fuel straight sex, gay sex and orgies and this lifestyle has many casualties.

The whole time I was in Miami, I lived out of my car. I went to a gym that was a fight club and this is where I exercised and showered and then left to go to work. The members at this gym were the bartenders and security for all of the clubs on the beach, and we took advantage of the many fringe benefits. They would come to the bar where I worked and the drinks were provided at no charge. When I got off of work, I went to their club and was given a VIP pass.

These are the places you see everyone from the young and old to the rich and poor, all hoping to realize the emotions everyday life has never afforded them. I've seen entertainers and athletes to high level government officials, all secluded behind roped-off and curtained doors doing things they hope the public will never realize.

Alcohol and drugs on every table and complete strangers indulge together in lewd acts of every kind imagined. Young girl's, barely legal, if at all, scream at and worship the fame of those who use their public image to score. I have never asked a famous person for their autograph and I never will. They put their pants on just like me and after watching these people doing the things they do, what makes me or anyone else want to emulate their lifestyle, other than pure ignorance? These people are cold and calculated, and knowing these establishments desire their presence and the money they bring, there is no code of conduct.

I was in this environment every night and the hopes I've seen shattered are too many to number. I eventually grew weary of this lifestyle and one morning after leaving the gym, I drove out of town. I didn't know where I was going; I just knew that I wanted to get away.

I have always had an issue with authority figures, especially when that authority was abused. All of my life another person's will had been forced upon me and my fuse was very short. One evening I found myself sitting at a bar listening to a live band and without any warning, a police officer threw me to the floor. I was then hand-cuffed and literally dragged to his cruiser. I did not cooperate because of how he had accosted me, and when he put me in the back seat of his car, he drew blood. My wrists were cuffed and I was unable to defend against his strikes. I was taken to jail and held in a processing cell. Nobody would say why I was arrested and because I was upset, I refused to give my name and let them take fingerprints.

Two officers entered the cell and threw me down, causing my head to hit a concrete divider. They took my wallet, removed my shoes and left me barefooted. I was dazed and when I stood up, there was blood everywhere from a big gash above my left eye. Now I was mad. They came back to see the extent of my injury and I said, "When you come in here, come deep." This was the second time they had drawn blood and I was ready to fight.

A few minutes later six officers entered the cell. As the door opened, I kicked the first one right in his mouth.....and the fight was on! It was not a fair fight at all. They beat me. Pepper spray, billy clubs, stomps to the groin, punches to my face, you name it, they did it and they taunted me the whole time.

While all of this was going down, the handcuffs were still on my wrists and they finally got shackles on my legs. When it was over, they took me to a local hospital and had to do a CAT scan to determine what injuries I had suffered.

One of the officers hit me so hard with a billy club that it drew blood on my neck and to this day there is minimal feeling in my left arm and shoulder. I was covered in blood and the doctor had to put stitches in my face and multiple bandages on my body. The police then took me back to jail and I went through processing. After everything that happened, there was still no explanation for the arrest.

Several hours later, they escorted me to a magistrate's office and said the charges against me were drunk and disorderly conduct. Bail was set at $100. I was furious. They pulled my personal belongings and I took money from the wallet to bail myself out. I then made a phone call to a woman who had given me her number at a bar a few days before and to my surprise, she came to pick me up.

This woman worked for a law firm and she made arrangements for me to meet with an attorney. I didn't have any money for an attorney and this woman was a single mother, so she didn't have any money either. So I looked up my adoptive mother's phone number and made the call. When I told her what had happened she sent me the $1,500 that would cover my attorney's fees. I was shocked. I hadn't seen or spoken to my mother for several years and I have often thought this was an expression of her penance.

Pictures of my injuries had been taken and pending charges against these officers began. A few days into this process, the attorney said an officer who was kicked during the fight pressed charges and there was a felony warrant issued for my arrest. He then advised me to turn myself in. I went through processing again and when they said my bail was $100, I could not believe it. This wasn't right; I knew they were covering up something

Because of the pictures, my statements and witness accounts, the officer's report was questioned and the police department had no defense for the charges of assault and battery filed by my attorney. So on the appointed court date, the attorney met with a judge and prosecutor to present my defense and within thirty minutes charges were dropped and a document was filed to expunge all records of the incident. But there was a clause: I had to leave the city and not return.

No apology, no compensation for lost work, no nothing. It's now well beyond the statute of limitations and I know that my vindication will never be satisfied but for my personal pleasure I want to say publically, the criminals guilty of this crime represented the city of Memphis, Tennessee.

The attorney said what had been documented was a case of mistaken identity. My profile fit a description of someone else they were looking for and the arresting officer admitted he "could have" been wrong. He then advised me a lawsuit would be difficult because I had no money, no witnesses willing to testify and it was the police department's word against mine about how the altercation went down.

And you wonder why there is so little respect for law enforcement today? This happens way too often, but what can one person do against a system looking out for its own? What could I do? I packed my car and drove out of town.

I had no idea what tomorrow would bring, nor did I care. Once again, I didn't know where to turn. I ended up out in the Midwest living out of a motel. I had a job as a waiter and I'd get drunk every evening. Then one day without any warning I heard a loud voice say, "NO!" It startled me. I knew who it was, so I went back to where I was staying and waited; it had been sixteen years since the last time God spoke to me.

Less than an hour later my cell phone rang and it was my adoptive father, the first and only time in my life he had ever called. He said his health was bad and he'd like to see me. That day I drove 1,500 miles to Fredericksburg, Virginia. I don't know why, but I wanted an opportunity to make things right with him. From that time on, until he passed away, we had a polite but distant relationship. Looking back, I am amazed at how everything that happened played itself out. God knew how I was living, but He reached out to me anyway.

> *All of us used to live that way, following the passionate desires and inclinations of our sinful nature. By our very nature we were subject to God's anger, just like everyone else. But God is so rich in mercy, and he loved us so much, that even though we were dead because of our sins, he gave us life when he raised Christ from the dead. (It is only by God's Grace that you have been saved!)*
>
> Ephesians 2:3-5

Once again, I was at my worst. I can't tell you how often I thought of crashing the car again or doing something stupid to end my misery. I would do anything to try to run away from what was in my past, but I could never outrun the memories. As a youth, people told me I was stupid and I would never amount to anything—I was worthless, a trouble maker, mean and hateful and I'd end up in prison. And to no one's surprise, I accomplished everything they said.

My school counselor told me I was no good and I'd never see twenty-one. You think what is said to a child doesn't affect their self-perception? The biggest lie you have ever told a child is the adage, *"Sticks and stones may break my bones, but names will never hurt me."* Do you remember telling your children that lie? The bruises went away, but words have haunted every day of my life. Like so many people of this present culture, a person's lifestyle reflects what they really think about themselves.

Shortly after coming home, I accepted a job at *Ristorante Renato*, and *The Prime Rib*, in Washington, DC. Both are nationally recognized restaurants. I worked seven days a week as a waiter and made really good money between the two jobs, but once again I smoked it, snorted it and drank it away. I lived out of my car or a motel room, and the restaurant I was at determined which city the car would be parked in.

One late night, having had several drinks with a maitre d' after hours and knowing not to drive, I laid the seat back and went to sleep. A couple of hours later a loud noise woke me up to see three police officers with flashlights telling me to get out of the car. I was honest with them about drinking, and I mentioned the restaurant that employed me was where my car was parked. It made no difference to them and I was handled quite roughly.

I did not want a repeat of my last meeting with law enforcement so they had their way. I was arrested and taken to jail. I had to spend that night and all of the next day in a holding cell with about fifty other foul-smelling, foul-mouthed, pissed-off people just like me. After the court hearing and being released, it was up to me to find the processing jail to get my personal belongings.

Upon arriving, I was greeted by a cocky, bodybuilder-type loud-mouth. He reminded me of a scrawny kid who was beaten up by the neighborhood bully and now he had some authority that went to his head. He was all up in my face talking about slapping someone so I got an attitude back at him.

I respect law enforcement's civil responsibility but not the person, especially when they act like this guy did. The mentality he had is the reason why most people don't like police officers. There is no denying the good many police officers have done for other people or that the job can be dangerous, but it does not give a public servant the right to be rude and arrogant. If you want to be respected you have to be willing to give some.

I made claim to what was mine and he followed me through the building running his mouth, telling me what he was going to do if one more word was said. So I turned to walk backwards while going out the door, and my way of saying goodbye was blowing a kiss at him followed with the middle finger. I didn't want to go back to jail but I wished he would have done something; I wanted to hit this guy. He didn't follow me outside.....and I figured as much. No words needed to be said. That gesture was my thought about him and life in general.

Why is the civil police force so aggressive, and why the disdain for the American people? This is a subject most people are unaware of and you better make the time to find out what police officers are being trained for. The term "peace officer" no longer applies. What's happening nation wide is militarizing the civil police and equipping them with military-grade armament and weapons in preparation for civil unrest. All of this is funded by Homeland Security.

One example is the events that took place in Waco, Texas. I think we all remember what happened, but only the knowledge of what a biased media reported was made known. Another place to witness the inhumane and brutal treatment of people are video websites. Officers are frequently taped abusing their authority by using excessive force to subdue an individual or committing outright assault on innocent people. With few exceptions these criminals are above the law they've sworn to uphold, and seldom held accountable.

That night after work we were drinking and the bartender was already drunk. For some reason he started running his mouth. I was still mad about the day's events and I said to him if he was so bad to come across the bar, and he tried. I reacted by grabbing the collar of his shirt and slammed him headfirst to the floor.

The other people there didn't know how to respond as I threw my drink back and headed for the door. I got into my car and left the city before something else happened. No explanation, I was gone. That was the last night I worked at The Prime Rib.

The next day I accepted a job at a river-front restaurant as a bartender and I broke up more fights than I made drinks. Every time alcohol and fools get together, stupid things happen. I've seen people shot, knifed and beaten by other drunks and even by the people that work bar security, who should use their position of authority to be diplomatic. But this is seldom the case. They are, in fact, ego-maniacs that get off on inflicting pain upon someone else.

It only takes a few drinks to drastically alter a person's behavior and I've witnessed really nice people become quite another person. I can't tell you how many times men have eyed an attractive woman sitting alone at the bar and as they make their move, the wedding ring disappears. Two complete strangers and quite frequently, next door neighbors.

It does not matter what their economic class or education, race, gender or sexual orientation is. People commit really vulgar acts and make very hurtful comments when influenced by a mood-altering substance. Most of the time other people find it amusing and will even encourage the situation. I have, on many occasions, asked all parties involved to leave.

I'm not referring to college-age kids. I'm describing the behavior of adults in their 30s, 40s and 50s doing what you would never expect from a person their age. And you wonder why each generation is a little more screwed up than the one before.

This is the environment I was working in the night my father passed away. After my stepmother called to let me know what had just happened, the manager let me clock out and started feeding me drinks. Bar patrons did the same and this went on for several hours. Any excuse was a good one.

My father had softened in his later years and my stepmother told me he had met with a friend who was a preacher and had made his peace with God. And that's when she told me what happened as he died.

He had undergone a major back surgery and while they were in the recovery room, my stepmother said he was talking to her. She said his eyes were closed and his complexion turned dark red. She then saw him reach up with one hand to point and he grabbed at something with his other hand, and a smile came upon his face as he flat lined. The doctors rushed in, but there was no bringing him back.

My stepmother believes he saw a glimpse of heaven and he was ready to go home. My father hadn't been to church in probably twenty-five years and based on her witnessing what he did as he died, it would make you think there is something else out there. I was happy for him because he was no longer in pain, and the realization of what he might have seen sat heavy on my conscience.

I worked at several different bars and would stay just long enough to get mad and then quit. I had no tolerance for people's arrogance or stupidity. My job made me an extrovert but when not at work I became an introvert. People often said I should smile more and my response was to tell them what they could go and do with their advice. What did I have to smile about?

In and around the party scene it was rumored I was rude and arrogant, and truthfully I didn't want to get to know anyone. I could care less what someone thought about me. By this time I had seen all of the ugliness in people I cared to see. I had made up in my mind I would never be hurt again.

My behavior was out of control and it wasn't just a buzz anymore; I was getting trashed. I went to work high and would leave intoxicated. At work I'd do a line of cocaine on the bar or in a bathroom with a customer or someone working at the restaurant, and I didn't care who knew about it. Days would be lost. I worked and would function, but I had no memory of what happened. I was doing my best to escape the painful memories that haunted me. I was inconsiderate to other people and I didn't understand or really care about what was happening. It was all about me and whatever I could do to not have to face what I thought of me. Sound familiar?

How I behaved during this time of recklessness, whether conscious or unconscious, was payback time for all that had been done to me. I wanted people to know what it was like to hurt and I was very good at it. Remember, hurt people hurt people.

Too often I would be found in situations where I should have been hurt or ended up back in jail, but there always seemed to be a presence that kept me safe. I would be wasted on a substance and come to myself later, not always knowing the surroundings I was in, but I was okay. This has happened way too many times to put on paper. It was not until I wrote this book that I understood the good that would come from what I had experienced.

The stories I could tell you! Until you have been there you will never understand what it's like to wish about a life you see other people live, believing the experience is something you do not deserve. To look in a mirror and see emptiness, hopelessness and hatred staring back is a loathsome realization.

People have no hope because they think so little of themselves. The majority of people you know, no matter how well they clean up live a lifestyle like this. And it's not a small number who have gone to an extreme like I have.

If you've had an experience anywhere close to this, you know what I'm saying is real. But for those of you still trapped in that place of self-gratification and doing what you can to provide for me, my and mine, I want to challenge you to take some time and look around.

All people really want is for someone to be nice and not try to get something from them. But in the day and time we live, with everybody's fast-pace life and doing what they can to survive, a genuine show of compassion for other people is a very rare commodity. So people stay stuck in what they think it will always be like and never have an opportunity to enjoy what could be.

Why do you think the industries catering to people's emotions are so successful? From government and universities to Hollywood, music and sports, casinos and nightlife entertainment venues, pharmaceutical drug companies, alcohol distilleries and pornography, it's all about money and fame, sex and feel-good. These people aren't stupid. They know what will sell and they use this platform to capitalize on your misery. Talk about the fleecing of America.

There is a purpose behind it and these corporations are run by people influenced by a greed for money at any expense. They do not care about how your life may end up. We the people have become this nation's most exploited commodity, and both government and institutions being run by their inner societies are reaping the benefits of our ignorance.

This is the reason why everyone you know has a scowl on their face. Hope has been shattered and people have been left alone to try to pick up the pieces with no knowledge of how to put it all together again. If you have really paid attention to the chronological order of these chapters, you will know they are an accurate account of how people now live. They base their perception of truth upon what feels good and tolerant only of those who are accepting of whatever lifestyle they choose to live.

Truth is a value few people give any consideration to and is seldom deemed relevant for the time we live in. Political and cultural correctness is now the rave affecting every aspect of American life and sadly, even Christian influence. This proves that our decision process has been greatly influenced by what a confused and depraved humanity has deemed relevant rather than by what the Bible teaches.

I wrote about these experiences for those of you who will surely criticize what I say in the following chapters. I know you, and I know why you act the way you do. I was you—casualties of choice who base their perception of truth upon how things are, will now be convincingly confronted with the truth, as it speaks for itself.

Nothing I say is in any way similar to the empty words that fill the pages of books on Christian living today. Nor will it be the same as the family member or neighbor you might have who tells you every time they see you that God loves you and you are in their prayers. They think this is a witness God is approving of, but in reality are disciples of another gospel and yet to realize God's love for His creation demands absolute obedience to His law.

The rest of this book describes what God did to lead a disobedient son back to His purpose. And it can be the example for you, if you so choose...

# TIME TO COME HOME
꙳ ꙳

It did not matter how inebriated I became or what sin I was laying in, my awareness of God's presence never went away.

*If I make my bed in hell, behold, You are there.*
Psalms 139:8b

It is not always what you know God did for you. In many of the situations you find yourself in, it's what you think God didn't do that can have the greatest impact when you realize He was right there all along.

I hated life and my dependence in substance abuse became repulsive. Nothing I did could satisfy the desire I had to get out of the mess I'd made of my life. I was miserable. There was no way for me to know what was happening at that time, but looking back, I believe God was deliberately making my circumstances uncomfortable.

One Sunday morning as I was driving past a new church that had been built in my old neighborhood, I turned around and decided to go in. I had no idea why. I was still drunk from the night before and walking in the door felt like I had come home, so I kept going back.

I had no fond memories from my childhood and I had no desire to stay in this area for any length of time because the pain was still very much real. But I knew I was here for a reason. I made an appointment to meet with the pastor of this church and I was honest with him about my life and what I thought of people.

The behavior I've witnessed in the past and how I had been treated should not have happened in a place of worship, but it did. For me to open up and tell people about myself in a church environment only to have them say I'm not welcome is rude and violates Scripture. Yet it's happened—ministry leaders have told me to leave and not come back. I don't care how tough you think you are…..that hurts. There are people like my father who will not go to church today because they were turned off by someone's arrogance, pride, or fear of being around people like me. It should not be this way! *Who are you to ever judge another person?*

> *For I was born a sinner—yes, from the moment my mother conceived me.*
>
> Psalms 51:5

In spite of how I had been treated in the past, it was not going to stop me this time. I didn't have to know the person or even like them to hear what God might say through them. I had often watched Christian TV channels hoping to hear something that would answer my questions but sadly, there were only a few ministers who said anything worth listening to. Most told a story irrelevant to my circumstances or the sermon was so deep I couldn't understand what was said. It seemed to me their only motivation was to encourage people to give money. It was the same stuff I'd heard twenty years ago and the people I knew that went to church on Sunday and Wednesday are the same now as they were back then.

Preachers are always talking about seven steps to this and twelve things to do that will change whatever. A humorous story or a yelping holler that did not challenge me in my circumstance is not something a preacher needs to be talking about. Never in all of my years had a minister gotten real with me. Everybody attempts to show they are loving and caring and will say only what they think will make a listener feel good. This is not how to communicate with people like me. A significant difference in the message needs to be made by actually doing something to help people right where they are. If what is said from the pulpit does not relate to or have an impact upon the current issues of today, then it's not the Gospel.

For there to be any lasting change in the hopelessness of people today, church leaders need to stop hosting baby-sitting sessions two and three times a week inside their four-walled comfort zone and get busy leading congregations in an outreach to those in their community who have a need they can help meet. This is the example that must be set before a depraved and godless culture will seriously consider the message of the Gospel of Jesus Christ. The time of talking about God is over. Either put up or shut up.

What I just said is my perception of most people in church, especially those in leadership positions. After working in bars as long as I have, I developed an eye for seeing what a person thinks, wants and is about to do. I can read a room like a book. I'm not above making a mistake but there was always something about a person's mannerisms that would cause me concern, and rather be wrong than right and have to deal with a situation, I would then have that person removed.

How church leaders choose to live speaks volumes, and people could care less about what they say if their lifestyle proves different. Give me specifics to look forward to, and don't just use stories from days gone by to say what God is getting ready to do. Tickling someone's emotions is not good enough. People are tired of the same old empty words. They need to experience what community leaders are prepared to do to help change their circumstances right now. A Christian's lifestyle witness is the example hurting people are looking to for direction. Their focus should be: "What can I do to reach people with this message?"

There were times when circumstances or my actions did not warrant God's attention, but often people who didn't know me would say things that left no doubt God had His mind on me. The following story is just one example. I knew the time of my running was over. It was time to come home.

One day at work on the river, there was an older couple eating by themselves and from time to time I'd stop at their table to check if they needed anything. Small talk was made and they were very nice people. I asked a few questions and the gentleman said he had just left a thirty-year high-level government job to pastor a church. He also said they were on vacation visiting family in the area.

I didn't say much about myself other than telling them I'd just recently started going back to church. My life was still a mess and I had no reason to believe it would be any different. While signing a credit card slip after paying, he looked at me and said, *"Billy, God doesn't call the qualified, He qualifies the called."*

I looked at him and asked, "How do you know this?"

He responded, *"I see it in you. You have something to say that people need to hear."* Tears began to run down my face as he talked. What he said made an impact on me and I will never forget it.

It always seemed like just when hope was fading, regardless of where I was, God would do something to get my attention. It was like dangling a carrot on a string in front of the donkey close enough to smell but just out of reach, and it frustrated me. Why did my life attract what kept me separated from God when so many people had said God was calling me to Him for a purpose only He knew? Throughout my life, God revealed Himself in so many different ways I could not deny His reality, and I had no clue what He was about to do.

I made it known to the pastor that my reason for attending his church was for the purpose of restoring my relationship with God. I told him I had no desire to get involved with the inner workings of his ministry. He agreed and said that would be okay. I went to this church off and on and about a year passed before we met again. As we talked, he said my problem was that I did not believe in myself and the healing I was seeking would come through my worship of God. I knew what he said was right. He then suggested I read scriptures in the New Testament that revealed who I was as a Christian, and it took me awhile to begin doing this.

Even though I was attending church, my self-image would not allow me to think I was worthy of God's love. I had lived an ugly existence and this shame dictated every decision I ever made. My escape was drinking alcohol and using drugs and every night a bottle of wine accompanied me to bed. I longed to change, but I did not have the courage to give up that comfort. This was an everyday attempt to find peace; it's what helped me get the little sleep I did.

I did not speak to anyone at church for quite some time; I came, I listened and I left. People stayed away from me because of my attitude and the unwillingness I had to allow anyone to get close. That's what I wanted. It was the only way I knew how to protect myself.

Since my youth I had wanted to live in the hope of what I imagined life could be like, and now at my age this was what I thought about most. All of my life I've never had anything of value to call my own or completed anything I could be proud of until this time in my life revealed why so many bad things happened to me, and what I was able to do with the experiences I have learned from.

What Curtis Gray had said to me about God allowing certain events in my life had happened, and now I wanted to experience whatever it was that I had to look forward to. I knew it would not be through a secular job. No job in my past had been meaningful or helped someone to live a better life, yet ever since the time in prison when God revealed Himself, this had been a hope of mine.

As a child, life never gave me an opportunity to dream about what I wanted to be when I grew up. It was not until the endless hours of being in isolation, reading books that were available, that I began to do this. Most of the books available to inmates in prison are no more than thoughtless entertainment and they would leave me fantasizing about a subject I'd read. But every now and then a good book came along that told a story of achievement and I would think, "One day I will do something significant." I could never have imagined my life's story would be my dream come true. (Think on this statement!)

> *"For My thoughts are not your thoughts, Nor are your ways My ways," declares the LORD. "For as the heavens are higher than the earth, So are My ways higher than your ways And My thoughts than your thoughts."*
> Isaiah 55:8-9

After my release from prison, I embraced the first industry to embrace me. And not really knowing why until now, I have gained a wealth of knowledge in understanding why the majority of people today gather at these watering holes called bars. The conversations are embellishments of who people are and where they come from, what they do, who they know, where they have been and how much they make.....all to impress. As drinks are consumed, masks come off, insecurities are made known and true emotions of shattered hope are revealed. Here is when you see a person for who they really think they are.

I have served drinks to tens of thousands, all of whom are lost in that place of not knowing: "Why did this happen to me?" The entrapment of self-gratification is why the masses who know no better happily escape to clouded justification. For this is a place of laughter with those who are just like you. Alcohol helps people feel good temporarily, but they are left with a sickening realization of being in that same circumstance another day. I have seen it break up homes, send people to jail and bury quite a few with no consideration of age or gender.

Misery wants company and attracts its own. Every day from the other side of a bar people would tell me stories much like mine and I was tired of hearing it. I didn't want to be like everyone else for the rest of my life and never have anything of value to offer another person. I knew in order for me to change there would have to be a willingness to let go of what was in my past and I would never have guessed how God would begin this process.

There are few things that have ever been of any significance to me, therefore very little is worth my time or attention. Reading the life-changing words of instruction in the Bible have helped me to overcome what has happened in my life so I can become the man God created me to be.

As I look forward to my thoughts being read, I'm overwhelmed at what God has helped me to express through this writing, and I have found what is to be a significant part of my future. All because of reading the Bible and asking God to help me understand what is expected of me.

There were times when I attended church and the person speaking would call me up front and say, *"God has a call on your life to preach the Gospel."* I would listen and then go sit down, thinking how badly he or she had mistaken me for someone else. Nothing qualified me to stand in front of people and give any advice on how to live their life, as messed up as mine was.

> *Christ Jesus came into the world to save sinners—and I am the worst of them all.*
> 1 Timothy 1:15b

There's not much sin I haven't known as a bed partner, and this is the shame I have had to overcome. To look in a mirror and hate the person looking back, knowing one does not have the ability to change, becomes crippling. For too long the worst enemy faced was the man in the mirror, and doing what everyone else does in an attempt to change the course of life makes it even harder to get out. When one can find no way to change, there is nothing to encourage hope.

> *Hope deferred makes the heart sick.*
> Proverbs 13:12a

I was tired of running to nowhere I wanted to be. It has taken a lifetime to understand my way was not the right way and I wanted out. I had come to my end and was willing to do whatever it took to find out who I was and why I was here? I can't speak for you, but I did not understand why I was going through the experience when it was happening, and it was not until years later as I looked back over my life that any of it made sense to me.

Seeing how the hand of God moves, protects and provides for you reveals His patience and plan to build a foundation of confidence and trust in His ability to hold you up until you learn how to do it for yourself. There are certain answers only time will reveal. I could not begin to imagine all of these events had been planned and God was setting up what has now become a deliverance from me.

My life's story so exemplifies the culture we have become. And like me, just how far down will a person have to go to realize the only hope they have is not in the god they want, but in the God who is?

The educational system in America is following the example of other countries by not only removing Christian influence from the classrooms, but also by taking away the students' right to express their faith in the only true and living God. Only to promote a humanistic ideology that has unquestionably far-removed any thought of God from today's youth culture, thus setting the precedence for the rest of their life...

I'd never really given this any thought until my study began, and this is when I realized the extent of damage done to a person's self-perception when they grow up having no consciousness of God. Now that God is foremost in my thought process, I realize just how important teaching the truths of Scripture is and its influence upon today's culture, or the lack thereof.

# GOD SPEAKS
80 C8

One thing I have learned about God is that He is a strategist. God will set things up and move other things around to accomplish what He wants done. And God does not have to ask your permission. If God has His mind set on you, there is nothing you can do nor any place you can go where He won't eventually get your attention. Some of us are more hard headed than others and that just means God has to use a more in-your-face approach...

The church I went to had a three-day conference meeting and Sunday was the only service I could make. The guest speaker was Pam Vinnett. As the speaker ministered, she would talk to people individually and just as the service was ending, she came to where I was sitting, took my hand and sang to me. She walked away and then turned around and said to me, *"Come here."* I walked to her and she asked, *"What is your name?"*

In a whisper I answered, "Billy."

She said, *"Billy lift up your hands before the Lord in the name of Jesus. Tonight is a night of surrenderance, total and complete surrenderance. Even as I held your hand as I was singing to you, the Lord said three times you have escaped death, literally. Am I telling the truth in this house?"*

I responded, "Yes."

She then said, *"Not your way, but its God's way or no way in this season. I see you putting your hands to so many different things, but God says, 'this time ask Me where, where it is that you are to put your energies and watch it work.'"* She walked away and I sat down and after about a minute, a copy of this recording was put into my hand.

She was from out in the mid-west and I had never met or spoken to this woman, and I hadn't talked in any detail with anyone else in church, so she could not have known about the events of my life. Yet she read my mail. God now had my attention! And to those of you who say it's wrong for women to preach the Gospel or that the gifts of the Holy Spirit have passed away, what would your defense be to this? I'll answer that for you. You don't have one!

After service was over, I drove to a Christian bookstore and bought eight different translations of the Bible along with an exhaustive concordance, an expository dictionary and several instrumental worship CDs. I stopped going to bars, sold the TV, canceled my gym membership and then I locked myself in the apartment.

For the next year and a half, the only places I went to were church, the grocery store and work. I had no association with anyone outside of church, and even they were few. If it did not have a positive impact on what I thought of me, no time or attention was given to it. Only God was qualified to answer my questions. I had to know, *would these words written in the Bible become reality?*

My study was the New Testament Bible. As an affirmation, I wrote out every passage of Scripture that told me how to live my life as a Christian. In the Gospels I read about how Jesus lived his life and realized this was to be my example. The epistles are the writings that give instructions as to how I am to witness to other people by the conduct of the affairs of my life. It was slow at first, but gradually my attitude began to change.

I would spend hours at a time reading, writing about and cross referencing all the different translations I had so I could get an understanding of what each passage of Scripture meant. I played instrumental music softly and I would get overwhelmed when realizing what God had to say about me. I'd weep, sometimes crying uncontrollably in release of the emptiness and anger I had known from my youth.

I made time for what would bring the change I needed and nothing was allowed to pull me away from my study. As I woke up every morning, the first thing that came to mind was: "How will God reveal Himself to me today?" I read from a daily devotional titled, *Pursuit of His Presence* and that's how each morning started. All of my life had been committed to finding a way to escape what I believed about myself and that's why I went after God with the passion I did.

What I thought was prayer in the past was no more than me complaining about a problem, and the conversation was all about me. Why do all of the talking when you haven't a clue of what to say or do, when God who knows everything is waiting for silence? I had no idea how to correctly pray and as I was telling God everything I needed, I realized it could never happen by my own ability, and that's when I shut up!

Sometimes hours would pass and nothing was said. I would just read, write about and meditate on a message of hope so eloquently described through each page of the Bible. As the months passed, this became the routine of my day and I could not wait to walk into my apartment and hear worship music that was never turned off. Each day there was an expectation of learning something new about God, and with this hope, I waited.

It was during one of these times when God spoke... *"I Am the Lord your God. I have brought you out of bondage. You will have no other god before Me. You will put nothing before your worship of Me. I Am the Lord your God and I Am a jealous God over you. I will show you mercy and I will love you all of your life. Love Me and live for Me."*

This was an audible voice but it was very soft. God's presence was overwhelming and it brought me to my knees. I began to weep because of how inadequate I felt with God's attention focused directly upon me. I was in awe of how real God's presence was.

When God speaks, what can be said in defense of your justification? I had no more excuses and I asked God to forgive me for being in His way. My efforts to try to make right everything that turned out for my wrong was the god of self, and that's why nothing ever worked for me. It took God stripping me of a self-willed motivation to begin the process of time and education He needed to bring healing to my soul.

For the first time in my life I began to understand it's in how I choose to live that my purpose is revealed. Now I no longer had to be concerned about how to provide for myself. When a person is in God's hand, everything of need will be provided. It may not happen when a person thinks it should, but take my word, it shows up right on time. This is God's way of showing He is in control.

In all of my years of alcohol and drug use, nothing had ever intoxicated me the way God's presence did that night. It was not something I read about or a story I heard, this happened to me.

> "Those who accept my commandments and obey them are the ones who love me. And because they love me, my Father will love them. And I will love them and reveal myself to each of them."

John 14:21

While reading this, you have probably come to the conclusion that my parents did not bring me up in a church environment, and I'm nothing like people who have had a Christian upbringing. I've been out there alone, no direction and no hope and I was looking for whatever was real. Church had jaded me and I'm not impressed with people who have never been stained with hard living or don't know what it's like to wish about something they believed they didn't deserve. This experience with God was face to face and as real as it gets!

Scriptures revelation of God is not some fairytale made up to tickle your emotions. God *is reality in its fullness revealed* and He longs to have a relationship with you. To do whatever is necessary to remove anything you're holding on to that would separate you from His presence, so He can then have the opportunity to reveal Himself through you. In truth, at the time I had no idea what was happening, but this experience brought reality to everything I have ever hoped for.

Several of the events that happen in my life are the type of things all of humanity longs to experience for themselves. Since God revealed Himself to me in this way, I am now obligated to say these things to you. There is no self-proclaimed atheist, humanist world-view or false religion that has a leg to stand on to try to tell me different. You have no defense.

The newly released documentary *Religulous* directed and narrated by Bill Maher, has received great reviews for its eye-opening interviews of people and their practices of several different world religions. In all honesty, it does expose the idiocy of what these people believe to be God. I watched this documentary online and understood it for what it really is. Of all the people interviewed, none were able to give a convincing account of their hope in the faith they proclaim. The underlying motive for this documentary is just another attempt to try to discredit the Gospel of Jesus Christ.

What Bill Maher didn't do was interview people who could give him a compelling and biblically-based testimony of how a personal relationship with Jesus Christ has transformed their life. I dare you to do this, Bill Maher! To allow the Spirit of God an opportunity to convict you of your sinful nature and see the stupidity of your humor.

God did not reveal Himself to me through Islam or other world religions like Buddhism and Roman Catholicism. These false religions are the apostate church that's emerging to create a one world religion of interfaithism, which is a belief that all religions, though different in practice, are valid pathways to God.

This was evidenced in 2000 when the United Nations hosted the first ever World Peace Summit, and brought together thousands of this worlds religious and spiritual leaders. It was the initial step towards creating a global religious body that will deceive the already confused.

Think rationally for just a moment—if God is real and this Supreme Being or conscience is what all of these religions want to attain, then why the confusion? Is God confused? I don't think so! God is revealed as the Father of creation, God among us in the redemption of humanity through the person of Jesus Christ and the Spirit of God who lives within each person who acknowledges Jesus as Savior. Apart from this, religion is nothing more than bondage to an ideal that will never be attained. Unlike what false religions teach as the utopic view of spirituality, the Bible reveals God's patient tolerance of His sinful creation through what is known as the dispensation of grace, and the coming judgment upon all of His creation. We have been given one lifetime to prepare for the day when God will judge each person for the life they chose to live.

Because of religious abuse over the eons of time, people have become skeptics of every religion under the sun. Until people are made aware of the kind of change only God can do in someone else's life, they really can't believe it for themselves. But now that I have told you my story, there is no excuse for you. It is beyond belief now; this is what I know to be true. You can argue in disagreement, but it's impossible to argue with conviction.

God is always talking, but so few people ever take the time to listen. There are several ways God will speak to you. One way is through His words of instruction written in the Bible. This is how God has communicated to all of humanity the revelation of His Self-Existence and the plan of salvation that made atonement for the sin and rebellion of His creation. The Bible is the most printed book in world history and has been translated into more than two thousand languages. Its message has endured the test of time.

Another way God speaks is through the preaching of the Gospel of Jesus Christ. This is what every person who claims to be a Christian is called to do, and not just pastors of churches and ministry offices. God also speaks to you through nature. As you look upon the beauty of what has been created, how can you deny God's existence?

As I mentioned earlier, I did not grow up around church and my exposure was very limited, but I knew there was something else beyond what I was seeing. I just couldn't figure out what it was. When I escaped to the woods, I felt safe and my imagination wondered at the beauty of what I saw.

I argued with my science teacher over the stupidity of evolution's theory and I never did my homework. I didn't believe what was being taught even though I had no answers. But now that I've had the opportunity to experience the things I have, I understand the real motive for the teaching of evolution. It is to dumb down a nation's people. It takes more faith to believe the Big Bang theory than to believe there is a God who meticulously created everything. If

Darwinian macro-evolution is your idea of truth, I really feel sorry for you, and the God whom you deny mocks you.

> *He Who sits in the heavens laughs; the Lord has them in derision [and in supreme contempt He mocks them].*
>
> Psalm 2:4

I have, on six different occasions in my lifetime, heard God speak to me in an audible voice that was no different than hearing another person speak to me. I really don't know why. I have never forgotten what God said to me and I remember each time as if it were yesterday.

I know people who have been Christians from the time when they were a child who have never heard the voice of God. Some have even made a doctrine of this. Maybe that's why people said I was crazy to think God would speak to me. If you are of this opinion, you're right. Because of your unbelief, God will never speak to you.

Several times I have had people say things to me that no one but me knew about. And then there were the times I should have died, and yet God protected me.

Why me? This is a question everyone has asked and as you continue to read, I will tell you why. God will also speak to you by the Holy Spirit who bears witness with your spirit—that knowing of when something is wrong or the peace you have when you just know it's right. I know this to be real. God has spoken to me all of my life.

As I studied to learn about what God requires of me, the less I desired to be the person of my past. I thought I had to be perfect before God would do anything, but that idea couldn't have been more wrong. God does not care about where you have been or what may be happening in your life right now. He accepts the gift of who you are. You, in all of your mess, are what God values most; the person you become is God's gift to you.

When that gentleman spoke to me at the river-front restaurant and said *I had something to say that people needed to hear*, it forever closed the door on memories that had robbed me of confidence and opened wide an imagination of what could be if only I believed. God waits on you, and then creates in you an expectation of hope. This hope comes by learning what God has to say about you and then speaking those words of thought-transformation as you pray, talk to yourself and witness to others.

> *And be constantly renewed in the spirit of your mind [having a fresh mental and spiritual attitude].*
>
> Ephesians 4:23

> *"And they overcame him because of the blood of the Lamb and because of the word of their testimony."*
>
> Revelation 12:11a

I have also learned you cannot mature in a relationship with God alone. You need to be receptive to spiritual gifting in other people and listen to what God will have them say. By doing this your convictions will grow stronger. Sometimes what another person might say will be an answer to a question you couldn't figure out. I believe God will use anyone if they will let Him. God is not concerned with your gender; it's your obedience He is seeking.

By this time, everything about me was beginning to change. When people saw me and I told them what was happening, their reaction was always surprise and that look of wonder... I cannot count the times people that know me have approached and commented on a change they see in my countenance and how attractive my smile is. All I can do is look up, and say what God has done for me.

> *This means that anyone who belongs to Christ has become a new person. The old life is gone; a new life has begun!*
>
> 2 Corinthians 5:17

God knows what He is doing and because of my life's experience I am fully persuaded that, if needed, God will set you up and allow things to happen for the purpose of turning your attention to Him, empty of self and broken in spirit. Only then can God be God in your imagination.

# CONFLICTING VIEWS

I have often wondered why God chose me. What of my life's experience did God find value in? I avoided mirrors for the shame of knowing what I've done. It was my belief that I would always live that way. I thought I was not deserving of anything good and that's why I made the decisions I did. No one had ever given me the time of day, and here I was faced with the realization of knowing my Creator wanted to have relationship with me. Talk about something giving you pause for thought.

In twenty years, more than a hundred jobs have come and gone as I tried to figure out what I could do to create a feeling of fulfillment. There was never any thought given to this until my writing began. Not liking people, why did I choose to work in an industry of public service?

Away from work, my personality was cold and aloof, but when at work I was warm and personable and this attracted people to me. It was my lifeline and I only had feelings of accomplishment when I was at work. I was very good at my job, and I began to listen to what I said and took notice of my attention to service. Over time I realized my intent was to do for other people what I hoped would be done to me.

What made me feel good about myself was knowing the good I'd done for someone else. This may be insignificant to a person who has been around family and friends all of their life, but for me it spoke volumes. I believe God was teaching me the importance of knowing what I do and how it affects the way another person is made to feel. In spite of the person I was.

> *"Do to others whatever you would like them to do to you. This is the essence of all that is taught in the law and the prophets."*
>
> Matthew 7:12

From the time I was old enough to understand how to communicate with people, I wanted acceptance and I longed to experience what it was like to know people respected me. As much as I disliked people, I went out of my way to try to be nice. I gave anything in my possession to someone if I thought it would help meet a need they had.

I was cold and indifferent, but at the same time I had compassion for a person when their situation affected me emotionally. I didn't understand why I was so willing to give of myself when people had been so unkind to me. I was kicked around all of my life and still was willing to give of myself, and I believe that is why God allowed me to come through what I experienced and to see from this new perspective.

From my childhood on, the events that happened to me created a negative expectation that influenced how I perceived everything. I was looking for a reason to not trust anyone based on what they said or by what they did. In my opinion, people were no good and I thought I had every right to feel this way, but as I read the Bible and learned about God's opinion of me, I realized just how wrong I was. No matter what I did, God still saw the potential that was in me. This is why God so willingly extends His mercy and kindness, and He forgives so readily. God does this for you to be the example of what He requires of you to do for other people.

> *Strip yourselves of your former nature [put off and discard your old unrenewed self] which characterized your previous manner of life and becomes corrupt through lusts and desires that spring from delusion; And be constantly renewed in the spirit of your mind [having a fresh mental and spiritual attitude], And put*

*on the new nature (the regenerate self) created in God's image,
[Godlike] in true righteousness and holiness.*

Ephesians 4:22-24

*Since God chose you to be the holy people he loves, you
must clothe yourselves with tenderhearted mercy, kindness,
humility, gentleness, and patience. Make allowance for each
other's faults, and forgive anyone who offends you. Remember,
the Lord forgave you, so you must forgive others.*

Colossians 3:12-13

From this point forward everything I say will prove no matter what you do, regardless of whether you want to believe it or not, you will be held accountable. But God has made the way of escape and that choice has been given to you.

Each of us was born with an innate God-likeness but so few are willing to endure the pressures of overcoming what has influenced their past, to then have an opportunity to realize. Should you choose to do things God's way, you will then have the opportunity for that goodness to be realized, by the rebirth of your spirit, once dead and separated from God. This is a spiritual law superseding any circumstance or situation you may find yourself in, and the only thing standing in the way of this discovery is you.

*Give, and you will receive. Your gift will return to you in
full—pressed down, shaken together to make room for more,
running over, and poured into your lap. The amount you give
will determine the amount you get back.*

Luke 6:38

You go through life thinking you're in control only to end up having to carry around stuff that does nothing but pull you down. You never realize God is right there waiting for you to let go, so He can then prove to you the Bible is true. You will never understand the Bible with your natural understanding. Only a born-again recreated spirit led by the Spirit of God can comprehend spiritual discernment.

*But the natural man does not receive the things of the Spirit of God, for they are foolishness to him; nor can he know them, because they are spiritually discerned.*

1 Corinthians 2:14

This is the reason why it's so difficult for people to accept the reality of what God has already done. The salvation of humanity was accomplished by the sacrifice of the person of Jesus Christ. "It is finished" leaves no room for what you think is the way it should be done.

*Therefore when Jesus had received the sour wine, He said, "It is finished!" And He bowed His head and gave up His spirit.*

John 19:30

God allows free will for you to choose. But you have been deceived into believing you have all of the answers, while oblivious to the reality of how your life has been negatively influenced by the lies you believed. And no matter how messed up your life becomes, you continue to do what you have always done, or you trust in the advise of someone who is just as confused as you are.

*Let them alone and disregard them; they are blind guides and teachers. And if a blind man leads a blind man, both will fall into a ditch.*

Matthew 15:14

The example we have been given to model our lives after was taught by Jesus when He told His disciples how to correctly pray. Nothing Jesus ever spoke was irrelevant. The example given in the Bible proves God is to be first and foremost in our lives, and we can be confident in knowing God is aware of what we have need of.

*For your Father knows the things you have need of before you ask Him. In this manner, therefore, pray:*

*Our Father in heaven, Hallowed be Your name.*
*Your kingdom come.*
*Your will be done On earth as it is in heaven.*
*Give us this day our daily bread.*
*And forgive us our debts, As we forgive our debtors.*
*And do not lead us into temptation,*
*But deliver us from the evil one.*
*For Yours is the kingdom and the power and the glory*
*forever. Amen.*

Matthew 6:8b-13

God is Holy and the conduct of our lives as Christians are to reflect this to an unsaved humanity in our words, thoughts and deeds. We are to live each day as if this is the day Jesus will return for those who are born again by the Spirit of God, to forever be with Him. We are told to live as if our inheritance has already been obtained. In God there is no time and as a born-again Christian, you are already living in eternity. There is a higher realm of living to obtain and it can only be realized when your lifestyle becomes conformed to the plan and purposes of God.

The first three examples are God-centered and give no allowance for the indulgence of whatever we want, unlike what today's easy gospel portrays. God is our provider and we are not to be concerned for the things we need. This is a direct conflict with everything you and everybody you know holds dear.

The next example is paramount. Forgiveness is not an option with God, it is a demand. For if a person violates this command, they have no hope of eternal salvation. Lastly, God does not do bad things to people, for He is the giver of life and everything good. Humanity's rebellion to God is the reason why there is so much evil in the world. People are tempted by choice when they succumb to the desires of their own wicked imagination.

*Let no one say when he is tempted, "I am being tempted by*
*God," for God cannot be tempted with evil, and he himself*
*tempts no one. But each person is tempted when he is lured*
*and enticed by his own desire. Then desire when it has*

> *conceived gives birth to sin, and sin when it is fully grown*
> *brings forth death. Do not be deceived my beloved brothers.*
>
> James 1:13-16

God allows these events to bring a person to realize the need they have for the transforming power of the Gospel to change their life. Thus God's sovereignty is revealed to the world.

I really want you to pay very close attention to what I describe in this chapter. I believe this is where you will see a very accurate and narrative description of everyone you know.....including yourself.

Why would you listen to a secular educator or someone claiming to be a spiritual advisor, when they have no absolute answers or definite convictions to explain why things happen? Nor do they know the answer to the question: "Is there life after death?" or how this is relevant to the life they live. Come on people! Don't even think that you can live and do as you choose and not be held accountable for what you have done. Every false religion or belief observed has a truth based upon Scripture, but somewhere within its expression there is always a way to escape being held accountable for what one says or does.

The only absolute that holds a person accountable to how they live and the choice they make is the Gospel of Jesus Christ. That is why every other false religion, belief or whatever it is you think you know, is endorsed by secular societies who are looking for any means of justification for their actions.

What more idiocy do we need to see to prove just how confused people really are? God created the desire for knowledge and fulfillment within each of us, but His Spirit cannot reveal to you the truth until you decide to do what is necessary to overcome what has influenced the way you think.

Take some time to think back over your life and be honest about the choices you've made that created the circumstances you are dealing with right now. It's my bet your dreams have yet to come true and each day is lived with a faint hope that maybe tomorrow will be better. And when today arrives, the same habits that created every yesterday will never allow your hope of tomorrow. As for those of you who appear to have achieved your personal and financial goals and are living the American dream, why are you so dissatisfied and angry all the time? Emptiness is lonely, isn't it?

My life was controlled by selfish emotions and what I did to try to satisfy every desire only kept me bound. I didn't have any natural gifts or skills God needed, but the one thing He did want was me.

God had to allow what I experienced in life to break my dependence of anything I would put before my worship of Him. Only then did I begin to see clearly. My spirit, which was created in the image of God, could not rule over my conscience until my reading of the Bible revealed who I really am and what God requires of me.

Everything you have experienced is stored away in the vault of your subconscious mind, and the only thing that can bring correction to how you think is knowing what God has to say and then acting upon it. As you meditate on these words and speak the truths that will be revealed, God will make happen things you thought you didn't deserve. Because you have watched it become real, no one can ever take this confidence from you.

> *So then faith comes by hearing, and hearing by the word of God.*
>
> Romans 10:17

The choices and decisions I made were a result of the mental programming of my childhood, and no positive change occurred in what I thought of me until this time of study revealed the person God created me to be. If only I had known. What the enemies of God have fought so hard for and don't want you to realize is that God created you in the image of the person of Jesus Christ to be just like Him.

> *And God said, Let us make man in our image, after our likeness.*
>
> Genesis 1:26a

What I have found to be so incredibly unique about God is the choice we've been given about the lifestyle we live. God wants to have a personal relationship with each of us, but He will never force the issue. I used to wonder why God who is Sovereign, would allow this. There is a reason and God will honor the decision we make, either good or bad.

> *"Now listen! Today I am giving you a choice between life and death, between prosperity and disaster. For I command you this day to love the Lord your God and to keep his commands, decrees, and regulations by walking in his ways. If you do this, you will live and multiply, and the Lord your God will bless you and the land that you are about to enter and occupy. But if your heart turns away and you refuse to listen, and if you are drawn away to serve and worship other gods, then I warn you now that you will certainly be destroyed. You will not live a long, good life in the land you are crossing the Jordan to occupy. Today I have given you the choice between life and death, between blessings and curses. Now I call on heaven and earth to witness the choice you make. Oh, that you would choose life, so that you and your descendants might live! You can make this choice by loving the Lord your God, obeying him, and committing yourself firmly to him. This is the key to your life. And if you love and obey the Lord, you will live long in the land the Lord swore to give your ancestors Abraham, Isaac and Jacob."*
>
> Deuteronomy 30:15-20

My testimony is for those of you who are in life where I have come from. You now have my life's experience as an example to believe God will do for you what He has for me. God's involvement in my life's transformation has created an awareness of self-worth I never had before. I'm confident that I can now do for someone else what was never done for me. What's needed more than anything else is a voice of experience that can relate to and has an answer for what the masses are asking of themselves.

If you have never struggled in life, you really don't know how to talk to people like me—we do not relate. I don't care what a secular education tells you is the reason for me feeling the way I do or a theology degree that is thought to qualify you to instruct me spiritually. Until you have walked in my shoes, you will never understand the world people like me live in and what has to be overcome to get out of that lifestyle. My suggestion to you would be to go to the places to meet the people you have avoided and become familiar with life experiences you can learn from. Only then can you understand how to deliver a message people will listen to.

> *When I am with those who are weak, I share their weakness, for I want to bring the weak to Christ. Yes, I try to find common ground with everyone, doing everything I can to save some.*
>
> 1 Corinthians 9:22

Your education or ministry title means nothing. It's having compassion and becoming involved. If the church would only realize that by helping people, no matter where they might be in life, it will attract those who are ready to hear about what being a Christian really means. When you can relate to someone in the realm of their emotions with a kind word and a firm conviction of knowing what God is capable of doing, it speaks volumes to encourage their process of change. I know this to be true because I've been there and come through it, and today I'm free from that image of the person I used to be. The statement I just made is the whole purpose for writing this book.

I know just how lost and confused people really are, and through the message of this book, I am describing what God did to help me find meaning in all that I've experienced. If you have not done this you need to listen to someone who has. Until you do, you have nothing of any real value to offer another person. The only thing that matters is what you do with the knowledge you have of Jesus Christ, and how a relationship with the Savior of your soul has transformed your life. Everything else is a waste of time.

I have yet to spend a lot of time studying the Old Testament Bible, but the first two chapters of Genesis describe God's creation of humanity and what rights and authority He gave to mankind. It is in the third chapter that humanity's fall is recorded. Every page after is God describing His willingness and plan to redeem mankind back to Himself.

The four Gospels give a description of Jesus' life, what He went through and how He lived during His time of ministry here on the earth. This is how the Bible proves God's awareness of what you are going through and shows the only way out of the mess your ignorance has made of your life.

> *For we do not have a High Priest Who is unable to understand and sympathize and have a shared feeling with our weaknesses and infirmities and liability to the assaults of temptation, but One Who has been tempted in every respect as we are, yet without sinning.*
>
> Hebrews 4:15

In the day and time we live, Americans have become a spoiled, arrogant and self-centered people whose main focus is what feels good and could care less about what is morally right. I believe the experience of my life has earned a platform for me to say this. Life for me has not been easy and I had to sleep in the bed of my choice. Living the way I have, and working as a bartender has given me an insider's view of just how ignorant people really are about their true selves. For twenty years I listened to people's inebriated justifications as to why they behaved the way they did.

You have a house, two cars and all the toys, a spouse if you're married, however many kids and a pet, your career, a part time job or two, financial debt and nine credit cards all maxed out and you are stressed. Is it any wonder why you drink, do drugs and pursue emotional ease the way you do?

You're a member of this club and that committee, basketball on Monday and the designated soccer mom on Tuesday. You would never consider a community outreach on Wednesday because it's ladies night with no cover charge for girls and domestic bottles are half price. Thursday is over-the-hump night as you corral with all of your buddies at a pub to watch soccer on a HDTV mounted over the bar, and here comes Friday. Everybody's living for the weekend date night out to dinner, big screen movie time and then you end up at a club to dance all of your frustrations away—girl hunting, boy hunting or whatever your sexual preference with cocktails flowing to inebriated bliss. You wake up hurting, about mid-morning on Saturday, and stumble into the bathroom to get rid of the poison in your system. You then begin to make calls planning the day's events to try to recapture lost youth. And that night, you do it all again. Sunday morning comes around and your head is swimming with vibes of the weekend, so you stay home to recuperate and pop a few tops watching ESPN. You're living life!

Man…..you have arrived and are proud of your accomplishments. Sacrifice to career has earned you great respect among vain peers as you strut around in a pompous show of confidence, having achieved the American dream. You're oblivious to reality and that everything of value has crumbled all around you. Your spouse or significant other cannot stand you and the kids are going to hell in a hand basket. Having no guidance, no discipline and no direction, they turn to the mentally-challenged individuals of today's arts, entertainment, music and sports industries to be the model of their dreams.

Youth in America are hopelessly lost in their search of social acceptance and self-expression, all because of the influence their culture's cliquish peer pressure has on young people today. The neighborhood where they live to the school they attend, what they wear to the car they drive and how many "in" people they know. And if someone is not like them, they are less than and made to know it.

Young people today are mean-spirited because the have no sense of purpose or self-respect. In school they are taught an evolution theory as truth, and look at the effect it's had on shaping the opinion of what they think of themselves. This self-perception is what has influenced how they treat other people.

How many times have I caught teenage girls in bars with fake IDs, and their parents have no clue where they are? They're being drugged and raped by adolescent men old enough to be their fathers while you sit back and discuss the lies of politicians with people as misguided as you are. The priorities of people in this nation are way off from where they need to be and something must be done to alter the direction it's heading. We have a government that intends to control and regulate the things that influence ethics in people, and this is the reason why so few have escaped the effects of moral decay that have now shaped a culture with no value for human life.

One of the greatest atrocities of our time is the estimated 1.4 million abortions every year in the United States. Women do this in the name of avoiding an inconvenience, but in reality it is one of the methods being used to depopulate the world. Margaret Sanger, who was the founder of Planned Parenthood, was an evil sadistic woman. Read the history about this woman and her writings. Those who work for this organization today are no different than her. Log on to the internet and do your research among the only nonbiased media archives to learn the truth about issues like this.

As difficult as my life has been, I am drawn to those who cannot defend themselves. And to the vulgar people committing this crime, either legislatively or in person, against the sanctity of human life, your day in court is coming. God will judge you.

Take a moment to reflect on the example being set for young people to follow. Do you really want your children to be just like you? What is more important, the justification of hiding from the shame of your past or maybe even the pride of what you have accomplished, or their future? What will you have to experience before accepting responsibility for the many wrong decisions you've made? What you should do is ask for your family's forgiveness, and then lead them in doing what is necessary to make things right with God. But no, this would point the finger of blame at you and that's why you allow your children to do whatever they choose.

Whether it's TV or video games, running the streets until late in the evening, experimenting with alcohol and drugs, sexual intercourse with another child or maybe even committing a crime, your children have watched you do nothing to try to model their behavior. They know you really don't care.

As they get older, you pull your hair out wondering why they behave the way they do and why they have no respect for you. Well.....

look in the mirror—they're a spitting image of you. To justify what you have done, you embrace the ideologies that claim a child's behavior is the result of a medical condition. You continually endorse those in public office who make laws to promote filth like Social Justice Education, which has removed from today's culture all conscience of accountability.

Look at how many entertainment venues there are for people to immerse themselves in while doing their best to numb that feeling of insignificance. Whatever the mind can imagine! The amount of alcohol consumed today by casual drinkers and alcoholics is staggering. Again, read the statistics about alcohol related deaths, spousal and child abuse, date rapes and all the violence resulting from excessive alcohol consumption. This is the environment teenagers can't wait to experience and by the time they turn twenty-one, most are well versed in self-indulgence. This is what America's enlightened culture is doing to your children.

The younger generations are mad and have no example to follow, and you Mr. and Mrs. Career, are the reason they will stand before God naked and ashamed. Their distrust of you will be the edifice that will condemn them to an eternity in hell because of their rebellion to God.

Like you, I enjoyed the feeling of being drunk because it was a temporary escape and the only place where I felt good about myself. The only problem is, it doesn't last and to get there again you have to drink more alcohol, and over time it becomes addicting. While drunk, you do things that you regret if you have a conscience, and most of the time these things can never be undone. I'll say it again, hurt people hurt people.

What the enemies of God have done to keep the American people focused on their survival has been played out with precision. They are puppets in the hands of other puppets, and we are all a part of a bigger plan. I know it will not set well with people who are both politically and culturally "correct" in their opinion when I say that, based upon my life's experience, there are only two possible beliefs. One is truth and the other is a lie. Every person has to choose between Divine Salvation or reliance on ones own conscience.

These are the only two choices humanity can make. Either people live their life in obedience to what the Bible teaches or they have made themselves god. One doesn't have to look very far to see what happens when humanity is left to their own self-indulgence. The proof of this is a nation of confused people who willingly embrace secular education and government intervention, these self-proclaimed spiritual advisors who are themselves deceived, and the entertainment and media spokes people claiming there is no God.

> *Only fools say in their hearts, "There is no God." They are corrupt, and their actions are evil; not one of them does good!*
>
> Psalms 14:1

Truth has been distorted by everyone's opinion of what they want it to be instead of trusting in what the Bible actually teaches. This has all happened because the seeker-friendly religious market, which makes up the majority of churches and so-called spiritual awakenings of today, have lost focus of God's command to teach the truths of Scripture and to not be offensive to anyone.

> *I charge you in the presence of God and of Christ Jesus, who is to judge the living and the dead, and by his appearing and his kingdom: preach the word; be ready in season and out of season; reprove, rebuke, and exhort, with complete patience and teaching. For the time is coming when people will not endure sound teaching, but having itching ears they will accumulate for themselves teachers to suit their own passions, and will turn away from listening to the truth and wander off into myths.*
>
> 2 Timothy 4:1-4

This is the time we are now living in. There are no absolutes in the minds of people and it seems as though everyone has been left alone to do whatever they desire without a thought of an impending consequence for the choice they make. Now that self-indulgence has shaped how we live, people refuse to be told or acknowledge their conduct of living is wrong, and that they will be held accountable by a sovereign God.

This is why there is so much wrong in not only America, but in every nation today. This mentality crosses every societal boundary, whether liberal, moderate or conservative, socialist or free. No one is beyond the reach of God's grace or the inevitable judgment of His law. Who do you think you are?

> *But who are you, O man, to answer back to God? Will what is molded say to its molder, "Why have you made me like this?"*
>
> Romans 9:20

The Bible is the only how-to manual revealing the foundation of truth capable of restoring self-worth and bringing about lasting change in a culture that has lost all sense of who they are. When all else fails, read the directions. It's really that simple.

During my years as a bartender I heard every story imaginable, from restaurants catering to social elite's to people just getting by. There is one thing that crosses every boundary and is not gender specific—when people are inebriated they reveal the truth of what they really think about themselves, their circumstances and everyone around. It would make you blush to know what the people you call a friend really think about you.

Alcohol consumption, or any form of substance abuse and the Bible are the two great equalizers. Alcohol is a short term, quick-fix to hide behind while still in the circumstance, but what God has to say will make right everything that turned out for your wrong. Both will make you more of the person you're trying to be. Alcohol abused will destroy, while acting upon biblical instruction will give life and bring restoration.

Like I did, many of you use what is easily purchased to cover up wounds and tolerate the thought, "I hate what my life has become!" If you are ready to listen, know that change is really not that difficult once you surrender self-will to God. Your opinion of what can be done will lead you to do more of the same, and only what God is allowed to do will bring lasting change. God can only do what you are willing to give Him. And He's waiting.

> *Give all your worries and cares to God, for he cares about you.*
>
> 1 Peter 5:7

> *So the LORD must wait for you to come to him so he can show you his love and compassion. For the LORD is a faithful God. Blessed are those who wait for his help.*
>
> Isaiah 30:18

God is very much aware of what it will take to bring healing to your soul. So wherever life leads, know that you are not alone. God will meet you in any circumstance when you let Him.

> *For no temptation (no trial regarded as enticing to sin), [no matter how it comes or where it leads] has overtaken you and laid hold on you that is not common to man [that is, no temptation or trial has come to you that is beyond human resistance and that is not adjusted and adapted and belonging to human experience, and such as a man can bear]. But God is faithful [to His Word and to His compassionate nature], and He [can be trusted] not to let you be tempted and tried and assayed beyond your ability and strength of resistance and power to endure, but with the temptation He will [always] also provide the way out (the means of escape to a landing place), that you may be capable and strong and powerful to bear up under it patiently. Therefore, my dearly beloved, shun (keep clear away from, avoid by flight if need be) any sort of idolatry (of loving or venerating anything more than God).*
>
> 1 Corinthians 10: 13-14

God made it clear He was calling me, and at this crossroad I had to choose God's provision or my own. It was not a hard decision, but I struggled with the commitment to changing a lifestyle that wasn't easy to let go of. Too many times my attitude created situations where God had to protect me, and I did not want to continue living this way.

> *For I do not understand my own actions. For I do not do what I want, but I do the very thing I hate. Now if I do what I do not want, I agree with the law, that it is good. So now it is no longer I who do it, but sin that dwells within me. For I know that nothing good dwells in me, that is, in my flesh. For I have the desire to do what is right, but not the ability to carry it out. For I do not do the good I want, but the evil I do not want is what I keep on doing. Now if I do what I do not want, it is no longer I who do it, but sin that dwells within me.*
>
> Romans 7:15-21

The more my thoughts were given to this the, more sincere my awe and appreciation of God became. GOD wanted to have a relationship with me. He told me to my face He was the reason I was no longer in bondage to the influence of my past. It has taken the writing of this book for me to understand what God has been doing and how it would happen. Just as my parents had spoken damning words that created a feeling of insignificance, God was speaking the prophetic truths of His will to me, and they have created an expectation that everything I hope for will one day become reality.

> *Who gives life to the dead and speaks of the nonexistent things that [He has foretold and promised] as if they [already] existed.*
>
> Romans 4:17b

Why would God continue to encourage what I was unable to do for myself? At that time I had no answer, but I was willing to find out because nothing I did in my own ability brought the change I needed to overcome a lifetime of ignorance and abuse. That's why I made the decision to allow God to help me overcome what is in my past.

*The weapons we fight with are not the weapons of the world. On the contrary, they have divine power to demolish strongholds. We demolish arguments and every pretension that sets its self up against the knowledge of God, and we take captive every thought to make it obedient to Christ.*

2 Corinthians 10:4-5

Why stay in misery when you have been given a lasting course of eternal change? This was my way out and I dove in head first. It reminded me of the day my father taught me how to swim. I was probably four years old when he took me fishing. I was sitting on a rock watching him, and for whatever reason, I slipped off the rock and sank to the river bottom. I sat there for I don't know how long. I remember watching a big turtle coming right at me and all of my air bubbles had stopped. The next thing I knew was the wrenching pain of being grabbed by my hair and yanked out of the water.

My father made a fuss over me asking if I was okay and then he told me what I needed to do to stay afloat. With no warning, he threw me in the river again. I hollered and kicked, spit and cussed at my father for what he did, but he just stood there and watched me with his hand held out. He was there waiting, but it was my effort that got me close enough to him, so only when I reached up and found his hand was he able to pull me to safety. The water was deep and there was nothing for me to depend on. It was through a struggle that I learned how to swim.

God is no different, at least for me. I came into this world fighting and I've been doing so every day of my life. God has been there from my childhood, offering His hand to help, but I would not take it. I was determined to do things my way…..and God let me.

The decisions I made created almost every experience I've had as an adult. Only when I came to my end by the act of repentance and made an effort to give God control of my emotions, did He meet me in the circumstances I chose to live. I was tired of fighting and I wanted to let my guard down to rest. I've heard preachers speak about a quiet place you find in God's presence and this is what I've longed for all of my life.

*Then Jesus said, "Come to me, all of you who are weary and carry heavy burdens, and I will give you rest. Take my yoke upon you. Let me teach you, because I am humble and gentle at heart, and you will find rest for your souls."*

Matthew 11: 28-29

The stuff you've carried around all of your life that has become a crutch will have to be left behind. There is a whole new set of rules to live by. God's way will earn you both spiritual and emotional freedom and your way is to stay in bondage. Change is a process we all have to go through. The attitude you have and your willingness to learn Biblical truth while in this time of your life directly affects how long it will take to get out. God will not allow you to enter His rest while still holding on to what is in your past. My advice to you is, "Let Go!"

My second year at that church, and a year into this study, I allowed something that happened to anger me and I almost missed the opportunity to write my book. My personality had softened but I wouldn't go out of my way to get to know anyone. On a few occasions people had invited me out to eat or to their home to try and get to know me. The conversation would inevitably be about church and I did my best to avoid these discussions. "This was going on and that had happened, someone said something to make another person mad and so and so had left." It was way too much drama.

There was an arrogance among the leaders of this church and I eventually spoke to one of the staff to suggest a change I thought might help other people not be offended by their actions. At the next service I was approached by an usher who said he wanted to speak with me. He told me they were not going to change what was being done and it was no concern of mine. How it was said crawled all over me and I wanted to slap him, and as I turned away to go to my seat is when I made a decision to not stay for the service. How inconsiderate can a person be? In church of all places!

When I entered the lobby I could see the usher in the office speaking to an associate pastor. I was close enough to hear what was being said, so I opened the door and went in. They looked at me like I was crazy. He finished with what he had to say and then my concern was spoken. The associate pastor said to the head usher, *"It never ceases to amaze that people who do nothing in church are the ones who want to make all the changes."* Then turning to say to me, *"If you don't like how we are running things here you need to find another church to go to."* I could not think of an appropriate response, so I walked out the door.

They must not have known about the conversation I'd had with the pastor, and that he said it was okay for me to come listen for however long it took to receive what I needed. Later that evening, I sent an email to the pastor describing my side of what happened. It was a month before he responded and to my surprise, the finger of blame was pointed at me and no comment was made as to what his associate had said.

This incident took place just a short time after Strong Tower Ministries had its tenth year anniversary celebration. At this meeting T.D. Jakes and Jesse Duplantis were guest speakers. It was a big event for the area. During the meeting, these men made statements about the significance of this conference, and what God wanted to do through the people making up the body of this church. But nothing they said came to pass.

Kevin Mihlfeld is the founder and senior pastor of this church and unlike what his website profile states, his life's expression for ministry at that time was not one of excellence, diversity, integrity and relevance. About the time of this conference Kevin took upon himself the title of, "Apostle." The arrogance that followed cost him his marriage and caused people to leave the church by droves. It was really sad and even more frustrating to once again have to sit and listen to someone talk about something his lifestyle contradicted.

I then spoke to someone who had been one of the founding members and a department head who had recently left the church. When I asked him about this situation, he told me it was an issue of them trying to get as many people in the building as quickly as they could before the offering was taken. He said the suggestion I had was not new and there had been a discussion among the staff about the same issue on several occasions.

He then said it was Kevin's opinion that collecting the congregation's money through tithe and offering was more important to ensure church expenses and its creditors could be paid. Once again it had been proven he was just like the other churched people in my past. I wanted nothing more to do with it, so I didn't go back.

I'm not implying this church wasn't making an impact in people's lives, because it did in mine. But somewhere along the way Godly motivation was replaced by self-indulgence. There is no place for this attitude in an atmosphere where people come to be encouraged and find strength to change their lives for the good.

Eight months passed and I was still mad about what had happened at church. At first my drinking was casual, but the angrier I became, the heavier I'd drink. I was frustrated and nothing about my life was as it should be.

At the bar where I worked it had always been busy, but it soon became empty. It seemed as though everything had come to a dead end and I was miserable. I had been down this road too many times and I didn't want to travel it again. I believe God did this to prove He was still in control, and He wasn't going to let me have my way.

So I went back to this church and made myself listen to a pastor I had no respect for. The incident that had caused me to leave has never been mentioned and no one came to me, as though it didn't happen. Even when Kevin went through a divorce, he never stepped down from the pulpit. It took about a year for me to understand why that was what God wanted me to do, and experience the change I needed to go through to be ready for what I now believe is God's intent for my near future.

I've been around enough churches and confused preachers to have learned what not to do when it comes to how my actions might negatively influence a person's opinion of God. When God reveals the knowledge of how He expects you to live, those of you in ministry positions should examine your conduct of living with scrutiny. If you cannot live it, you have no right to try to teach someone else.

In prison, among people who have committed crimes and atrocities, there is a code of honor that, when kept, earns you respect, but if violated can cause your death. I am amazed at people, churched and unsaved, who will tell you one thing and then do something completely different.

> *Every good gift and every perfect gift is from above, and comes down from the Father of lights, with whom there is no variation or shadow of turning.*
>
> James 1:17

Do not stand behind a pulpit and say one thing, while ignoring issues of legitimate concern when they are brought to you. It will nullify every good thing you do in the eyes of the people who have a history of feeling insignificant.

How you treat other people is what proves the faith you proclaim. If how I am made to feel is not important, then I can't follow you. Actions speak louder than words. Ministry leader, live what you preach.

All of my life, I have reacted to situations negatively or ran away from the confrontation because I had nothing convincing to say. Not any more. From now on I am going to stand up for what is right and confront everything that can be judged by the Word of God and proven to be wrong. I don't have to be liked to be obedient to an order God wants my life structured to.

After going back to church and submitting my ego to God, I began writing the manuscript for this book. In these last two years, more significant change has taken place in me than the three years before. Truthfully, I did not want to be at that church but until God released me, that is where I learned to submit to a purpose bigger than mine.

> *Jesus answered, Will you [really] lay down your life for me?*
>
> John 13:38a

This is a place of consciousness God wants to bring every person to, but so few ever choose to go through the struggle of leaving behind "me, my and mine" and "what about me"!

*For many are called (invited and summoned), but few are chosen.*

Matthew 22:14

I had walked away from church once again, but God still reached out to lead me back to His provision. Had I not come back this time, only God knows what would have happened, but it's my belief that I'd probably be dead.

*"When an evil spirit leaves a person, it goes into the dessert, seeking rest but finding none. Then it says, 'I will return to the person I came from.' So it returns and finds its former home empty, swept and in order. Then the spirit finds seven other spirits more evil than itself, and they all enter the person and live there. And so that person is worse off than before. That will be the experience of this evil generation."*

Matthew 12:43-45

When that woman minister called me out and said, "Not your way, but its God's way or no way in this season," it was God telling me He had had enough with my antics. God will not call you to His purpose as long as your motivation is solely to achieve what you want. And there comes a time when God will remove His hand of protection from you.

I am convinced this is the reason why so many people die young. The gift of salvation made available by God's indwelling Spirit is offered to all, but few ever realize because what we want is always in conflict with His omniscient nature.

*Then the Lord said, My Spirit shall not forever dwell and strive with man.*

Genesis 6:3a

Through my study of the Bible, I overcame what I thought would be all I would ever know. Today my hope has been restored and I see in myself what God describes in His Word. This is God's challenge to every person and to accept His call is to obligate God to make happen what only He can do. Now that I know who I am and what God requires of me, my obedience to His calling has become a lifestyle of worship and God honors this.

> *God blesses those who are poor and realize their need for him, for the Kingdom of Heaven is theirs.*
> *God blesses those who mourn, for they will be comforted.*
> *God blesses those who are humble, for they will inherit the whole earth.*
> *God blesses those who hunger and thirst for justice, for they will be satisfied.*
> *God blesses those who are merciful, for they will be shown mercy.*
> *God blesses those whose hearts are pure, for they will see God.*
> *God blesses those who work for peace, for they will be called the children of God.*
> *God blesses those who are persecuted for doing right, for the Kingdom of Heaven is theirs.*
> *God blesses you when people mock you and persecute you and lie about you and say all sorts of evil things against you because you are my followers. Be happy about it! Be very glad! For a great reward awaits you in heaven.*
>
> Matthew 5:3-12a

What God has to say is the determining factor in how your life will be lived. It does not matter what someone else has said, even if it is a fact. What's written in the Bible is the highest law and everything else is subject to God's authority.

> *Sky and earth will pass away, but My words will not pass away.*
>
> Matthew 24:35

> *Who is the image of the invisible God, the firstborn of every creature: For by him were all things created, that are in heaven, and that are in earth, visible and invisible, whether they be*

*thrones, or dominions, or principalities, or powers: all things were created by him, and for him: And he is before all things, and by him all things consist.*

1 Colossians 1:15-17

Everything in life is paralleled by a biblical truth that will either explain why you are going through the experience or what you need to do to overcome the things that have influenced the way you think. The knowledge of your true self is what the enemies of God hope you will never come realize.

I was like you when God spoke to me face to face. Lost and confused in the midst of all the things I had allowed to influence the lifestyle I chose to live, God challenged me to do the one thing I didn't understand. *How to live my life for His glory.* Through an in-depth study of the New Testament, I learned about what God requires of me, and that my purpose could only be realized by doing something good with the experiences of my life.

*For I know the thoughts and plans that I have for you, says the Lord, thoughts and plans for welfare and peace and not for evil, to give you hope in your final outcome.*

Jeremiah 29:11

I gave more thought to this chapter's message than any other, because of its focus on the hardest decision you will ever make. Which is choosing between the lifestyle you want to live, or answering God's call. The best wisdom is to learn from someone else's pain.

# ADVERSARY OF YOUR SOUL

## ಚಿ ಅಶ

C hange is not easy because it goes against a selfish nature that wants to be in control and make decisions that are comfortable. And honestly, until you want to change you never will. Life happens to all of us. No two circumstances are the same, but there are similarities we have all faced.

Your life's experience can be a double edged sword, and I believe the side you fall upon is of your own choosing. I believe what happens in everyday life-circumstances is to lead you to the revelation of God and your need of His divine help. But most of you have chosen the path that keeps you from living out the purpose God created you to influence. What is believed to be all you will ever know creates a repetitious thought process you'll struggle with until you learn how to renew your mind. This is where your fight will always be.

I was born fighting and I've been doing it all of my life. Street fights, prison fights, ring fights and bar fights; it was the one thing I was good at. I have been stabbed, I've broken both of my hands, most of my fingers, several ribs, a foot and my nose three times and I've lost count of how many stitches. But I have never been in a fight that has cut me open like the one I am in right now. To live out what God requires takes a determination to overcome at any cost. *What are you willing to let go of?*

*And from the days of John the Baptist until the present time, the kingdom of heaven has endured violent assault, and*

*violent men seize it by force [as a precious prize—a share in*
*the heavenly kingdom is sought with most ardent zeal and*
*intense exertion].*

Matthew 11:12

You cannot use compromising terms to overcome the lies that
have influenced the way you think. As a child, you were given no
choice and how your life has been played out is what the adversary
of your soul intended. I strongly believe you will stay in a place of
bondage, always mad, having no hope, no vision and no joy, until
you make a decision to overcome the lies that have manipulated
what you were made to believe about yourself.

As you make time to study the Bible, God will reveal His plan
for you through each stage of your emotional surrender. This will
not happen overnight. You are where you are in life because of the
many wrong decisions you've made and if you're ever to realize
truth, the way you think must change. Do you really want things to
change, or have you, like I did, accepted what happened as the way
it will always be? The choice is yours, my friend!

Working as a bartender gave me the opportunity to hear people's
thoughts on good and evil, and to hear their personal opinions of
who they think God is. Based upon these conversations, I know most
people outside the Christian faith give very little thought, if any, to
Satan, whom they think is no more than a fable. Few people, even
in a state of inebriation, deny the existence of God, but they have
nothing to say when it comes time to explain why there is so much
evil in the world. Why is this?

*And you were dead in the trespasses and sins in which you*
*once walked, following the course of this world, following the*
*prince of the power of the air, the spirit that is now at work*
*in the sons of disobedience—among whom we all once lived*
*in the passions of our flesh, carrying out the desires of the*
*body and the mind, and were by nature children of wrath,*
*like the rest of mankind.*

Ephesians 2:1-3

The Bible says Satan is the god of this age, a liar and the deceiver of the whole world. Satan longs to be worshipped by all of humanity and it was pride that cost the most powerful angelic being, to be cast down and stripped of heavenly authority, only to then be condemned to an eternal punishment.

This is why Satan hates God and has, since the beginning of time, perverted what God created to be perfect. From the time of Adam and Eve, who were created perfect and enjoyed the presence of God's fellowship, Satan has twisted the truth with lies and half-truths to deceive the mind, the will and the emotions of mankind.

Since Adam's act of disobedience and humanity's fall from God's grace, every person to ever be born is spiritually separated from God because of the sinful nature we are born with. This is not something you or I have any control over and to the shock of many, God created both Satan and humanity, knowing what would happen, for the purpose of revealing His Christ. As I read the Bible and reflected on the words that were written, I came to this resolve: Satan has been given a time of influence to allow God to sift through the masses of humanity, with the intent of drawing to Himself those who want to know Him."

It's time for the church to stop compromising the message God intended for the lost people of this world to hear. I believe the church has focused way too much on worldly issues and not on what the Bible actually says about humanity's fallen condition and what must be done to overcome the satanic deception that has led every person to live a lie. Instead of these endless motivational pep-talks, church leaders need to return to teaching biblical doctrine. They need to educate people on the difference between God's directive on how we should think and what our liberal education system has led the masses to believe. Humanism is the conscience of self-reliance being taught to children from the onset of their education, and this is the true battleground for the souls of humanity.

This was the lie Satan used to have all of humanity forever question the validity of God's Word. Every false religion falls under the category of humanism, the lie of trusting in our own ability to make things right with God.

*Now the serpent was more crafty than any other beast of the field that the LORD God had made. He said to the woman, "Did God actually say, 'You shall not eat of any tree in the garden'?" And the woman said to the serpent, "We may eat of the fruit of the trees in the garden, but God said, 'You shall not eat of the fruit of the tree that is in the midst of the garden, neither shall you touch it, lest you die.'" But the serpent said to the woman, "You will not surely die. For God knows that when you eat of it your eyes will be opened, and you will be like God, knowing good and evil." So when the woman saw that the tree was good for food, and that it was a delight to the eyes, and that the tree was to be desired to make one wise, she took of its fruit and ate, and she also gave some to her husband who was with her, and he ate. Then the eyes of both were opened, and they knew that they were naked. And they sewed fig leaves together and made themselves loincloths. And they heard the sound of the LORD God walking in the garden in the cool of the day, and the man and his wife hid themselves from the presence of the LORD God among the trees of the garden.*

Genesis 3:1-9

Eckhart Tolle and Deepak Chopra have been given a lot attention for their books and what they teach about spiritualism. They add to a host of influential celebrities and Oprah Winfrey, who claim there are many pathways to God. This is why there's such an awakening in people for the truth. During a webinar event, Oprah made public a personal observation after endorsing Eckhart Tolle's book, *A New Earth: Awakening to Your Life's Purpose.*

Oprah said, *"God is a feeling experience and not a believing experience. If your religion is a believing experience, then that's not truly God."*

Nowhere within the teachings of Scripture does the Bible allow her New Age humanistic beliefs. But because of a person's unregenerate mind, they cannot see that these men and women are false teachers who are themselves deceived and leading people astray.

There are roughly nine thousand known false religions in the world that people from every nation and culture observe. Is it any wonder why people are so confused about the topics of God and spirituality. In the Bible we are told the only way to God is through Jesus Christ.

> *Jesus said to him, I am the way, the truth, and the life. No on comes to the Father except through me.*
>
> John 14:6

Every other way will lead to spiritual death—eternal separation from the presence of God. Do you really want to take that chance? You are a fool if you do.

> *"Enter by the narrow gate. For the gate is wide and the way is easy that leads to destruction, and those who enter by it are many. For the gate is narrow and the way is hard that leads to life, and those who find it are few."*
>
> Matthew 7:13-14

Let me explain this in a way everyone can understand. If I follow the teachings of the Bible and you do not, and we both do good things for other people and live our lives to the best of our ability, it would be reasonable to believe that we are both good people. I know a lot of people who are kind and friendly and have helped others through difficult situations, and should be commended for what they have done. There is nothing wrong with living this kind of life and it's something we should all want to attain, but sadly we do not. Being a good person is the argument all of humanity uses to justify how they live. But to whom do you compare your perception of being a good person? A fallen humanity just like you, or Jesus Christ?

If your way is right and there are many different pathways to God, be it through works, conscience or the practice of another religion or no religion at all, you have lost nothing. But if the teachings of Bible are in fact true and you have lived the way you wanted to satisfy your conscience and rejected God's gift of salvation through Jesus Christ, you have lost everything.

This is why Satan has deceived all of humanity regarding the authenticity of Scripture. There are several religions that claimed a virgin birth, the resurrection from the dead and many other similarities to that of Christianity. But none have endured the scrutiny of time that proves authenticity or are capable of transforming a life.

Satan, who was created by God and now is a fallen spirit, is void of all creative thought and expression. The same tactic Satan used to deceive in the Garden of Eden is the same method of operation being used today. Because of humanity's fallen condition and attempts to feel justified is why so many false religions are practiced in the world today.

From the day Satan fell from God's grace until the day Jesus died on the cross, no human had a revelation or the knowledge of how to resist demonic oppression. But when Jesus raised Himself from the dead, the Bible states all authority was stripped from Satan and the fallen angelic hosts suffered an eternal defeat. From that day until the end of time as we know it, the only power Satan has is through the thoughts you think and the words you speak giving life to the lies you believe.

> *Be of sober spirit, be on the alert. Your adversary, the devil, prowls around like a roaring lion, seeking someone to devour. But resist him, firm in your faith.*
>
> 1 Peter 5:8-9a

This fight for your conscience is with a spiritual adversary who has but one intention—*for you to be ignorant of who you really are.* Satan does not fight fair and don't think for a moment demonic spirits are not real. I saw into this realm once before and even though it was thirty years ago while I was in a drugged stupor, I remember it as if it were yesterday. The being reeked of death and evil, and I will never forget the evil I saw as I looked into its eyes.

I don't know why God allowed me to see into the spirit realm, but I did and it's real. Now all these years later, I understand why I experienced in life what I have. My ignorance of biblical truth made me susceptible to the whims of influence, and you are no different than me. This has been Satan's tactic from the beginning and I know of no other world religion other than Christianity that reveals God's eternal enemy. From now on, if I ever hear anyone ask why there is so much evil in the world, I'll know what to tell them.

Humanity's deception is believing they are less than who God created them to be. This is why so many atrocious acts have been committed against people as far back as time has been recorded. We are created in the image of God, and because Satan hates God, we are seen as the reflection of Him through the eyes of a lost and unregenerate humanity. Apart from God's Spirit indwelling our lives, there is no defense against demonic oppression. You can do nothing other than what your sinful nature desires. If you don't know who you are fighting, you cannot prepare a defense or look for weaknesses to know where to attack.

Should you make the decision to join this fight, everything you were ashamed of or regretted doing will come to mind as if it is the day it happened. Any weakness you've ever had will revisit and people you don't even know will be unkind to you. The areas you've struggled in will be where the most damage is inflicted— *the uneducated man within*. Until you make the time to learn about the person you really are, you can never become the person God created you to be. You need to make a choice about what you allow to influence how you think of yourself.

> *Dear friend, I pray that you may enjoy good health and that all may go well with you, even as your soul is getting along well.*
>
> 3 John 2

Why was I never given an opportunity to enjoy the better life so many people have taken for granted? Here is the answer. *Until in my mind was the belief that God had a purpose for my life and that He was willing to lead me in the discovery of that purpose, the prison of my past is where the hope of my imagination would've stayed forever locked away.* This is why God challenged me to study His "Will and Testament" to discover truth and to learn about the lifestyle He requires of me.

It was during this study that I realized there was no time limit for the process of change I had to go though. It began when God revealed Himself and He proved to be much more patient than me.

When God spoke to me the first time in prison and said, *"Pick up my Bible and read it,"* His intent was to show me what I needed to do to change my future. But no, I chose to do it my way. My own self-perception and my observation of those who said they were born-again Christians, yet behaved just like people who had no knowledge of God, made me think the instructions written on the pages of my Bible were expectations I could never live up to.

God knew the paths I would choose and I believe He allowed my experiences so I would realize the need I have for Him. The answers have been right there, but I had to be willing to give my time to learning what they are. *God has made the way of escape, but He will not do it for you!*

> *All scripture is inspired by God and is useful to teach us what is true and to make us realize what is wrong in our lives. It corrects us when we are wrong and teaches us to do what is right. God uses it to prepare and equip his people to do every good work.*
>
> 2 Timothy 3:16-17

Nothing I did made any difference in the circumstances of my life until my first priority became the study of Scripture to find out who God says I am. And only then did change begin to take place in the circumstances my mind had created. It will be the same for you. *Change the way you think, and God will change how you live.*

> *Then Jesus said to the disciples, "Have faith in God. I tell you the truth, you can say to this mountain, 'May you be lifted up and thrown into the sea,' and it will happen. But you must believe it will happen and have no doubt in your heart. I tell you, you can pray for anything, and if you believe that you've received it, it will be yours."*
>
> Mark 11: 22-24

I often wondered what qualified a person to tell someone else what to do having never done it for themselves? People do not want to hear about a theory a person has on a subject of matter they have never experienced. People want to know what you have overcome and stayed free from. There is no text book other than the Bible that can be used to teach people how to overcome the demons they fight every day.

Emotionally soft, secular counselors and naïve pulpit orators who compromise the truths of Scripture are incapable of reaching beyond pain to provoke a desire in people to change. It takes experience or at the least a willingness to get down in a person's mess and offer a strong hand of encouragement to help them up. This is something many of today's safe-church pastors and congregations are not doing.

As I look back over the events of my life, I see that most of what happened to me was the result of circumstances I thought I had no control over. But when I made a decision to study the Bible and find out for myself about the person God created me to be, there was no influence from my past that could stop the change I was seeking. This is when I understood it's not the people in my past I should be angry with, because they were influenced by the same evil. Now that I've learned the truth, I have the confidence to make these statements to challenge you.

I will never again give place to what I know is not God's will for me. When someone like me has overcome an experience that relates to one you may be dealing with, learn from what they have done. It just might be the push you need to step out into the unknown. Here is when the renewed man within is revealed. *"God in you"* brings to light the knowledge of what demonic oppression has done to manipulate the truth of who you really are.

This will be the most uncomfortable, yet self-revealing and exciting time of your life. It will be a spiritual fight for not only you, but also the people God has called you to reach. You can, with the influence of what is written in the Bible, overcome a lifetime of lies that controlled how you thought. Listen and learn…

# WATCHMEN'S NEGLECT
ℰ ℭ

Learning the truth has made it very clear to me as to what I am called to do. I was not qualified to even think I could lead another person until I allowed God to lead me into my freedom.

*"You are truly my disciples if you remain faithful to my teachings. And you will know the truth, and the truth will set you free."*

John 8:31a-32

There is no treading lightly here and certain groups of people will not like the statements I'm about to make. I believe you will either stand in applause or try to crucify me when I tell you the motivation behind these agendas.

I speak from a viewpoint that does not come from either a secular or theological education when I say both government and the religious market of our time are deceiving the masses. Man's government, though necessary, is not an answer for what plagues the modern world today. It goes much deeper and cannot be corrected by the local, state and federal programs that attempt to only change what a person does. And sadly, the watchmen of men's souls have neglected their call.

We have become a nation of people divided by religious beliefs, or the lack thereof, and political views that are just as sharply divided. Moral relativity—the belief that what's right for each individual should be based upon their point of view, regardless how the behavior is viewed by someone else—is widely accepted as truth.

Being culturally correct is now the safe zone and no one dares to confront behavior that's offensive, for fear of the consequences to follow. I've seen the ugliness in people, from the older generations set in their ways to the youth that have no self-respect, who choose to live this way simply because they do not know any better.

I was never given the opportunity to realize my true self as a young man because of the environment I was brought up in and how that shaped my thoughts. Now that I know why, it is my passion to educate those who will listen. So being either politically or culturally correct is not a concern of mine.

American culture has become so self-absorbed that it's nearly impossible to wake them up to what is actually happening without people criticizing me and labeling me a right-wing conspiracy theorist. It goes against everything they have been taught by their parents, education, the governing elites and every other person they know. Until people have been challenged, what is to keep them from acting out who they think they are? It's time for truth to stand up against the flow of humanity.

There are other people way more qualified to provide documented proof of the events of 9/11 and the many crimes both Republican and Democrat administrations are guilty of. These men and women have dedicated their lives to finding out the truth about organizations like the Bilderberg Group, Trilateral Commission, the Counsel on Foreign Relations and the United Nations. They also research how these organizations have quietly manipulated the world into becoming what we are witnessing today. The people heading up these organizations are the enemies of God, yet we listen to their rhetoric as if they are doing what is good for humanity. Their sin has become so rank that God is now exposing them for who they really are. And you had better take heed...

> *He began to say to his disciples first, "Beware of the leaven of the Pharisees, which is hypocrisy. Nothing is covered up that will not be revealed, or hidden that will not be known.*

*Therefore whatever you have said in the dark shall be heard in the light, and what you have whispered in private rooms shall be proclaimed on the housetops."*
Luke 12:1b-3

The mainstream media is owned by people who are members of these groups, and that's why most of you have no clue what is going on. But because of the Internet and alternative means of media, the evidence is now available if you will only take the time to look for it. If you choose not to believe what these people have discovered, you deserve what is coming.

Now, keep in mind I am a convicted felon and even though I was incarcerated twenty-seven years ago when I was a child, I do not have the right to vote. So I am not partial towards any political party. I have never given any thought to try to regain this right because of corruption in the government, and now that I've had time to study history and world events while writing this book, I realize just how correct I am.

I have to question whether the people in powerful government positions are placed there by an electoral vote, or by those who control the financial interests of the nations. Just as a child has no choice in what they are subjected to, I believe the American people have no say in who becomes president of the United States. It's been proven by documentation and congressional hearings that the computerized ballot box can be manipulated.

The person to best implement what the financial elites want done is the one placed in office. People get so caught up in this political circus and think an individual's opinion means something to their corporate masters. This proves just how clueless people really are.

I blame this on a government that is being controlled by people who are unwilling to submit their lifestyle of self-indulgence to the moral standards God requires of every person. Politicians tell the American public what they want them to believe and not what is good and beneficial for the people they're supposed to represent. In my opinion, they have become corrupted and are deceiving the masses because of their greed for money, power and control.

What is taught in the Bible is not comfortable and it exposes all the areas in a person's conduct of living that are incorrect. This is why for the last fifty years or more there has been a never-ending attack against biblical doctrine in a country whose forefathers were greatly influenced by Judeo-Christian values. Read the documents these men wrote to establish the Charters of Freedom: The Declaration, The Constitution and The Bill of Rights. To read these documents, it is impossible to deny that the founders of this nation were not Christian. History proves none of these men were perfect, but they were definitely used by Divine Providence to create a nation whose God was the Lord Jesus Christ. But sadly, look at what the governing elites have been allowed to accomplish because of the ignorance of their constituents.

Men and women who we thought were elected to safeguard our rights do not have the backbone to do what is necessary to correct what has undeniably shaped the current culture. And to ensure main street remains unaware, principles are compromised for personal gain as policies are created and laws passed to encourage behavior that produces more of the same evils.

The root of moral erosion in this country is because of what people have been made to believe about themselves and since people have very little self-respect, they have an alarming amount of disregard for others. I'm not a historian and I won't even try to explain this in depth, but in my lifetime I have seen moral conscience become almost nonexistent. I was too young to remember these events, but it is a proven fact that political leaders used the momentum of the evolution theory, the hippie movement, sexual freedom and Roe vs. Wade to set the standard we now live by today. This brainwashing is the reason why there's so much negativity in the lives of people today. *If you take away the conscience of accountability, ignorance will run rampant.*

If you are willing to take the time to research the increase of cultural negativity within this time frame, it will shock you. And what have these public servants done to try and cover up the idiocy of their agenda? They have deceived generations with a deliberate education of humanism and the freedom of expression, which is being hammered into the minds of people from the cradle to the grave. All you have to do is be observant and you will see the evidence. The result of a socialist world-view in the political leaders of this nation and our parents, who became their prodigies, is a youth that has no self-respect or consideration of another person.

These same children are now being diagnosed with all kinds of mental sicknesses. I'm not a doctor or a psychologist, but I do know how to read. The most common diagnosis is a psychological condition known as ADHD, and everything else that goes along with it. A known cure has yet to be found only the numbing of symptoms with amphetamine medications like Ritalin, which are no more than a nervous system jumpstart very similar to cocaine. I should know. I have used illegal drugs for thirty years to not have to deal with my issues.

The problem is not a child's genetic makeup, and it's not even their fault. In my opinion, parents of today are the reason why their children are so screwed up. Instead of doing what is necessary to be a good example, children are drugged so that the adults won't have to deal with their own issues or the child's. It is widely publicized by the medical profession that these diagnoses are genetic in nature and passed down from parent to child, and for the most part this is correct. But if you will research just a little bit deeper, it will be revealed that what is said to be genetic cannot be validated by the medical community.

Taking into consideration the children that do have a serious medical condition and the influence it has over their behavior, the majority of children have had no say in what has been allowed by the ignorance of misinformed people to influence what they think of themselves. Something I find to be the epitome of stupidity, is the way people and agencies scream inhumane treatment at the parents that do discipline their children, when these are the very same people who have legislated for legalized abortion. Which is more humane, correcting a child or killing the child?

> *Whoever spares the rod hates his son, but he who loves him is diligent to discipline him.*
>
> Proverbs 13:24

Read the statistics for yourself and they will prove what I say to be true. ADHD, and all the symptoms associated with this condition, is a problem that is said by medical professionals to have a negative effect on the entire family. According to the surveys that have been done and are available for you to read, nearly fifty percent of children are in some way affected by this dis-ease. In reality, this suggests about half of the adults in America today are screwed up mentally. Based on my twenty years of work experience in the restaurant industry, I would even say this percentage is actually much higher. This begs the question: "How can a psychologically challenged parent think they know what is best for their child?"

An estimated fifty billion dollars a year is spent on medical costs, as well as on both the legal and expected drug addiction of adolescent children, in order to avoid the true issues creating these problems. Ignorance of these agendas has not allowed people the opportunity to realize they are a highly marketable commodity. The medical industry has lied to people to prolong sicknesses, and is endorsed by bipartisan politics because of the monetary benefit to all parties included. Now children have become legalized drug addicts because no one wants to accept responsibility for the ethical rape of a people's conscience.

A government controlled by those who are relentless in their attempts to remove all consciousness of God from the public sector, is why the majority of people now exist at a standard of living thought to be normal. This is why children grow up to be just like their parents. It's been happening as long as I can remember and it affects everybody in some way today.

The result of this act of stupidity is shoved down our throats morning, noon and night, every time the news channels are turned on. Murder, rape, domestic violence and every other wrong that can be imagined is acted out in the lives of people you know, and nothing is being done about it!

The committees, AA's and TV talk shows are doing nothing to alter how people think, and if there is not a radical change in what the masses have been made to believe about themselves, it will only get worse. If the mayhem and blatant disregard for other people seen in the youth of today is a forerunner of what is yet to come, that's a scary thought. It's a vicious cycle so few ever find a way out of, and they say there is no known cure. Well, I disagree. I've learned the truth.

The education I was given, and I'm not referring to just my public schooling, is why I experienced the things I have in life, and that is wrong. While growing up, I was never told about a God who loved me for the person I was, what good I could accomplish or that anything I set my mind to do was possible—it was just the opposite. I'm not the only one to have had an experience like that. Almost every person I know has a story to tell about the harshness of life and as people get older and more set in their ways, what they're familiar with just keeps pounding away. Because people don't know how to change, is why they lash out in pain.

Ask yourself why does this accepted behavior permeate today's societies? I can say from my own experience that once you've made the decision to take your head out of the sand and look around, the answers are right in front of your face. Should you understand these special interest agendas for what they really are, it will anger even the dumbest of the dumbed-down. This is why our governing body writes documents in a language few people can understand, and within these documents they've hidden agendas that are then voted into law without the approval of the American people.

Their tactics to divide people have led to a nation no longer unified and it seems everyone has forgotten what it took to give us the liberties we have enjoyed. Everything you hold dear is being taken from you with each new policy and law that is passed, and we are not far away from the slaughter of the American dream. The deliberate influence of both humanism and socialism being taught in schools and universities has robbed people of their destinies. Children that grow up having no consciousness of the only true and living God have no guideline for morality, and these are the people who are now and will be in the future leading this nation.

Just look at the results. If those working in government positions are not appalled at the economic and living conditions people are subjected to, they should be ashamed of themselves and should resign their office. But with the current state of how people think today, this is not about to happen.

The American public has been duped by the lies politicians tell and ignorance continually applauds those who in reality are wolves in sheep's clothing. These people are paid six figure salaries they did not earn, while so many people can't even make it to the next paycheck. There is an ever-widening gap between the classes of people—those with power and everyone else. If we do not wake up to the real issues that have been taking place for quite some time, we will soon find ourselves in bondage to socialism. The European Union has already led the way in becoming this example.

This world's financial elites and America's governing elites are doing the same to us. With President Clinton signing into law North America's Free Trade Agreement and President Bush's Security and Prosperity Partnership with Canada and Mexico, the North American Union could very well happen. The strong arm behind this push is the United Nations Coalition.

For those of you who are not familiar with the NAU proposal to dissolve national borders and have all of North America be controlled by an unelected government and their imposing of new laws, means our constitution and our bill of rights would be dissolved. A new currency called the Amero would replace the US dollar. Have you ever given any real thought as to why current and past administrations have done so little to enforce the immigration laws. They know what they are doing but sadly, most of you do not.

The United States is now facing a very dangerous time and world history has every potential to repeat itself. Do your research on FEMA, the Federal Emergency Management Agency. This fascist agency is not what we have been told it is. If martial law is ever enacted because of civil unrest, people will be herded into FEMA's camps, strategically located in almost every state. If you do not believe this, then ask the victims of Hurricane Katrina what they think of FEMA agents, and how these displaced people were treated by both military and law enforcement personnel. If you are stupid enough to think a holocaust could not happen in American, then explain to me the millions of plastic coffins stacked on both government lands and private lands being leased by the Centers for Disease Control.

> So the four angels who had been in readiness for that hour in the appointed day, month, and the year were liberated to destroy a third of mankind. The number of their troops of cavalry was twice ten thousand times ten thousand (200,000,000); I heard what their number was. And in [my] vision the horses and their riders appeared to me like this: the riders wore breastplates the color of fiery red and sapphire blue and sulphur (brimstone) yellow. The heads of the horses looked like lions' heads, and from their mouths there poured fire and smoke and sulphur (brimstone). A third of mankind was killed by these three plagues—by the fire and the smoke and the sulphur (brimstone) that poured from the mouths of the horses.
>
> Revelation 9:15-18

I seriously recommend everyone read an article called *The Haig-Kissinger Depopulation Policy* made available by Lonnie Wolfe in March of 1981. An investigation by the Executive Intelligence Review learned about the plans to reduce the world's population by two billion people through military conflict, starvation, disease and any means necessary. I'm not going to even try to add anything to this because the article is sufficient enough. But when you read something like this and then compare current world events to the end-time teachings in the Bible, you would have to be willfully ignorant to not realize what is happening.

A one—world government is spoken of in the Bible during this time. Taking into consideration the current affairs happening with the devaluing of the American dollar and the impact it would have on the entire world, this could be the beginning to the end of the world as we know it. Read the entire book of Revelation and pay very close attention to the events unfolding in chapters thirteen and eighteen. Another account of biblical prophesies describing the end time's events is the book of Daniel. If what is happening is a part of

God's plan for the end times, what in the world do you think a group of confused and godless people can do to change it? This nation's administration, regardless of party are not your friends.

You would think the people who have been educated at the most prestigious universities this nation has to offer would know the difference between right and wrong. But it's quite evident that neither Democrat nor Republican pundits have any clue as to what they are doing.

What more will we have to see before the people decide to hold those in public office to a higher standard of accountability to the laws they swore to uphold? In spite of what everyone might think, the only people qualified to police the actions of others are those who adhere to the moral standards of Scripture.

I do not believe God intends for Christians to sit idly by and do nothing as these events unfold, but neither do I believe we are to allow the world to influence us the way it has... So many times I had hoped to see an example of how I should live in people who went to church but sadly, this was an expectation never realized. Any person who claims to be a Christian has an obligation to be a light of hope in the midst of a depraved and godless culture.

> *"You are the salt of the earth. But what good is salt if it has lost its flavor? Can you make it salty again? It will be thrown out and trampled underfoot as worthless. You are the light of the world—like a city on a hilltop that cannot be hidden. No one lights a lamp and then puts it under a basket. Instead, a lamp is placed on a stand, where it gives light to everyone in the house. In the same way, let your good deeds shine out for all to see, so that everyone will praise your heavenly Father."*
> Matthew 5:13-16

The introduction of modernism that gradually brought complacency and the eventual compromise of biblical truth into the great cathedrals of nineteenth century Europe decimated Christian influence. The events of the Holocaust and the other ethnic cleansings of recent history are examples of Europe having become a godless society. A government that can take moral conviction from its people can then easily disarm them of their will and the ability to fight.

This deception is happening in our schools and universities where the youth of this nation are being trained up to accept the philosophy of Marxists socialism. It also comes from the pulpit of churches whose pastors have been recruited by Homeland Security to try to quiet any unrest in the event of martial law being instituted. They cite the Bible as the authority telling people to obey their government.

> *Let every person be subject to the governing authorities. For there is no authority except from God, and those that exist have been instituted by God. Therefore whoever resists the authorities resists what God has appointed, and those who resist will incur judgment.*
>
> Romans 13:1-2

This nation's government, military or law enforcement agencies do not have the authority to impose any laws or regulations upon the American people that are in contradiction to our constitutional rights. They are God-given rights and yours by birth. History proves that atrocities are committed when a government enforces rigid control over the political, economic and social life of its population, better known as a "Police State." Probably the most well known example of this in modern history was Nazi Germany.

A couple of questions you might want to ask yourself are: why are the police being trained and equipped in such a manner, and what must you do to be prepared if martial law is imposed? The vast majority of Americans are either clueless or just plain scared, and rather than being educated and equipped, you have buried your head in self-satisfying pleasure. What's even worse is when you criticize those who are trying to educate you. Don't be one of the sheeple. No pity will be afforded you or your family if you are ever unjustly taken away.

I can't find anything in the New Testament that tells me to take up arms against a tyrannical government or rogue police force, but I'm not about to be taken to any camp of any kind when I've done nothing wrong. What about you? Will you become one of the informed?

I would hope enough people will come together, once they have been made aware of what is happening, to speak out against this aggression and remove from public office the robbers of men's souls. It is without any reservation that I say President Barack Obama and his administration, Nancy Pelosi as Speaker of the House, and Harry Reed as the Senate Majority Leader, are leading the assault on American sovereignty.

When I worked behind the bar, I heard many discussions suggesting all congressional seats, both Senate and the House should be limited to two terms, just as the presidency has its limitation. This would make room for a new generation of public servants who will uphold the rights so many have bled and died for, and who will expel the United Nations from the borders of this country. I do not think any person in their right mind would want an unelected group of internationals dictating how and what standard of living we can obtain. As a people, we must not allow our constitution to be rewritten in favor of government control.

Any person not willing to submit their lifestyle to the moral guideline of the Ten Commandments written in the Bible should never be allowed to hold public office or make decisions that would influence the education of a child. No one has the qualifications to even think they can lead another person, much less a nation, if they won't even allow themselves to be led. Ted Kennedy now believes in the God his lifestyle and political advocacy opposed. I do not believe the acronym "RIP" is applicable...

I don't want you to take my word for these statements; I want you to research the statistics so you can then come to your own educated conclusion. Try to crucify me if you want, but I am right and you cannot deny it. The proof is the ignorance of today's culture.

The evident decline of American culture is the result of what church leaders in modern yesterday, and many holding this position today have not done. They are avoiding the inevitable confrontation of issues that have shaped cultural trends. In fear of the loss of financial stability or being sued by someone whose ego has been challenged. I've watched preachers on TV talk shows say it's not as important to adhere to biblical doctrine as it is to reach out to all people with a message of love and acceptance. What's even worse is when a minister is caught up in some immoral scandal that mirrors the behavior of those who are to be reached.

If this, is in fact, the beginning of the end of time before God's judgment, the Christian community must allow the Spirit of God, by the teaching of biblical doctrine to drastically change their representation. As Christians, we have an obligation to influence every aspect of life. If we don't, then the evil in those who do not know the Lord Jesus Christ will.....and have. This world is not our eternal home, but for the time we live here, God's law must be proclaimed to capture the attention of those who will listen.

> "Do not think that I have come to abolish the Law or the Prophets; I have not come to abolish them but to fulfill them. For truly, I say to you, until heaven and earth pass away, not an iota, not a dot, will pass from the Law until all is accomplished. Therefore whoever relaxes one of the least of these commandments and teaches others to do the same will be called least in the kingdom of heaven, but whoever does them and teaches them will be called great in the kingdom of heaven."
>
> Matthew 5:17-19

Christianity is mocked by the masses today because of a unanimous division in what is taught as divine truth, and the many different displays of human emotion seen in churches of every denomination. I have been in meetings and witnessed things that had me questioning the sanity of these people, and you wonder why faith in the Christian lifestyle is made fun of. The message has become so empty and weak it no longer has an appeal.

The many pulpit orators who have grown up among the ranks of churches and Bible colleges are way too naïve to have any concept of what is really happening in not only America, but the entire world. Not having the personal experience, these spineless wimps try to tell someone else how to live their life. Most of the people I've met in Christian leadership couldn't beat their way out of a wet paper bag.

If I am going to be in a fight, whether physically or spiritually, I want someone in my corner who can coach me through the fight. If a person doesn't know what to look for in my opponent's tactics, how can they lead me? This is the reason church leaders and the congregations they coach are so pathetically weak in their representation of such an awesome God.

The time for playing church is over. People are going to hell by the masses and very little is being done about it. My personal view of main stream denominations and the independent churches of today is that they are more concerned about ego and race issues, who's interpretation of the Bible is right, congregational numbers and making money, than in speaking the truth and meeting a person at their need.

Every time Christian television is turned on, someone, if not everyone, is asking for my best offering. "One hundred, five hundred, twelve hundred dollar love offering for such and such ministry is a breakthrough seed you need to give for your dreams to come true!" No offering is going to make anybody's dream come true. Only a life submitted to the plan and purpose of God can truly know what happiness is.

Nothing irritates me more than a preacher who hollers and screams in an attempt of putting on a show describing a theoretical point of view. All the while they have no concept of the audiences struggle within of hoping to hear something that brings healing and closure to what is in their past. "Been there and come through it" instruction of how to bring about this change is what people need to hear. It takes a lot of money to meet the needs people have today, but it should never be at the expense of a person's eternal salvation.

I am not opposed to giving to a church ministry, as long as I know the money I give is going to meet a need. Until those who are preaching "the money message" are willing to meet people at their need, they have no right to ask for support.

This give to God through the church money market is what most modern day ministries are being built upon, and I believe it's being taught way out of context. God's Gospel is free, but a false gospel is being packaged and sold to people for the profit that can be made.

There are ministers who won't even upload their sermons online for people to hear, but they will sell the CD for $12. People buy this trash as if it's something they've got to have to learn how to live a successful Christian life. I refuse to waste my money on lies when God has revealed truth through each page of His book of divine authority.

> *Grace and peace be multiplied to you in the knowledge of God and of Jesus our Lord, as His divine power has given to us all things that pertain to life and godliness, through the knowledge of Him who called us by glory and virtue.*
>
> 2 Peter 1:2-3

This problem needs to be addressed and corrected before people will trust in what Christian leaders have to say. There has been too much abuse. Someone must confront these false teaches and educate God's people as to the lies they have been told. And only when these false teachers are either removed or repent, will God bring about the change needed to attract people who are hurting and looking for what can only be offered through the person of Jesus Christ. It's called having hope that things can really change.

People have been quick to tell me what they thought my problems were and few have ever had anything to say that helped me understand how to live differently. Because of this, I am now very selective in who I allow to speak to me. If you have never been through anything tough or experienced the struggle of overcoming that demon within, listen to what I am saying and you just might learn a language no university or book on Christian living can teach.

One of the more beneficial things I experienced while writing this book was coming to an understanding of the importance of Bible study. I am not going to go into great detail about this because I'm really not qualified. But now I understand why there is so much confusion about false world religions and especially about Christianity today.

Almost every preacher I have ever listened to picks topics that, for the most part, are what they think people want to hear. Anyone can make the Bible say just about anything they want it to say. I cannot count the times I have attended a church service or listened to a TV broadcast and never once heard the speaker quote from the Bible. Church today is all about programs and stories filled with humor and drama, and full of compromise to try to make the audience comfortable. Well, I have some news for you—there is nothing *comfortable* about the Bible's message of how to transform a person's life. You have to be willing to die to what you want if you are to ever discover what God has planned for you.

To understand what the Bible is saying, you must do an expository study of the entire context of Scripture, and not just a particular verse or group of verses saying the same thing. In my opinion, the majority of people running their mouth from the pulpits of American churches today have lost focus of what the Bible really teaches.

God doesn't change, but eras and people do. To avoid all of the confusion surrounding everybody's different interpretations of what they think the Bible says, we need to understand the life application teachings of Scripture and how they apply to our present day situations. And I want to make this statement again: should the message you hear preached not give answers to the questions you have or the situations you face, then what was said is not the Gospel. If the church is ever to prove to an unsaved world that the Bible is a living revelation of God, there must be unity in the message presented. The walls of denominations must be brought down.

> But Jesus knew their thoughts, and said to them: "Every kingdom divided against itself is brought to desolation, and every city or house divided against itself will not stand."
>
> Matthew 12:25

All of the different denominations and independent churches making up the religious market of our time need to return to the message of God first, the denying of what you want and focusing on the welfare of other people, like Jesus taught in the Gospels. I would be lying if I were to say I don't want to make money and enjoy the good things this world has to offer, because I do. As I earn the money, it's my hope that I'll have the opportunity to enjoy it.

Today's easy gospel presented from the pulpit and media programs hosted by charlatans like televangelists Mike Murdock and Robert Tilton, must be stopped. I waited on Mr. Tilton and his "third wife" at a restaurant in Miami, Florida. His demeanor in person is not what you see on television. They had lunch in the bar area and neither he or his wife were nice to me and they didn't tip. I won't listen to anything he has to say, and neither should you.

It is not my or anybody else's responsibility to pay their bills and provide for their extravagant lifestyles. If they are asking for money so that their programs can continue to be heard, it would be better for everybody if the shows didn't air.

It's bad enough to know that the people working for this nation's political system enjoy all the perks that come along with doing nothing of value for those being represented, and even worse when I hear a preacher ask for money. What a mess they have made by playing with the emotions of those who are needy. And if they do not repent and change their representation, those who preach the buying of God's time and provision are not far away from His judgment.

*For the time has come for judgment to begin at the house of God; and if it begins with us first, what will be the end of those who do not obey the gospel of God?*
1 Peter 4:17

*"Therefore, you shepherds, hear the word of the LORD: As surely as I live, says the Sovereign LORD, you abandoned my flock and left them to be attacked by every wild animal. And though you were my shepherds, you didn't search for my sheep when they were lost. You took care of yourselves and left the sheep to starve. Therefore, you shepherds, hear the word of the LORD. This is what the Sovereign LORD says: I now consider these shepherds my enemies, and I will hold them responsible for what has happened to my flock. I will take away their right to feed the flock, and I will stop them*

*from feeding themselves. I will rescue my flock from their*
*mouths; the sheep will no longer be their prey. I will search*
*for my lost ones who strayed away, and I will bring them*
*safely home again. I will bandage the injured and strengthen*
*the weak. But I will destroy those who are fat and powerful.*
*I will feed them, yes—feed them justice!"*

Ezekiel 34:7-10, 16

I know there are untold ministries and individuals doing what God has called them to do and who are successful in reaching out to other people to make a difference, so please understand I am not being critical of the true Christian church. I am, however, confronting those who have compromised God's mandate to reach the unsaved. This is the reason why entertainment venues draw tens of millions of people every week in their pursuit of self-satisfying pleasure and never be challenged on their conduct of living.

I have never been to a church building that once I was inside its doors, I didn't see everything I wanted to leave outside. Don't tell me what I should be doing when you aren't living it. I see you every day at lunch or at evening dinner praying over your food and then treating a waiter or waitress rudely and leaving no tip. And you have the audacity to leave a witnessing tract on a table or on my bar. You have no right to be in ministry of any kind when how you live is for your own self-indulgence.

*I appeal to you, brothers, to watch out for those who cause*
*divisions and create obstacles contrary to the doctrine that*
*you have been taught; avoid them. For such persons do not*
*serve our Lord Christ, but their own appetites, and by smooth*
*talk and flattery they deceive the hearts of the naive.*

Romans 16:17-18

Jesus reached out to the outcasts and proved His love by providing for their needs, and He never judged. His issues were with the religious leaders of that time and I believe it would be the same today. You are so much like those who have no knowledge of God that it's often hard to tell the difference. You are not a living epistle to the message of hope and life-transformation I read in the Bible. My question to you is this, "What will it take for you to change so people can then see something appealing in the message you present?" I hope what I've said in this book will point you in that direction.

> *If you claim to be religious but don't control your tongue, you are fooling yourself, and your religion is worthless. Pure and genuine religion in the sight of God the Father means caring for orphans and widows in their distress and refusing to let the world corrupt you.*
>
> James 1:26-27

Until you are willing to do what God requires and then actually live it out, people will not listen to what is said about a God you don't even know. I firmly believe religion teaches a theory of God rather than about a relationship with Him. It is a bondage to an obligation that will never be fulfilled, as long as you think God exists only in a box you're comfortable with. God is as tired of religion as are the masses.

When I made a decision to separate from the influence of my past and I began to read the Bible with an expectation, that is when God met me where I was. This was not an emotion I worked myself into. God's Spirit was a tangible presence that brought comfort and helped me to feel at peace. In this atmosphere, God proved who He is by what He did to help me overcome the influence of my past, and to reveal the purpose of my life. This has given me a lot of thought as to how Jesus presented His Gospel, and now I understand the example He left me to follow after.

I don't believe God is opposed to me or anybody else being successful in any area of life, because there are too many scriptures in the Bible telling me this is His desire. If I don't have the means, I can't help anybody. But a separation from what the worldly mentality holds dear must come first.

This is where the religious market has grossly misled people. The Bible teaches a lifestyle of selfless giving and service to humanity, not the deception of compromise Christian psychology churches are full of today. The Biblical challenge is to become like Jesus and live your life in a way that attracts people to the message of eternal salvation. God's calling is for something much higher than what a false religion and the modern day secular church are presenting.

> *"His purpose was for the nations to seek after God and perhaps feel their way toward him and find him—though he is not far from anyone of us. For in him we live and move and exist. As some of your own poets have said, 'We are his offspring.' And since this is true, we shouldn't think of God as an idol designed by craftsmen from gold or silver or stone. God overlooked people's ignorance about these things in earlier times, but now he commands everyone everywhere to repent of their sins and turn to him."*
>
> Acts 17:27-30

I want my lifestyle as a Christian to be changed to reflect the fullness of the person of Jesus Christ for all people to see. God's approval is our reward.

> *"Look at my Servant, whom I have chosen. He is my Beloved, who pleases me. I will put my Spirit upon him, and he will proclaim justice to the nations. He will not fight or shout or raise his voice in public. He will not crush the weakest reed or put out a flickering candle. Finally he will cause justice to be victorious. And his name will be the hope of all the world."*
>
> Matthew 12:18-21

Now that I understand what God expects of me and I am willing to answer the call upon my life, it has created an expectation that everything I've hoped for will one day become real. God's commitment to me is the indwelling of His Spirit, who will confirm my sonship by His evident blessing upon all I put my hands to do.

> *"Therefore, obey the terms of this covenant so that you will prosper in everything you do. By entering into the covenant*

*today, he will establish you as his people and confirm that
he is your God."*

Deuteronomy 29:9, 13a

There are so many things to do and experience now that I believe
God has a plan for my life. But my greatest desire is to realize the fullness
of what God can do in and through me to advance His Kingdom here
on this earth, as I lead people to the saving knowledge of Jesus Christ.
This relationship comes through a study of the Bible, Spirit-led prayer, a
lifestyle of worship and going to a church where God's presence inhabits.
Once you have been in the presence of God, nothing else satisfies.

*Seek the Kingdom of God above all else, and live righteously,
and he will give you everything you need.*

Matthew 6:33

*You will show me the way of life, granting me the joy of your
presence and the pleasures of living with you forever.*

Psalms 16:11

Run away from a church that has become a social club and find a
work of ministry where God's Spirit and His uncompromised Word
have the freedom to challenge you and bring change, so you can
then be an example to those God will have you influence. People are
not perfect and we all need help. This is why God wants us to come
together so we can draw from each others strengths. Something
you've been through just might be what I need to hear to help me
overcome what I'm dealing with.

*As iron sharpens iron, so a friend sharpens a friend.*

Proverbs 27:17

Slowly and thoroughly God is changing my perception of
people because I have asked Him to do this. Every day I am learning
and discovering things about God that helps me want to express
forgiveness, kindness and compassion towards people for God has
been all of these to me. I am still very reserved around people and

probably will be for the rest of my life. But I have finally come to realize I'm not an island and it's going to take the gift in each person to accomplish what God wants to do in the time we live.

The only thing I had to give to God was me. My study of the Bible that led to the writing of this book is why I now believe I can accomplish what I've always hoped for. My lifestyle has become an expression of worship and knowing God has my back, I'm confident that everything I need will be provided.

> *Faith is the confidence that what we hope for will actually happen; it gives us assurance about things we cannot see.*
>
> Hebrews 11:1

If you believe only one thing I have written, believe this: God is making every effort to reach out for the purpose of bringing you to a maturity of what salvation provides. God has called you to be an example of His willingness to love unconditionally as He leads people out of their mess.

> *The eyes of the Lord search the whole earth in order to strengthen those whose hearts are fully committed to him.*
>
> 2 Chronicles 16:9a

Knowing God's at work to make real what you have wished for and watching it happen, is the most addicting intoxication you will ever experience! What you entrust to God, He will do.

> *For whatever one sows, that will he also reap.*
>
> Galatians 6:7b

When you finally realize the person you have become through a process of overcoming the negative experiences of your life and knowing what you now have to offer other people, it makes it all worthwhile. Whether you want to admit it or not, what God will teach you is the only education of any real value.

Don't you think that just maybe the right thing to do and the only option we really have left is to turn to the only source of strength capable of making it all right again? What happened to you is not important when compared to the people God can now reach and lives that can be changed through your brokenness.

> *The sacrifice you desire is a broken spirit. You will not reject a broken and repentant heart, O God.*
>
> Psalms 51:17

# BRIDGING THE GAP
ഇ৩ ୧ଓ

Apart from salvation, the most significant event to happen in my life was the time I spent reading the Bible those years ago in prison. That was the seed that gave birth to the hope I would someday become who I am today. Because of this, I can tell you where God has brought me from. I've been where you are and the process of describing what I did to overcome the feeling of insignificance I'd had from my earliest memories has given me vision and a better understanding of what to do with the experiences I've learned from.

> Then the Lord said to me, "Write my answer plainly on tablets, so that a runner can carry the correct message to others. This vision is for a future time. It describes the end, and it will be fulfilled. If it seems slow in coming, wait patiently, for it will surely take place. It will not be delayed."
>
> Habakkuk 2:2-3

Never did I imagine this study would become what it has. It just goes to prove that God can do what you cannot.

> Jesus looked at them intently and said, "Humanly speaking, it is impossible. But with God everything is possible."
>
> Matthew 19:26

It was not my intent to write a book about the transformation God took me through that brought healing to my soul and through that, discover my purpose in life—it just happened. I have no theological training and the highest year of public school I completed was the eighth grade. When you were graduating from middle school to high school to college, I was being moved from juvenile lockdown to jail to a state penitentiary—two completely different influences. And from that time until writing this book, I lived in a state of inebriation to avoid dealing with my issues.

Another struggle I had to deal with is the memory I had of being told I was stupid. This has taken me a lifetime to overcome. The whole time I was writing this book I did not feel as though I was qualified, and to even think someone would want to read it was beyond my expectation. Now, reading what I have written, I see how wrong they were.

This is the existence I have lived and I believe it's why God inspired me to write about my experience. If I can overcome the deceptive lies condemning me to a lifetime of ignorance, wouldn't you want to do the same? I am not proud of what I've done, but the wisdom I gained from having been through so much far outweighs any regrets, since I know what I now have to offer other people has the potential to help only God knows how many.

> *Now all glory to God, who is able, through his mighty power at work within us, to accomplish infinitely more than we might ask or think.*
>
> Ephesians 3:20

Popular opinion will lead you to think differently, but what's really important is taking the time to ask someone in sincerity, "How are you doing?" and then listening to what they say. You don't have to listen long to learn about the issues people are dealing with and become overwhelmed when you discover their problems are just the same as yours. And in many cases, they're worse off than you.

You think that because of your circumstances there's nothing you can do to help, or perhaps you really don't care. This selfish indifference to the needs of others must be confronted with the Gospel of Jesus Christ to restore an awareness of your true self and bridge the gap between God and what He values most.

As I read the structure of my thoughts, it became very clear how people could relate to the message of hope these words are describing. Doing this has helped me find the peace that at one time was so elusive. I've often wondered why my life happened the way it did and created in me the personality I have and all these years later, I now understand. I hold no punches when it comes time to challenge what's wrong and provoke a desire in someone else to change.

What I've been through has built a backbone in me that will never again bow down in defeat to secularism. This time around it's a new fight and I have a confidence no one can silence. As for what happened to me, God has turned it around and is using it for what I believe will be a challenge to a nation that has lost focus of its calling and the encouragement people need while going through their process of life transformation.

Now you have seen for yourself how a hopeless and shattered life can be transformed by doing something as elemental as reading the Bible and becoming aware of the lifestyle God requires. This is the example that takes everyone's excuse away.

> *God knew what he was doing from the very beginning. He decided from the outset to shape the lives of those who love him along the same lines as the life of his Son. The Son stands first in the line of humanity he restored. We see the original and intended shape of our lives there in him. After God made that decision of what his children should be like, he followed it up by calling people by name. After he called them by name, he set them on a solid basis with himself. And then, after getting them established, he stayed with them to the end, gloriously completing what he had begun.*
>
> Romans 8:29-30

The image I now have of myself is a result of knowing God accepts me for who I am, and being willing to express His creative ability in this writing while bringing me out of the mess I made of my life. Don't ever listen to someone when they tell you God cannot use you right where you are. They're a liar and the truth is not in them.

There were nights when my study first began and all through the writing of this book that I was wasted on alcohol or drugs of some kind. I wasn't ready to give up my comfort but even while under the influence of whatever state of inebriation I was in, I read the Bible, hoping the promises would somehow all come true. And I can honestly tell you they have!

It's not what you can do for God, it's what you allow God to do in and through you that proves to people who He really is. Now I understand what true humility feels like. It's a humbling experience to know God is using the life you have lived in order to give people hope. The more I learn of God, the more I expect of myself. Knowing what I am now capable of has created in my imagination the hope of living a life to honor what Jesus has done for me. This will be an ongoing, life-long realization of the fullness of God's creative ability, being expressed through the lifestyle I live to capture the emotional attention of people. There is no higher calling. To whom much is forgiven, much is required.

> *[But what of that?] For I consider that the sufferings of this present time (this present life) are not worth being compared with the glory that is about to be revealed to us and in us and for us and conferred on us!*
>
> Romans 8:18

What an eternal future God has given every person to help establish the hope of doing something significant. Let come what may, I will praise God anyway! I do not allow anything to move me from this confidence. I have become very much aware of my thoughts and what I say. If my actions are wrong, I'm easily convicted and quick to ask God for forgiveness. If it involves anyone else, I will admit my wrong and ask that person to forgive me. I'm not perfect, but I will not allow pride or anything else to separate me from the presence of God I so desperately desire.

> *But if anyone does sin, we have an advocate who pleads our case before the Father. He is Jesus Christ, the one who is truly righteous. He himself is the sacrifice that atones*

*for our sins—and not only our sins but the sins of all the world.*

1 John 2:1b-2

God gave His best. Give Him yours.

*"For God loved the world so much that he gave his one and only Son, so that everyone who believes in him will not perish but have eternal life."*

John 3:16

*I appeal to you therefore, brothers, by the mercies of God, to present your bodies as a living sacrifice, holy and acceptable to God, which is your spiritual worship.*

Romans 12:1

This begins when you make a decision to accept Jesus as your Savior, and the representation you become through a process of transformation, will take the rest of your natural life. True Christianity is a relationship with Jesus, not a religion. A willingness to worship God by how you live is what gives you access into His presence.

Here is that coveted place where your imagination is restored to its innocence and you understand why God allowed what you had to experience. This is the question you need to ask: "Was the experience because of my choice, or is it for my purpose?" Knowing what it's like to not be ashamed of myself anymore, I refuse to give any place to an image of my past. That person no longer exists. God has promised to not hold what is in my past against me, and neither will I.

*If we confess our sins, He is faithful and righteous to forgive us our sins and to cleanse us from all unrighteousness.*

1 John 1:9

*For I will be merciful and gracious toward their sins and I will remember their deeds of unrighteousness no more.*

Hebrews 8:12

Let's get real. Your way hasn't worked yet, so give God His chance. Like me, many of you have wasted years chasing an elusive dream and are so caught up in the emotion of everyday life that your true calling has been neglected. Stop defining who you are by what you do for a dollar amount and realize it's the good you do for someone else that reveals true character and value. My hope is to live every day in a place of intimacy and oneness with God. And as I change, this will attract people to me so I can then lead them into what God saved me to do.

> *But whenever someone turns to the Lord, the veil is taken away. For the Lord is the Spirit, and wherever the Spirit of the Lord is, there is freedom. So all of us who have had that veil removed can see and reflect the glory of the Lord. And the Lord—who is the Spirit—makes us more and more like him as we are changed into his glorious image.*
>
> 2 Corinthians 3:16-18

> *And Jesus said to them, "Follow Me, and I will make you become fishers of men."*
>
> Mark 1:17

If you have never accepted Jesus as your Savior or you really want to know what it means for Jesus to be Lord, today you can ask God for help and begin your process of an eternal transformation. Everything as you know it will change.

> *For he says, "In the time of my favor I heard you, and in the day of salvation I helped you." I tell you, now is the time of God's favor, now is the day of salvation.*
>
> 2 Corinthians 6:2

The definition of salvation is an encyclopedia by itself. The purpose of what I am saying is to make you aware of a condition affecting every person to ever be born. Sin is not something we chose to do; it is in our nature to do evil. No one is exempt.

*"This is the judgment, that the Light has come into the world, and men loved the darkness rather than the Light, for their deeds were evil."*

John 3:19

Until you come to know the truth and ask God for forgiveness by accepting Jesus as your Savior, you are spiritually dead and separated from God. An unregenerate soul is what dictates the circumstances of your life and blinds you to the truth. It is only by the Spirit of God that a human spirit can be reborn and have the Bible come to life as its words transform your soul. Salvation is something you walk out every day. The choices you make, the thoughts you entertain, the words you speak and the things you do through the opportunities of each day proves an awareness of what you have been saved from.

Twenty years ago in prison I asked God to forgive me for how I had lived, but I was unable to live in the freedom of what salvation provided because what I thought of myself hadn't changed. I believe if anyone is in a life and death situation and you sincerely call out to God, spiritual salvation is instantaneous. But the soul's transformation may take a lifetime. This is where so many people have been caught unaware. I believe this subtle ignorance has cost an untold number their eternal destiny. I don't know everything there is to know about this subject but one thing is very clear, no one can fall away from something they have never obtained.

*For it is impossible, in the case of those who have once been enlightened, who have tasted the heavenly gift, and have shared in the Holy Spirit, and have tasted the goodness of the word of God and the powers of the age to come, and then have fallen away, to restore them again to repentance, since they are crucifying once again the Son of God to their own harm and holding him up to contempt.*

Hebrews 6:4-6

The "once saved always saved" ideology taught in many churches is something I am not in agreement with. It is true that only God knows a person for who they really are, but I cannot say with confidence if I had died the night I drove my car off the cliff I would not have been eternally lost. That would have been murder and the Bible plainly states those who commit murder and are unrepentant cannot enter into the Kingdom of Heaven. And to look at the church today in all of its worldliness, I would have to say most of the people claiming to be Christians are playing roulette with their eternal destinies.

When I hear a preacher give an alter call and they ask if there's anyone who wants to be saved to just raise their hand and God will welcome them into the family, I want to scream. That is not true biblical salvation.

This is where seeker friendly churches and movements like the Emergent Church have compromised the true Gospel of repentance, which is the turning away from whatever it is you are doing and embracing a lifestyle submitted to the plans and purposes of God. Only then can God lead you in the journey of obtaining His wisdom and the knowledge to live a life He will honor.

> *Work hard to show the results of your salvation, obeying God with deep reverence and fear. For God is working in you, giving you the desire and the power to do what pleases him.*
>
> Philippians 2:12b-13

I would never have come to this place in a relationship with Jesus Christ had I not given myself time for the recreative work done in my imagination. When I started this study my intent was to find out what the Bible says about how a Christian lifestyle is to be lived, but what I found was closure to the memories of my past and this has now become my healing. What happened to me doesn't matter anymore; what matters is the opportunity I have now been given to help someone else.

I believe this to be one of the next great moves of God in the lives of those who make up the body of churches today. I also believe what is happening with the policies and laws that are being passed in favor of these special interest agendas, is to purge the body of

Christ of its compromise. How can you be the Christ like example to other people when what you are supposed to represent is not yet evident in yourself?

I have never in my lifetime witnessed anything that appealed to me in the lives of religious people. In many circumstances, they did not represent God in a favorable light. The people you are to influence need to see something in you that they do not have in their own lives. Why would a person give up what they find comfort in when they can see you're just as confused as they are?

> So we are Christ's ambassadors, God making His appeal as it were through us. We [as Christ's personal representatives] beg you for His sake to lay hold of the divine favor [now offered you] and be reconciled to God.
>
> 2 Corinthians 5:20

I cannot find any teachings in the New Testament to support what the evangelical movement now calls church. Scripture teaches those who profess to be Christians are to be the example for nonbelievers to want to experience the hope, the peace and the joy that should be the motivation behind the faith we proclaim. But if you are honest with yourself, this confidence has been far removed. Many church leaders today do not adhere to biblical doctrine, but have instead introduced secular psychology and every other kind of worldly influence to present themselves as socially acceptable. Instead of being the standard people would respect and want to emulate, many of you in church today are no different than those who are dead in their sin.

What God has done in your life is for the purpose of representing Him and not to be an embarrassment. Sadly, church as we know it in America has done a very good job of the later. The church I attended after coming home was much like other churches in my past. I experienced what should never happen because of someone's ego, pride or whatever the reason. This kind of self-centered behavior does nothing but turn people off. It grieves the Holy Spirit of God. Unless you repent, you will be held accountable for these actions.

*"And the King will say, 'I tell you the truth, when you did it to one of the least of these my brothers and sisters, you were doing it to me!'"*

Matthew 25:40

I attended Strong Tower Ministries for three years and I honestly believe it is where God placed me for a time of emotional healing and spiritual growth. During the spring and summer as I was writing what became the manuscript for this book, I was one of a few men who came on Saturday mornings to cut grass, but that was as active as I chose to be. I had no desire to be involved with any of its drama.

I hope in my near future there will be a man who has earned people's respect by the manner in which his lifestyle has been lived, who I can learn from as he helps me find my place in the body of Christ. Church is a place for people to come to be healed and like everyone else, this has been a process for me. I am not fond of some things that have happened, but I've matured enough to know this is where God intends for there to be spiritual instruction and the restoring of a persons confidence.

*And He Himself gave some to be apostles, some prophets, some evangelists, and some pastors and teachers, for the equipping of the saints for the work of the ministry, for the edifying of the body of Christ, till we all come to the unity of the faith and of the knowledge of the Son of God, to a perfect man, to the measure of the stature of the fullness of Christ; that we should no longer be children, tossed to and fro and carried about with every wind of doctrine, by the trickery of men, in the cunning craftiness of deceitful plotting, but, speaking the truth in love, may grow up in all things into Him who is the head—Christ.*

Ephesians 4:11-15

If you have been offended or hurt by churched people, it's time to quit feeling sorry for yourself and find a God-ordained pastor you can submit to and learn from. To those you outside of church who call everyone else a hypocrite, at least they are in the will of

God. You have no right to criticize someone else when you lack the courage to do it for yourself.

> *In the same way you younger men must accept the authority of the elders. And all of you serve each other in humility, for "God opposes the proud but favors the humble."*
>
> 1 Peter 5:5

Everyone needs a spiritual covering and God requires this obedience, but no person will ever replace the personal relationship Jesus desires to have with you. Giving your time every day to a study of the Bible and communicating with God in prayer is the foundation of strength you need to turn away from every influence that does not edify the image of who you really are. Only you can make a decision to do this.

> *Don't copy the behavior and customs of this world, but let God transform you into a new person by changing the way you think. Then you will learn to know God's will for you, which is good and pleasing and perfect.*
>
> Romans 12:2

The church collectively will never be more than what each person becomes in the privacy of an intimate and personal relationship with Jesus Christ. What is done when no one else is looking is who you really are. I have always thought there was more to serving God and being a Christian than what I've witnessed in the lives of people in my past. This time of study has revealed to me what a lifestyle of worship is capable of doing.

There is a higher realm of living to obtain and it cannot be done alone. I know from experience that God can create in you an imagination filled with the expectation of becoming the person you have always hoped be, by studying the Bible and learning how to live each day submitted to the leading of God's Holy Spirit.

> *May He grant you out of the rich treasury of His glory to be strengthened and reinforced with mighty power in the inner*

*man by the [Holy] Spirit [Himself indwelling your inner most being and personality].*

Ephesians 3:16

I have done what few people ever take the time to do for themselves, and that is why I have experienced such a radical change in how I think of myself and what I now believe I'm capable of doing. Your understanding may be different than mine and that's okay. My testimony is meant to provoke your imagination and encourage a study of the Bible that brings understanding to who you are, while learning about the lifestyle of worship God requires of you.

# CONFIDENCE RESTORED

Most of my life I was in bondage to substance abuse because of what I thought about me. People who saw me at work or out in public would never have thought I was buzzed. I carried it well. Working behind a bar for so many years taught me what to drink and how much I needed to keep a constant feel good.

Substance abuse is not something you will easily let go of. It's comfortable, it's relaxing and you can laugh. Only when I was sober did I have thoughts about the person of my imagination and as hard as I tried, never more than a few days passed before I had to have another drink.

There were times when I'd pour myself a drink behind the bar or be in a wine store making a purchase and God would convict me. I had no peace about this. It was not a feeling of condemnation but of realizing in everything I chose to do, God's Holy Spirit would be involved.

> *And what union can there be between God's temple and idols? For we are the temple of the living God. As God said: "I will live in them and walk among them. I will be their God, and they will be my people. Therefore, come out from among unbelievers, and separate yourselves from them, says the Lord. Don't touch their filthy things, and I will welcome you. And I will be your Father, and you will be my sons and daughters, says the Lord Almighty."*
>
> 2 Corinthians 6:16-18

I will never tell a person it's wrong to drink alcohol because I would be in violation of Scripture. What you will never hear a preacher expound upon is that the Bible does tell us to drink wine for its antioxidant benefits.

> *Drink water no longer exclusively, but use a little wine for the sake of your stomach and your frequent illnesses.*
>
> 1 Timothy 5:23

It's been proven medically that moderate wine consumption has health benefits and I believe this is why we find a command like this in Scripture. God made us and food we are supposed to eat, and everything we really need to live healthy lives grows naturally from the earth.

God is not concerned with you having a drink. What He's concerned with is the drink having you. And the drink had me! It was my kryptonite. The older I got, the angrier I'd become and it was because I had finally realized alcohol was keeping me from living out my purpose. So don't ever let anyone make you feel guilty, but know your limits and understand what you do could hinder yourself or someone else. This is when it becomes sin.

> *Do not, for the sake of food, destroy the work of God. Everything is indeed clean, but it is wrong for anyone to make another stumble by what he eats. It is good not to eat meat or drink wine or do anything that causes your brother to stumble. The faith that you have, keep between yourself and God. Blessed is the one who has no reason to pass judgment on himself for what he approves.*
>
> Romans 14:20-22

There were times when I would serve a cocktail to someone with tears running down my face. My awareness of God's presence was so real it overwhelmed me. People often asked me what was wrong and my response was, "You wouldn't understand." It was not time for me to talk about what God was doing.

There's a time for everything and then there is a time to do nothing. It was not the right time for me to speak to anyone about the change I was going through. If I had told someone what was happening and a derogatory comment had been made, I would have cussed someone out or worse. During this time I didn't talk much because I was still trying to figure out me. But knowing God did accept me and that wherever I went His presence was right there, was the most significant encouragement of my life.

> *Even before he made the world, God loved us and chose us in Christ to be holy and without fault in his eyes. God decided in advance to adopt us into his own family by bringing us to himself through Jesus Christ. This is what he wanted to do, and it gave him great pleasure.*
>
> Ephesians 1:4-5

God wants to be everything you need in this natural life and even if you won't let Him, He will do it anyway. I so appreciate God's mercy and patience when dealing with me. He has become everything never given to me as a child. What I missed learning, God has taught me through this time of study. The way God has corrected how I think makes me want to live a life that honors the gift of salvation and my soul's peace given to me by Jesus' sacrifice.

I have finally come to realize the Bible is not a book written to tell me what I can and can't do. Its message is to help me understand what I am to believe about Jesus Christ and myself, how I'm to live and those I am to reach. So whatever has happened, the circumstance you are in right now is leading you to God for a purpose He created you to influence.

> *But God is so rich in mercy, and he loved us so much, that even though we were dead because of our sins, he gave us life when he raised Christ from the dead. (It is only by God's grace that you have been saved!) For he raised us from the dead along with Christ and seated us with him in the heavenly realms because we are united with Christ Jesus. So God can point to us in all future ages as examples of the incredible wealth of his grace and kindness towards us, as shown in all he has done for us who are united with Christ Jesus. God*

*saved you by his grace when you believed. And you can't take credit for this; it is a gift from God. Salvation is not a reward for the good things we have done, so none of us can boast about it. For we are God's masterpiece. He has created us anew in Christ Jesus, so we can do the good things he planned for us long ago.*

Ephesians 2:4-10

Everything that's happened in my life is not for me to understand. I believe my life's experience was orchestrated by God and then used to break me. As I look back over everything I've come through, I realize God was leading me by His unseen hand to a willingness of surrender in spirit, soul and body. Coming through this process of change and overcoming the negative experiences of my life gives me the confidence to say to you what I do. God now has a voice in this culture who understands the cries of people wanting to believe their life has purpose.

*And we know that all things work together for good to them that love God, to them who are the called according to his purpose.*

Romans 8:28

Most of the problems you will face in life are not what Satan or another person is doing to you. There's no denying the evil in people who are influenced by Satan or that people do bad things. But what most people have failed to realize is the circumstances we face in life have been ordained by God to prove whether we are worthy of His Spirit indwelling our lives.

*Now there was a day when the sons of God came to present themselves before the LORD, and Satan also came among them. The LORD said to Satan, "From where do you come?" Then Satan answered the LORD and said, "From roaming about on the earth and walking around on it." The LORD said to Satan, "Have you considered My servant Job? For there is no one like him on the earth, a blameless and upright man, fearing God and turning away from evil." Then Satan answered the LORD, "Does Job fear God for nothing? "Have You not made a hedge about him and his house and all that he has, on every side? You have blessed the work of his hands, and his possessions have increased in the land. "But put forth Your hand now and touch all that he has; he will surely curse You to Your face." Then the LORD said to Satan, "Behold, all that he has is in your power, only do not put forth your hand on him." So Satan departed from the presence of the LORD.*

Job 1:6-12

God is the creator of your circumstances and He knows how to push your buttons. So instead of complaining about what you think you have no control over, begin thanking God for what He is leading you through to reveal the purpose you are here for. All of the other situations are what you have ignorantly brought upon yourself! An idle mind and compromised truth is the devil's playground.

The time I've given to reading, study and writing about something I didn't understand was difficult at first. But staying consistent and truly seeking change has allowed God the time He's needed to heal to my soul and restore my confidence, as I witnessed this transformation happening right in front of me.

*Come close to God, and God will come close to you.*

James 4:8a

*But to as many as did receive and welcome Him, He gave the authority (power, privilege, right) to become the children of God, that is, to those who believe in (adhere to, trust in and rely on) His name.*

John 1:12

God's patience with me while I was in my mess has allowed the time I needed to overcome what had held me down from my youth. What was once an elusive dream has now become reality in knowing God's love and acceptance of me is unconditional. I'm now learning how to express an emotion I don't yet fully understand by my lifestyle of worshiping God, not only for what He has done, but for who He is. God will never give up on you.

> *"I will never leave you nor forsake you."*
>
> Hebrews 13:5b

As far back as I can remember, my imagination was damaged to the point of having no confidence and I believed I did not deserve to live a successful life. I saw myself being a sixty-five year old bartender trading stories with all the other wishful thinkers and that sobered me. This is why I made a decision to take God at His Word and I am searching the Bible to discover what God expects of me.

There are numerous books available to read on this subject. But choosing to do the research for myself has created a confident expectation of seeing what I hope for become reality, as I experience a significant change in how I think and the way I live taking place in such a short time period.

> *"Then you will experience for yourselves the truth, and the truth will free you."*
>
> John 8:32

God desires for you to be confident and at peace, so the lifestyle you live will then reflect this inner beauty to those who have no hope.

> *What shall we say about such wonderful things as these? If God is for us, who can ever be against us?*
>
> Romans 8:31

I have given much thought to what I am about to say and reading the structure of my thoughts, I feel this chapter is an appropriate place to write about it. This is a subject men refuse to talk about because of the pain they have had to endure. Forgiveness and healing have yet to be experienced, and the memories of what happened years ago influence the life they know.

You may wonder why church has so few men active in its outreach programs and why the sanctity of their families are no more secure than those who have no knowledge of God. In their minds they are still wounded little boys who have never had a chance to grow up free from the trauma of their violated innocence.

I have carried this shame from my childhood and I believe it is why I have been so bitter in response to how people treated me. On the news you see this same thing taking place in every class of people, crossing nationalities and both genders, and it is sickening. My childhood was not easy and I reacted the only way a child could, given the experiences I had.

It was not until I was sexually molested that I withdrew into a make-believe world where everything was perfect and nobody was trying to hurt me. I don't know if the man who did this to me is still alive and I really don't care. What he did, though, was transfer an image he had of himself to me. The demonic influence controlling his imagination was now familiar to me.

> *This is not the wisdom that comes down from above, but is earthly, unspiritual, demonic. For where jealousy and selfish ambition exist, there will be disorder and every vile practice.*
>
> James 3:15-16

I believe it was that demon I saw staring back at me from the mirror. It twisted my self-perception and from that time, I have had to fight this influence to not let it take control of me. From my youth I have been around gay men and I remember an uncle who slept with a man every night. I didn't know why and never asked—I had no feelings either way. It was not until prison that I began to resent homosexual men, because that was the reason for every fight I was ever in while incarcerated. Every time I look in a mirror, the scars of those fights stare back at me, and these memories have never gone away.

I was born into an abusive environment and over time a resistance to my feelings developed. I believe this is why I was able to resist a relentless influence of homosexual emotions. All through my adolescence and into my adulthood, the image of what that man did to me, what was experienced in prison and everything else I've had to deal with pressured me to give in. I've had to fight off thoughts, images, people approaching me, being touched and even worse...

When I came home after my father called to tell me about his sickness and I met up with people I used to work with, the lifestyle I was living never changed. One night I was with a group barhopping as we waited for someone to get off work. When he arrived, we closed the last bar open that night.

About ten of us went to his apartment. We continued to drink alcohol and were doing drugs. It was early morning when I excused myself and went into another room to pass out. I had crashed at his apartment on many occasions and never once did anything bad happen.

All of my clothes were on when I laid down and I have no memory of anything until someone woke me up. I remember waking to a feeling of discomfort. There was this man who I'd thought was my friend on top of me, having sexual intercourse. I pushed him off, and he went into another room. I got up, gathered my composure and stumbled into the other room and asked what his problem was.

Fortunately for both of us, I was too inebriated fight, but as I left his apartment I warned him if he were to see me in town, he had better avoid me. My car was parked at a restaurant where I worked several blocks away and as I walked in that direction, the tears started flowing. I had been raped. The emotion was overwhelming. I wasn't a child this time—I was a grown man.

Memories of what happened almost thirty years before that I'd tried so hard to suppress flooded my mind and I became furious. I went back to his apartment and just as I was reaching for the door, I turned around and walked away. It was one of the better decisions of my life.

The city where I lived was small enough that it wasn't unusual to see someone several times a day, especially when the restaurants we worked at were within a block of each other. It was a year before we saw each other again and I don't know how God did this, but I never attempted to hurt him. That was a miracle in itself.

What happened really messed me up. I wanted to react, but instead I chose to pickle my emotions. My day was twisted from the time I got out of bed to when I passed out, only to wake up and do it all again. It's a bitter cycle so many people are caught up in today and sadly, few ever find a way out of.

The morning after I was raped, I drove past a new church in my old neighborhood. I had not been to a church service in five years and when I passed the building, it felt as though I needed to be there to hear what was said. I was still drunk from the night before and when I walked in and heard worship music, I stood on the back row and cried, tears running down my face. What was I doing here? I thought God would strike me dead. The shame I felt was almost unbearable.

The music and atmosphere was very quiet when a woman came over and whispered in my ear, *"There is still a ministry in you if you stay faithful."* I never looked up to see who she was. Why would God continue to love me when all I had ever done was be someone that no one else could love? Why did my life have to be this way? Would it ever end? These were questions I kept asking myself, and it has only been through a process of soul-searching prayer and writing this book that answers have now been revealed.

The statements I'm making here will upset people but because of what happened to me and the untold victims who think they don't have a voice, I have every right to say what I do. I want to make you think about what has been done and its effect on the culture we have now become.

I'm nothing like a book-smart psychologist or theologian rationalizing why someone behaves the way they do based on a proposed thesis or an ever-changing scientific theory. What I have learned is by living it and knowing a person makes the decisions they do based on how they think. It's no secret that people today are influenced by education and what is marketed to make them feel good, and when left to their own self-willed imagination, truth becomes what they want it to be.

184 LIVING IN THE HOPE OF MY IMAGINATION

*All of us like sheep have gone astray, Each of us has turned to his own way.*

Isaiah 53:6a

America's infatuation with civil tolerance is being pushed so hard upon this culture that the youth have fallen prey to its deception. Just turn on the TV or log on to the internet and you will be inundated with every kind of immorality you can imagine. These media outlets glorify what people now praise as their newly-won freedom of expression.

From attention-hungry adolescent adults engaging in every kind of lewd pornographic behavior on the internet, to inappropriate content produced by both the music and entertainment industries, and everything in between. We are fed trash like the Jerry Springer Show and This Evening's News, and a diverse menu of sitcoms to promote social acceptance and amuse an empty mind. And you think there is not a purpose behind the preachers of immorality.

The US Department of Education, Planned Parenthood, the National Organization for Women, the Human Rights Campaign and the American Civil Liberties Union are among the top ranks of institutions deceiving the minds of the weak. These are the groups that tell people, "It's your body and no one has the right to tell you what is right or wrong," that homosexuality is normal behavior, and they even do profiling in schools to determine how easily a child will conform. Young people are the targets of these attacks and if left unchallenged, it will wreck their lives.

I have no choice but to do what few people today are willing to risk their social and financial reputations, by telling you the true motive behind the homosexual movement. I will also explain what their agenda has done in leading the way to so many lives being shattered.

The *"gay"* lifestyle is not the happy and committed family environment they and the media portray, or the culture image Hollywood has spent billions of dollars propagating. In reality, the homosexual lifestyle is a very harsh reality. It is a moral perversion expressed by those who have a blatant disregard of God and His Bible. I have been in restrooms where homosexual men have propositioned me and even exposed their genitals. If this behavior is normal, then why are the participants of pride events so blatantly vulgar in their displays of sexual expression? I have witnessed homosexual men having sex at these public venues with no consideration of who might witness their behavior.

Homosexuality is a sin that shakes its fist in the face of God and dares the Christian to confront its destructive agenda. This is why so many people who indulge in this lifestyle choice are dependant upon substance abuse to numb their emotions and to not have to deal with their own accusing conscience. STDs are widespread because of the high number of sex partners. Domestic violence is common and suicide has taken many lives. There are too many verifiable accounts by people who have been delivered out of this lifestyle describing how degraded they were made to feel. And sadly, the stories of many infected with Aids have told on their death-bed of regret and the fear of dying to then face the judgment of God.

Yet the homosexual agenda hopes to convince the American people that their love and fidelity for each other is the reason behind their insistent and argumentative litigations. This is not the real reason. There's a wealth of knowledge available for those of you who want to know the truth behind this agenda. The question is, will you seriously weigh the facts?

I can speak from experience when I say a person is not born with a homosexual gene. It's a choice they can be influenced to make due to home life or environment, and what another person has subjected you to. I believe the weaker a person's mind is the more susceptible they are to any influence.

As I mentioned earlier, children are not being corrected but rather numbed in their emotions and allowed to do whatever they choose with no thought of an impending consequence for their actions. I hated my parents for the whippings and beatings I was given, but today I am so thankful for the pain they inflicted on me because it made me angry enough to fight. That's why I chose not to be "gay" when all of my life I had to resist those memories and their influence upon my self-image.

Those men had no right to do what they did to me. A person who has any compassion has to wonder why someone would violate a child's innocence or another person's body in that way. What if they had been diseased? What was their childhood like? Had they been molested as a child? How confused is a person's mind to make them want to act out something so vulgar? Whether you want to agree with this or not, here is God's opinion:

> But God shows his anger from heaven against all sinful, wicked people who suppress the truth by their wickedness. Yes, they knew God, but wouldn't worship him as God or even give him thanks. And they began to think up foolish ideas of what God was like. As a result, their minds became dark and confused. Claiming to be wise, they instead became utter fools. And instead of worshiping the glorious, ever-living God, they worshiped idols made to look like mere people and birds and animals and reptiles. So God abandoned them to do whatever shameful things their hearts desired. As a result, they did vile and degrading things with each other's bodies. They traded the truth about God for a lie. So they worshiped and served the things God created instead of the Creator himself, who is worthy of eternal praise! Amen. That is why God abandoned them to their shameful desires. Even the women turned against the natural way to have sex and instead indulged in sex with each other. And the men, instead of having normal sexual relations with women, burned with lust for each other. Men did shameful things with other men, and as a result of this sin, they suffered within themselves the penalty they deserved. Since they thought it foolish to acknowledge God, he abandoned them to their foolish thinking and let them do things that should never be done. Their lives became full of every kind of wickedness, sin, greed, hate, murder, quarreling, deception, malicious behavior, and gossip. They are backstabbers, haters of God, insolent, proud, and boastful. They invent new ways of sinning, and they disobey their parents. They refuse to understand, break their promises, are heartless, and have no mercy. They know

*God's justice requires that those who do these things deserve to die, yet they do them anyway. Worse yet, they encourage others to do them, too.*

Romans 1:18, 21-32

President Barack Obama claims to be a Christian, but recently he said on national television it's his opinion that what is written in this passage of Scripture is obscure and irrelevant for today. He wants the support of the religious right, while at the same time being sympathetic to a homosexual and lesbian lobby by stating he is in favor of civil unions. Now, by presidential proclamation, he has declared June as the official lesbian, gay, bisexual and transgender pride month. Where does it end? Or is this just the beginning? Like so many times before, he continues to avoid taking a hard stand on any issue considered to be divisive. I have to question his sincerity of the faith he proclaims.

Either you believe the Bible is the inspired Word of God or you do not. If you really think about the context which he was referring to, his comment is the epitome of ignorance. This passage of Scripture is a very real and definitive description of what the American culture has become. And this man is heralded by the advocates of change to be the one who knows what is best for you and me. That's a scary thought.

What you haven't taken the time to do is find out what this man really stands for. Based upon my research and to the best of my understanding, Mr. Obama adheres to ideals much like that of the Fabian Communitarian socialist agenda. Founded in 1884, individuals who adhere to Fabian doctrine plan to implement world socialism incrementally through legislation. They believe individualism has no relevance, and private ownership of business and lands should be relinquished for the good of the state and the welfare of other people.

We all remember the now famous "Joe the Plumber" question and what Mr. Obama's response was. He wants to spread the wealth around. If he is the man you have based your hope of change upon, you are exactly what the ruling class has created. A people unaware of the reality that awaits.

The enemies of God despise an individual's creative ability to think and govern successfully over their own affairs, and thus being an example for everyone else. Now the real purpose for Mr. Obama's placement in office by those who are truly in power is being witnessed by the great influx of governmental control over the financial and business industries. Through the control of money through credit and lending, the government will eventually control the people.

With leaders like these making decisions affecting every person's life, it's very clear why America's foundation has been ruptured. Truth has been banished from the scales of justice only to allow lies for the intent of deceiving the masses. There has been so much neglect and abuse to the needs of humanity that God's judgment is to allow His people to be led by men and women with no moral ethics. I believe God has given the American people not only what we want, but also what we deserve.

The Bible commands us to pray for those in authority, and my prayer for Mr. Obama is to come to the saving knowledge of Jesus Christ. His stand alone on politics proves he has no knowledge of the life transforming power of the Gospel.

I do not have a right to judge a person for the lifestyle they choose to live. Nor do I care what a person does in the privacy of their home. God's holy and righteous sovereignty will judge you! But I do have the right to confront behavior that has caused so much pain in my life when it's blatantly paraded in my face. Because we have become so desensitized and culturally divided as a nation, there's now a tolerant fear of the militant homosexual movement.

Advocates claim ten percent of this nation's population is gay when in reality it's more like two percent. But there is nowhere the homosexual agenda does not have influence, including education, arts and entertainment, and corporate management. It influences the work force, every aspect of government and even the church. Yet all of Scripture teaches homosexuality is an unacceptable behavior.

Their screams of injustice and a demand for equal rights, same-sex marriage and benefits, and the education of alternative sexual lifestyles to school-age children is all a part of the planned-out initiative to force tolerance of their behavior upon everyone else.

They claim their unjust treatment as a minority group is in violation of their civil rights. This is a slap in the face to black Americans who fought for and won their equality. Yet we are all too quick to forget about the decimation of Native Americans by this nation's government. Confusion with one's sexual identity is not the same as a person being born to a certain ethnic group. The color of a person's skin is not something you can change, but you do have a choice in your sexual preference.

In October of 1998, everyone was inundated by their local and national news media with the brutal beating and slaying of Wyoming resident Matthew Shepard. The media said this twenty-one year old college student was the victim of a hate crime because he was open about his homosexuality. The two young men guilty of this crime were rightly convicted and sentenced to consecutive life terms in prison.

What the media didn't report then or even now, were the implications giving evidence that the crime committed against Matthew Shepard was not because of his sexual orientation, but a robbery or possibly a drug deal gone bad. Only the people who committed this heinousness crime will ever know the real motive. Regardless of why, the life of Matthew Shepard was tragically taken as a result of the violent rage in these two young men. Read about their life stories. They are products of the American culture.

Less than one year later, in September of 1999, a thirteen year old boy was abducted and drugged, bound and gagged and then repeatedly raped, tortured and murdered by two admittedly open homosexual men in the state of Arkansas. They too, were sentenced to life terms in prison. But there was very little media coverage of this crime outside the state where it was committed, and most people to this day have never heard the name Jesse Dirkhising. No legislation, movements or movies were made in memory of this young boy whose life was taken in as brutal a manner, if not more so, than Matthew Shepard's.

The media was silenced by advocates of political correctness so as not to hinder the advancement made by homosexual and lesbian activists who used the death of Matthew Shepard to propagate the hate crimes legislation. This is biased and unfair treatment committed against a boy whose civil rights were truly violated in order to not offend the perception of a protected minority. Actions like this prove the real motive behind the LGBT agenda.

This is why I have to speak out in defense of people like Jesse and the untold victims violated by homosexual pedophiles. If the advocates of gay rights are as tolerant as they claim of everyone's freedom of expression, opinion and speech, then what gives these people the right to force upon me and everyone else an acceptance of behavior God calls sin?

Now June is a month where the American people are to "celebrate" the homosexual lifestyle. This is not something I can do, nor will I be silent. Am I and others like me, who know the harm being done to young people today, supposed to keep silent and remain within the safe zone of being culturally correct to not offend someone in their sin? I cannot and will not condone this behavior. The homosexual lifestyle other men chose to live damaged so much of my life that for me to be respectful of this behavior is to be untrue to my convictions.

When a child is taught same-sex unions are traditional and to be accepted, what is to keep them from acting out who they think they are upon another child? If truth be told, training up a child in this manner is creating nothing less than a breeding ground for the sexual predators of tomorrow. Ask a person living this lifestyle if they were ever molested as a child, and the number who have been will shock you. Or the children without a mother and a father concerned and active in their training. When left alone, inquisitive young minds mimic what they see other people doing.

To know my tax dollars are being used to not only promote, but also protect this special interest group angers me. But in this charged atmosphere of political and cultural correctness, my feelings as grounded upon the truth as they are have been labeled religious intolerance.

There are so few free thinkers among today's "enlightened" societies. The enemies of God want people to believe their freedoms of expression earned by a perceived intellectual advancement makes them above and beyond the need of any help.

American culture is being influenced by a relatively small group of elitists. The ruling class wants complete control of their subjects and these limp-wristed government officials, whom you put so much of your hope in, are being controlled like puppets by these same people. Who have worked relentlessly to implement their liberal socialist agenda of keeping the masses from ever becoming the people God created them to be.

These people looked too as leaders have been deceived by Satan and are themselves deceiving weak-minded generations. Having grown up dazed and confused, people now look in any direction they can to find acceptance outside their ever increasing dysfunctional family environment. What people fail to realize is the breakup of the traditional family unit has over time destroyed the basic fundamentals of this nation. This is the reason why we are witnessing such a concerted effort to redefine marriage, and the beginning of restrictions it will bring upon Christian beliefs and its influence upon our culture. The homosexual agenda is deftly being used to silence our First Amendment.

The ignorance of misinformed people, who have been trained up and recruited to embrace these special interest agendas designed to stupefy, is the reason why the masses are living a lie and will never realize their full potential. It's sad to realize just how little people have been made to actually think of themselves and have no desire to know the truth.

If you do not question the evident purpose in the demoralizing of people today, you have never in your lifetime thought an original thought. You have become one of a culture of people happy in their blissful ignorance, and like dumb animals being led to their slaughter; you have no clue of the reality that awaits.

The anger acted out in what the media now calls "The Culture War" is not because homosexual and lesbian couples are treated unfairly and denied certain privileges heterosexual couples have always had. Their anger is a result of an ever-increasing depravity in the minds of godless people without hope, and from being intolerant of those who oppose this behavior from a biblical world-view. The truth offends.

God's abandonment is His judgment upon a culture refusing to acknowledge Him as God, and turn from the wickedness of their pleasure-seeking. What we are witnessing is, in fact, the corrupted character of human nature being affected by moral evil. The homosexual culture is a people oppressed by demonic spirits and are driven by a selfish motivation, always in conflict with their natural affections.

These are the progressive steps leading a person to demonic oppression:

***Suppressing the truth in unrighteousness*** – (Rom 1:18) A person's conscience void of conviction when behavior and thought are in opposition to God's law, and would rather indulge in the pleasure of satisfying the sin of their desire.

***For even though they knew God, they did not honor Him as God*** – (Rom 1:21) God has revealed Himself through creation and no one has an excuse to deny God's existence. This is proven in the fact that people from every nation observe some form of a higher power, though ignorant of who God really is. The failure to honor the Lord Jesus Christ as Savior and Sovereign Judge is humanity's greatest reproach against their Creator.

***Professing to be wise, they became fools, and exchanged the glory of the incorruptible God for an image in the form of corruptible man and birds and four-footed animals and crawling creatures*** – (Rom 1:22-23) All of humanity substitutes the worship of God with animals, nature, people and ideals, and every kind of idolatry that can be imagined. This is in violation of the first of the Ten Commandments: ***You shall have no other gods before me.*** (Ex 20:3)

***Therefore God gave them over (abandoned) in the lusts of their hearts to impurity, so that their bodies would be dishonored among them*** – (Rom 1:24) When a person consistently rejects the knowledge of God, God will in time reject this person. This is evidenced when whatever sinful desire a person might have becomes the predominate influence upon their life. This is, in fact, what has happened in the new sexual revolution currently influencing every aspect of American life.

*For they exchanged the truth of God for a lie, and worshipped and served the creature rather than the Creator* – (Rom1:25) Denying God's sovereignty by thought, word and lifestyle, people now emulate every humanistic ideology to try to propagate self-righteousness.

*For this reason God gave them over* (abandoned) *to degrading passions* – (Rom 1:26) Practicing homosexuality is the farthest away from God a person can be. All of my life this lifestyle choice was forced upon me by other people. Despite what I've experienced, I knew this sexual act was wrong. I have never condemned a person for living this lifestyle, but often I wondered why they chose to become a homosexual and I didn't. All of Scripture condemns homosexuality and calls the act an abomination to God. This is a harsh realization to know the God that created you finds the acts you commit of extreme dislike.

*God gave them over to a depraved mind* – (Rom 1:28) Useless, of no value and unable to have God express His life and nature through you, is the sum of a person's life who indulges in the homosexual lifestyle. This is an indictment that any person in their right mind should never want to be accused of but when God has removed His Spirit from you, there is nothing to stop a person from being oppressed by a demonic spirit.

This is the reason why so much of what is written in the first chapter of Romans defines what the American culture has now become.

*Their lives became full of every kind of wickedness, sin, greed, hate, murder, quarreling, deception, malicious behavior, and gossip. They are backstabbers, haters of God, insolent, proud, and boastful. They invent new ways of sinning, and they disobey their parents. They refuse to understand, break their promises, are heartless, and have no mercy. They know God's justice requires that those who do these things deserve to die, yet they do them anyway. Worse yet, they encourage others to do them, too.*

Romans 1:29-32

It's not just the people living the homosexual lifestyle that are the reason why this nation is now judged by God. It is because we as individuals have chosen to do what we want to do in hope of realizing the approval of those whose sinful lives we want to emulate. But, in fact, the only life worthy of emulation is that of the Lord Jesus Christ. And if the Bible is an obscure writing, then why does it so accurately describe the moral state of a person's unregenerate mind today? The Bible is the mirror to your soul...

*For if anyone is a hearer of the word and not a doer, he is like a man who looks intently at his natural face in a mirror. For he looks at himself and goes away and at once forgets what he was like. But the one who looks into the perfect law, the law of liberty, and perseveres, being no hearer who forgets but a doer who acts, he will be blessed in his doing.*

James 1:23-25

I believe the greatest need in this nation today is not an economic or housing reform, but for the true Christian community to boldly stand up and speak the truth. Not to condemn or criticize, but with compassion to try to persuade those who will, to seek the knowledge of Jesus Christ for themselves and realize just how concerned God really is with their eternal salvation.

This needs to happen everywhere, from schools and universities and places of employment, to the court rooms and the highest government offices. Then God will be given the opportunity to convict people of their sin, receive the forgiveness they need and learn how to forgive others for what may have happened in their past. Only then can there be a change in what people think of themselves, so they can find significance in what they have experienced. Get the soul of a person right and their natural desires will then act out who they were created to be. My own life is an example of this.

I do want to make a point very clear so as to not be misquoted or have someone accuse me of saying something I'm not. I am not implying everyone who lives a homosexual lifestyle is a pedophile. I have worked with gay people all of my adult life and I've befriended many, but to live this lifestyle is to put your eternal salvation at jeopardy. God created man to be with a woman, and this is revealed all through Scripture. The difference between male and female sex organs is irrefutable evidence of the natural process of reproduction. And if the human race is an advanced species like the proponents of evolution teach, then explain to me why male animals only breed with female animals? If we were once animals like they say, wouldn't animals do the same things we do? *In and of itself, nature proves the will of God.* But you have been deceived into believing you were born with a homosexual gene to keep your attention focused on a lie and its influence upon the lifestyle you have chosen to live.

It's not the ideas you embrace or the sexual act you commit that will get you in trouble with God. Your past is not an issue with God. What is important is the choice you make to either live the life you want or the life God expects of you. In my opinion, the only sin that will condemn a person is their rejection of what Jesus did by the shedding of His blood on the cross to make atonement for the sins of humanity. Jesus came to be the bridge between God and what He values most.

We are all bad and in need of a Savior. If you are one of the masses living whatever lifestyle you choose, I've written this book to challenge what you believe. A life without God is empty. Apart from the life-transforming power of the Gospel of Jesus Christ working in you, there is nothing to base your hopes of a better life upon.

> *Remember that you were at that time separate from Christ, excluded from the commonwealth of Israel, and strangers to the covenants of promise, having no hope and without God in the world.*
>
> Ephesians 2:12

I have made known the events of my life to help you understand there is nothing you have experienced or anything you've done that God cannot make right. I have lived through so many negative experiences in my lifetime to tell you anything different, and I've been violated in too many ways not to believe the validity of what I say is true.

I was abused and rejected as a child, sexually molested and shamed, lied to, drugged, beaten and left for dead, incarcerated, harassed and verbally slandered, forced to react in violence, stabbed, I hated people and I hated myself, countless fist fights, involved in multiple car crashes, homeless, attempted suicide, divorced, I struggled inwardly with the influence of what happened in my past, had a lifelong alcohol and drug dependence, I prostituted, I was assaulted by those who have sworn to protect others, raped as an adult man, hopeless and everything else...

And you think God can't make right the wrong done to you? When put into perspective, what problems do you really have? Better yet, what are you willing to do about it? There is nothing bigger than God. He will forgive, heal and restore and then use your experience to give hope to someone else. All God wants is you.

That is a picture of how I was living when God reached out and proved His willingness to love unconditionally. By leading me to a decision of submitting to something I didn't understand, God has forever changed my expectation of becoming the man of my imagination.

What I never had was for someone to be real with me, especially in a church environment where everybody wore their game face and said what was thought to be accepted. Because of my experience and God doing what He has, I have no choice but to say to you what was never said to me.

"I know why you feel the way you do, what you think of yourself and the lie you are living!" A naïve person can be fooled but when I look at someone who knows pain, your life is an open book. I see it in the faces of people every day. I hear it in the words you say and I can smell it on you. Ignorance is rampant and misery attracts its own. Only when you are willing to sever all ties to what is in your past by surrounding yourself with a positive influence—whether it's the Bible, someone who lives an ethical lifestyle you admire or like me, running to Jesus Christ who is the true source of where all goodness comes from—does life begin to take on meaning and your healing process begins.

Only by the hand of God and the experience of His mercy and grace, His unconditional love and compassion and His willingness to forgive you regardless of what you have done, can there ever be a significant change in the will and the imagination of a human being.

> *The king's heart is in the hand of the Lord, Like the rivers of water; He turns it wherever He wishes.*
>
> Proverbs 21:1

You don't know what you don't know, so stop judging another person when you have never lived a life like theirs. I've committed too much sin to ever look down on anyone and I have made my life an open book for you to read. I hope you will meditate on what has been written and use this experience as a bridge to cross over through a discovery of your true self, as you step into the eternal future of what God has in store for you.

> *"No eye has seen, no ear has heard, and no mind has imagined what God has prepared for those who love him." But it was to us that God has revealed these things by his Spirit. For his Spirit searches out everything and shows us God's deep secrets. No one can know a person's thoughts except that person's own spirit, and no one can know God's thoughts except God's own Spirit. And we have received God's Spirit (not the world's spirit), so we can know the wonderful things God has freely given us.*
>
> 1 Corinthians 2:9b-12

I know the statements I've made will draw criticism and if you're offended at what I've said, I hope it gives you pause for thought. I am not talking from a perspective I know nothing about. These events happened to me. Nor will I back down to the blatant lies that have damaged not only mine, but so many other people's lives.

I was a hard case, like most people today, and through God's willingness to meet me at my sin and by His gentle persuasion, my life has forever changed. And in this race of life, I have just passed the baton to you. Please run to win!

> *If my people who are called by my name humble themselves, and pray and seek my face and turn from their wicked ways, then I will hear from heaven and will forgive their sin and heal their land.*
>
> 2 Chronicles 7:14

I was willing to change and today I am free from the man of my past and the dependence on a substance that I used to bring comfort. There is nothing to hide behind or be ashamed of anymore. This chapter of my life is finished. To wake up every morning without a hangover and not have to think regrettably or wonder about what was done the night before is a great way to start your day. I highly recommend it. I dare you to give God control of your imagination. What He can do will shock you.

> *O taste and see that the Lord [our God] is good! Blessed (happy, fortunate, to be envied) is the man who trusts and takes refuge in Him.*
>
> Psalms 34:8

The greatest gift you will ever be given is an awareness of God's Holy Spirit, whose indwelling of your recreated spirit and a renewed mind is to help you to believe in what seems so unreal by the experience of a life forever changed.

> *And we have received God's Spirit (not the world's spirit), so we can know the wonderful things God has freely given us.*
>
> 1 Corinthians 2:12

*All things can be (are possible) to him who believes!*
                                                    Mark 9:23b

I wrote this when I finally realized no matter where life takes me, God is always near...

*"Jesus, lover of my soul; you give me strength to overcome where you lead for the experience of knowing it's in you I depend. The foundation upon which I have established my faith is in the acceptance of your sacrifice; I am a man now redeemed. You became salvation and took upon you my sin to suffer and die that I might live again. In you do I trust; your Words have I hid in my heart. Oh, the joy of knowing I am your friend. Washed and made clean by the blood of the Lamb, you are my hope everlasting in this peace I have found. Shame cast away in a river of grace; confident, I stand upright in your presence, my King. Free from the bondage and slavery to sin, being healed in my body, mind renewed and made whole. Innocence once lost has now been restored; you are my God, my Savior, my Lord."*

# PURPOSE REVEALED

𝕏 ෬

A nything is possible with God, but there is a process of healing and self-discovery you will have to go through. It is much like the planting of a seed and the time it takes for the plant to grow. Deliverance like mine will not be instantaneous.

You have experienced years of verbal, physical and emotional abuse, and only by diluting a negative expectation of the person you think you are with a learned knowledge of everything good written in the Bible, will you ever believe this is something you deserve. Anyone who tries to tell you different is either naïve or is playing with your emotions to try to get something from you.

This was not written with the intent to tickle your emotions or paint a pretty picture to ease the thought of unknown change. What I've done is describe a process of learning about Jesus Christ and His expectation for how you are to live your life. My life has been what it was and the experience I had as a child set certain things in motion that have followed me all of my life. My way of escape was alcohol and drug use from the age of ten until the completion of this book.

There were a couple of times when I really tried to do what was right and live the way I should but my past always revisited me. And without a solid foundation to stand on, I fell. I did, however, do the one thing I'm telling you to do: "Get Up!" However many times it takes for you to stand on your own, God will hold you in His hand until you can. Don't ever let anybody tell you differently.

As my book was coming to its completion, I made the decision to turn away from this dependence with a lofty goal of staying sober today. For thirty-two years I escaped to that place of clouded justification to finally realize its emptiness, and now I have but one purpose alone. I want to learn about the person of Jesus Christ and live my life in a way that I become like Him. When you make the decision to do this is when you will begin to live in your destiny...

> *Dear friends, we are already God's children, but he has not yet shown us what we will be like when Christ appears. But we do know that we will be like him, for we will see him as he really is. And all who have this eager expectation will keep themselves pure, just as he is pure.*
>
> 1 John 3:2-3

> *And when I am lifted up from the earth, I will draw everyone to myself.*
>
> John 12:32

I refuse to live an ordinary life and be like those churched people of my yesterday. I want to be different and now I understand the price I'll have to pay. Any substance, the person you're with or situation you might be in, pales in comparison to what God can do once He has removed what is not pleasing to Him, so that His purpose can be fulfilled through the life you live.

The expectation I now have is a result of learning about the man I've become and a mental transformation God has led me through. I can only imagine what God will do by the power of His Spirit who now lives in me as my lifestyle and conversation are pleasing to Him. This is the significance of life I have hoped for since my youth.

Now I understand what it means for Jesus to be Lord. I am willing to let go of any influence that would limit my possibilities, by allowing God to do in and through me what will benefit the lives of people I now have an opportunity to help.

Unlike everything else, this feeling of self-worth can never be taken away from me. It is as much a part of me as the air I breathe. I have discovered the purpose of my life and I enjoy this confidence of being at peace. In the time we live, too many people die having never played their song. Don't let this be you. Who might your story help change the course of their life? You owe it to yourself to experience what this is like. I now live with an intimate God-consciousness, always mindful of His presence while becoming more aware of my gift and my calling each day.

These are truths revealed in the Bible that have had the greatest impact on establishing the foundation of my Christian witness.

Jesus is the only way to both your soul's transformation and you spiritual salvation:

> *"For Jesus is the one referred to in the Scriptures, where it says, 'The stone that you builders rejected has now become the cornerstone.' There is salvation in no one else! God has given no other name under heaven by which we must be saved."*
>
> Acts 4:11-12

Jesus is the example for all people to live by:

> *"Truly, truly, I say to you, he who believes in Me, the works that I do, he will do also; and greater works than these he will do; because I go to the Father."*
>
> John 14:12

There's peace in your lifestyle of worshiping God for who He is:

> *And God's peace [shall be yours, that tranquil state of a soul assured of its salvation through Christ, and so fearing nothing from God and being content with its earthly lot of whatever sort that is, that peace] which transcends all understanding shall garrison and mount guard over your hearts and minds in Christ Jesus.*
>
> Philippians 4:7

There's emotional healing in God's presence:

> *He heals the brokenhearted and binds up their wounds [curing their pains and their sorrows].*
>
> Psalms 147:3

Happiness and contentment will overtake you as you experience everything you've ever hoped for becoming reality:

> *May the God of your hope so fill you with all joy and peace in believing [through the experience of your faith] that by the power of the Holy Spirit you may abound and be overflowing (bubbling over) with hope.*
>
> Romans 15:13

God can restore what life took away:

> *He refreshes and restores my life (myself); He leads me in the paths of righteousness [uprightness and right standing with Him—not for my earning it, but] for His name's sake.*
>
> Psalms 23:3

God will take the mess you give to Him and make a life of significance with it. You can overcome what is in your past to become the person so vividly described in the Bible if you first have a willingness to be stripped by God of what He hates.

> *These six things the Lord hates, indeed seven are an abomination to Him: A proud look [the spirit that makes one overestimate himself and underestimate others], a lying tongue, and hands that shed innocent blood, A heart that manufactures wicked thoughts and plans, feet that are swift in running to evil, A false witness who breathes out lies [even under oath], and he who sows discord among his brethren.*
>
> Proverbs 6:16-19

Who does this remind you of America? This will not be a quick and easy process. God wants to remove from the vault of your subconscious mind the years of deception and shame that condemned you to a standard of living you thought would be all you would ever know. Through a process of time much like what a pregnant woman experiences, God is giving birth to the greatest Christian witness this world has ever seen.

You are called to be a world changer. I believe its people like me, who have walked away from everything familiar, to answer God's call and run with it. What, in the hell you have come out of, would you ever want to embrace again? How many people do you know who have had an experience in life like yours? Just look at the American culture today. People are mad and confused and they suffer from the infamous "me, my and mine" syndrome. The pursuit of money and self-gratification has become this nation's god, which only leads to the loss of their eternal destinies.

> *And what do you benefit if you gain the whole world but lose your own soul? Is anything worth more than your soul?*
> Mark 8:36-37

What I say here I've been as guilty of as you are. Everything you have given attention to is what has influenced the lifestyle you are now familiar with—your childhood and education, social life and choice of entertainment, political opinion and countless hours wasted in front of an idiot box fantasizing about a fake life that will never become reality. What on TV today is truly worth your time, other than the few programs focusing on the good deeds people do for each other?

I have worked in an industry that attracts people who want to or have made entertainment their career, and I've witnessed how twisted many of their lives are. If I were to name them, you would know who they are. Just turn on the entertainment news channels and they will tell on themselves. These people are mentally confused and yet the American public has made them rich by worshiping the idiocy of their role play.

Without a doubt, the people on the Hollywood "A" list are the most liberal voices for their cause and just about everybody today, especially the younger generations, envy this lifestyle. Why do you think these stupid reality shows have so inundated our culture? People are living a lie, and the picture of happiness and success portrayed by entertainment and media, to liberal education being influenced by the governing elites, has led the masses to their demise.

> *I appeal to you, brothers, to watch out for those who cause divisions and create obstacles contrary to the doctrine that you have been taught; avoid them. For such persons do not serve our Lord Christ, but their own appetites, and by smooth talk and flattery they deceive the hearts of the naive.*
>
> Romans 16:17-18

Cities I have worked in and clubs I've been to are known for their entertainment money and political power. I have personally served and drank with performers and decision-makers of both industries to the point of inebriation every day of the week. I've talked with these people and overheard conversations about things most of you are unaware of.

Policies made into laws we live by and pay taxes to are, with some exceptions, made by people who are alcoholics, and only God knows what is done in private to shape how they think. They have no awareness of God and no one challenges how they live because everyone in their realm of influence is just as they are. And the sheeple blindly follow this example.

The masses are angry and confused, egotistical, arrogant and full of pride, and are being driven by a self-willed motivation to remove all thought of moral conscience. Any religion or belief that gives you freedom to live and do as you choose is openly accepted and highly thought of by people today, and it's only when confronted with a moral compass do tempers flare. This alone should convince even the staunchest opponent that the Gospel of Jesus Christ is true.

I'm not going to try to be someone I am not, but I do speak from a platform that's heard what every inebriated culture group have said to me from the other side of a bar, whether rich, middle-class or poor, white, black, yellow and brown, male and female, gay or straight, republican, democrat and undecided, and the religious or just confused.

Everyone is looking for what will never be found until the Christian lifestyle is expressed in a way that will attract people who long to experience for themselves the true source of all they could ever want—Jesus, who is the revelation of God and the Savior of lost souls. People today are not receptive to the words you speak when your life paints a different picture. Church of America, it is time you stand up to answer God's call.

> *Dear brothers and sisters, pattern your lives after mine, and learn from those who follow our example. For I have told you often before, and I say it again with tears in my eyes, that there are many whose conduct shows they are really enemies of the cross of Christ. They are headed for destruction. Their god is their appetite, they brag about shameful things, and they think only about this life here on earth.*
>
> Philippians 3:17-19

Many of you attending church are as confused as the people God wants you to be a witness to. The demonstration of God's redemptive plan of salvation is expressed by how you live. Infidelity and divorce are as epidemic in the church as they are among the unsaved. Financial debt is just as high and you're stressed and mad. At the weekly church service I'm told how blessed you are, but no one pays attention to the person behind a bar watching how you treat other people. I serve you drinks to inebriation and watch you act a fool. I have watched you live a lie and the time has come for you to choose. Whose side are you going to represent?

> *This is the message from the one who is the Amen—the faithful and true witness, the beginning of God's new creation: "I know all the things you do, that you are neither hot nor cold. I wish that you were one or the other! But since you are like lukewarm water neither hot nor cold, I will spit you out of my mouth!"*
>
> Revelation 3:14b-16

I recently learned that Richard Dent, who is a graduate of Rhema Bible College, and the pastor of Trinity Family Church, was convicted of embezzlement in 2009. This was really disappointing to me. I knew Richard for several years. We attended Valley Word Ministries together. I remember when Eddie Crabtree, who himself is a graduate of Rhema, announced that Valley Word Ministries was going to pay for Richard's ministry training at Rhema. I even saw Richard at the Rhema church in Tulsa, Oklahoma. This was after I had left Miami and drove out west, not really knowing where I was going. I stopped in Memphis, very briefly, and then I ended up in Tulsa. I knew that the Rhema church was in Tulsa, so I went. I had been to this church several times before I saw Richard.

The Rhema church is massive and people from all over the world attend these services. Many are students of the Bible College and the rest are Tulsa residents. When I was there, I had the opportunity to meet Kenneth Hagin Sr, who at the time had given control of the ministry to his son Kenneth Hagin Jr. I can say nothing against the elder man who is thought by many to be the father of the *"Word of Faith"* movement, but if the graduates of this Bible College are anything like Eddie or Richard, I have to question whether the Lord Jesus Christ is the God of this ministry training facility.

After meeting Richard and attending several more services, I thought I would attend the Bible College that next year. I was lost and confused, and I thought that because Eddie and Richard had both attended Rhema, it would be good for me. But God did not approve of my thoughts. I remember the Sunday morning when I walked up to the sanctuary doors, and just as I began to pull the door open is when I heard God holler *"NO!"* It startled me so badly, that I turned around and left the premises. And I never went back. It had been sixteen years since the last time I heard God speak to me, and His intention was very clear. That day was when my adoptive father called and said he wanted to see me.

For so many years I thought the preachers who headed the mega ministries like Rhema were God's generals. I have come to believe something quite different. When I attended Valley Word Ministries, I had the opportunity to meet many of the well known TV preachers of today. I've met Kenneth Copeland, Jerry Savelle and Charles Capps, Crefflo Dollar, Rodney Howard Brown and Jesse Duplantis, John

Avanzini, Mark Chironna and a host of others. I've watched Leroy Thompson land his private jet and then taxied him to the church for the evening's service. I was on Phil Driscolls airplane once as Curtis Gray and I talked with him, and helped to remove his luggage to be taken to the hotel room. All of these men live very comfortable lives.

I know of only one of these men to have been involved in a scandal. In 2007, Phil Driscoll was sentenced to federal prison for tax evasion. But in recent years, many of these ministries have come under the scrutiny of government crooks who want to share in the spoils of a churches tax exempt status. Those who are named and everyone else, who preaches the same message, look at the damage you have done to God's humanity. I used to think the Trinity Broadcasting Network was God's media portal to the world, but I can no longer listen to the charlatans who spew the heresy they claim is the gospel. This is what the ignorant evangelical church body of today embraces as the Gospel of Jesus Christ. I hope this book slaps you in the face!

To those of you finding comfort in the surroundings of a safe church environment discussing topics of no relevance for the time we live, you should be ashamed of yourself. There is very little Gospel, if any, in the evangelical church message today. Leroy Thompson's rants on *"money cometh to me now"*, the endless motivational pep talks, and what is being taught about tithing ten percent of your income cannot be validated by Scripture in the New Covenant. Not one time! Yet the majority of people in these churches happily throw their hard earned money at the feet of these slick charlatans. Who have studied Scripture well enough to know what verses they can use to manipulate spiritually dumb people into believing their money is needed by God.

If you would ever take the time to research the history of the tithe you will discover it was a tax paid by the people to the Levitical Priesthood, who were the theocratic government of Israel at that time. The tithe was used to provide the needs of the priesthood and for the welfare of people. There were two different tithes given each year and a third tithe was required every third year totaling not ten percent, but nearly thirty percent, much like this nation's tax system.

There are commentaries you can read to gain a better knowledge of this subject from Doctors of Divinity who have studied God's law for a lifetime, so don't take just my word. And what you might not have realized yet, there is always the Bible. You have been fed a lie that has corrupted the true message of the Gospel of Jesus Christ, and it's time you study the Bible for yourself to then have God reveal His truth.

When speaking to religious and legalistic leaders, Jesus taught on the subject of God's law in order to create an awareness of their sinfulness and the need they had for a Divine Savior. This is what the evangelical church is not doing today. Another gospel proclaiming God's acceptance of anyone who makes a decision to become a Christian without evidence of genuine repentance is what the sinner hears. I like to call this the seeker-friendly gospel.

Topics of grace and mercy, unconditional love and forgiveness are what we hear to try to attract new converts. These are accurate descriptions of God. But Jesus only taught on these subjects when the person was repentant or broken and of a contrite spirit. Messages like this will never reach the calloused sinners of our time who think religion is beneath them.

This is the great deception of the modern-day church. What these teachings have done is create a superficial and morally-weak person who, when faced with temptation or persecution, denies the Gospel of Jesus Christ by the lifestyle they live. Nor is God's presence in the display of emotions, time-sensitive choreographed sermons, or the people falling down every time someone lays hands on them. Read the account of Jesus' ministry. Jesus always met the person at their need. Today's culture is the result of what organized religion has neglected to do, and as to the cost of those eternally lost.....God weeps.

People's lives are more important than your fears. Your responsibility as a Christian is to be intimate with God and realize your gift so that when you speak, people will listen. When people see in you what they cannot find anywhere else, then you will be given their undivided attention to teach them about true repentance and the need of studying the Bible to learn how to live out their salvation each day.

*Brothers, my hearts desire and prayer to God for them is that they may be saved. I bear them witness that they have a zeal for God, but not according to knowledge. For, being ignorant of the righteousness that comes from God, and seeking to establish their own, they did not submit to God's righteousness. For Christ is the end of the law for righteousness to everyone who believes. But what does it say? "The word is near you, in your mouth and in your heart" (that is, the word of faith that we proclaim); because, if you confess with your mouth that Jesus is Lord and believe in your heart that God raised him from the dead, you will be saved. For with the heart one believes and is justified, and with the mouth one confesses and is saved. For the scripture says, "Everyone who believes in him will not be put to shame." For there is no distinction between Jew and Greek; the same Lord is Lord of all, bestowing his riches on all who call on him. For "everyone who calls on the name of the Lord will be saved."*

Romans 10:1-4, 8-13

*Work hard to show the results of your salvation, obeying God with deep reverence and fear. For God is working in you, giving you the desire and the power to do what pleases him. Do everything without complaining and arguing, so that no one can criticize you. Live clean, innocent lives as children of God, shining like bright lights in a world full of crooked and perverse people. Holding firmly to the word of life.*

Philippians 2:12b-16a

Turn off the TV and change the secular beat to music that will usher you into the presence of God. Open the Bible and study the truth of what God has to say. Quit doing what has always brought you to familiar circumstances and distance yourself from those who will only try to pull you down.

As this change is seen in you, people will react in ways that can hurt you, if you allow it to. But when they see consistency in a manner and conduct of living they want to believe is real, conviction then takes over and you will be given an opportunity to act out what you are created to do.

*And Jesus said to Simon, "Do not be afraid. From now on you will catch men."*

Luke 5:10b

When you reach out to someone who wants to change, who has witnessed this transformation in you, is when they will allow you access into their world of isolation. And together, you can begin tearing down walls that have kept people from experiencing all of who God created them to be.

There is no defense against compassion. As people experience this, significant change will take place in communities and a move that's desperately in need will begin to turn reluctance and the ignorance of unbelief to a passion of knowing and learning about the person of Jesus Christ for who He really is. I'm not asking you to do anything I haven't already done for myself and if I can do this, there is no excuse for you.

This is the message church leaders should be preaching today. In spite of popular Christian opinion, it's not about what you can do to enjoy your best life now. Nowhere in the New Testament will you find this being taught. Joel Osteen is a great motivator but motivation will not deliver the church-going sinner from the eternal wrath of God. The uncompromised Gospel of Jesus Christ is the only message that will deliver.

People do not care how much you have or what you know, until they experience how much you care. You can't help anybody until God has delivered you. The first thing you must do is allow what God has to say in Scripture to change how you think and be evidenced by the transformation of your life.

*For the word of God is living and active and sharper than any two-edged sword, and piercing as far as the division of soul and spirit, of both joints and marrow, and able to judge the thoughts and intentions of the heart.*

Hebrews 4:12

Only then will God equip you for the work He's called you to do. When you live each day not for yourself but to reach out and help meet the immediate needs of those in your community, people will have no other option but to respond.

They will be influenced by your acts of compassion and a show of kindness not present in the life they know. When they experience for themselves the inner peace and happiness available to those who honor God first, everything else that's needed, whether it's time, talent or resources will be gladly given.

> *Wherever your treasure is, there the desires of your heart will also be.*
>
> Matthew 6:21

As the people come, so does everything they have. So instead of asking someone to give their money as an expression of their faith, challenge them to trust God by being this example.

Of all the churches I've been to, I have personally seen this happen only twice. The first time I witnessed this example was at the church I attended that eventually hired me. Curtis Gray was still there and it was during a Sunday morning service when I witnessed something I will never forget.

The pastor announced a newlywed couple was moving out of state and they wanted to do something for someone. They came to the front of the church and Curtis then asked me to join them. As I walked up front, I had no idea what was about to happen. I was doing a lot of volunteer work at the church but I did not have a vehicle at the time, and I depended upon public transportation. I stood beside this couple and to my shock, they handed me the keys and title to one of their cars and said God wanted them to give it to me. It blew me away.

The second time I saw something like this was at the church I was going to when I first began to write this book. At this particular service, the guest speakers were Don and Mary Colbert. Near the end of the service there was a line for people to come up front and be prayed for, and I remember Mrs. Colbert stopping everything. A small child had asked her to pray for their mother to find a job so they could have money for food. Mrs. Colbert then asked the ushers to direct everyone to come up front and put money in the hands of this young mother. Hundreds of people responded and it moved everyone to tears. It was a beautiful thing.

This is what many churches lack today and its people are missing out on the true meaning of the Gospel. The only thing of significant value are the people Jesus paid such a great price for, to bring them back into a relationship with Himself, for He is the Creator and the Savior of all.

Are you willing to become the person Jesus is looking for to influence people in your community, state, nation and all the countries of this world? Compassion will capture their emotions and a selfless act of kindness will win their confidence. This will not be done in the confines of the four walls we call church.

This ministry will be lived out among people in whatever state their lives may be in. Forget your parents' and your grandparents' religion, and look beyond what church as we know it has become. This is a completely different mindset you are called to influence. Only by meeting the physical and emotional needs in your community will people be receptive to what God might have you say. People do not like being confronted with the truth. But the good news is you don't have to be the way you are any longer, because I'm going to help you learn how to stand upon the confidence of knowing what God has done for you.

This is the example people are waiting to see, and as lives are changed, they become emotionally involved and will graciously give of their recourses to others who are in need.

*And all the believers met together in one place and shared everything they had. They sold their property and possessions and shared the money with those in need.*

Acts 2:44-45

Here is where I believe one of the greatest injustices has been committed against the American people. It was never God's plan to have a nation's government provide for either the welfare or the "*healthcare*" of its people. The welfare of those who need help should come from the community outreach programs of local churches and the goodwill of others, and given only to people unable to do for themselves. It should never be given to able bodied people who refuse to work and have learned how to manipulate the system.

> *It was not because we do not have that right, but to give you in ourselves an example to imitate. For even when we were with you, we would give you this command: If anyone is not willing to work, let him not eat. For we hear that some among you walk in idleness, not busy at work, but busybodies.*
> 2 Thessalonians 3:9-11

This system has been grossly abused since its inception to fund the government and create a dependant voter base. If you research the history of The Social Security Act of 1935, you will see just how badly it has been abused.

In the Gospels we are given the example of how Jesus ministered to people. In the times when He taught, there were always people in need. Many times before teaching, Jesus provided for the needs people had and it drew great numbers to Him. I am convinced this is what churches should be doing today. When you do something for someone else and it is not motivated by getting something in return, the sincerity of what you do is noticed. It's not preaching alone, but your service to people that penetrates their callousness so they become receptive to the message you present.

It all begins with doing what God expects, resulting in your life's transformation. Only then can help be given to someone else. Having come out of a life of despair, you are now a voice of experience and the example people need to change the course of their eternal future.

It has taken everything I have been through to finally make a decision to surrender my will to God and have Him reveal what my purpose in life is. Don't be as stupid as I was. Of all the Christian books I've read, few, if any, have ever been as forward about the inappropriate behavior permeating churches today. I hope you take notice of what you do and the influence it has upon the people you know.

There is so much to be done in order for the message of hope and eternal salvation through Jesus Christ to regain trust in the day and time we live. People do not want to see the sin they struggle with in a place of refuge where they go to find help. What churches have done is point the finger of blame at everyone else instead of crying out to God for help. The moral conscience is the battle ground where truth contends for the salvation of a lost humanity. Sometimes the hardest to reach are those who adhere to religious beliefs.

> And I said: "Woe is me! For I am lost; for I am a man of unclean lips, and I dwell in the midst of a people of unclean lips; for my eyes have seen the King, the LORD of hosts!"
>
> Isaiah 6:5

It's my prayer that when this book is read and its message convicts, that you do what I have done and witness what God will do. If you have read to this page, there is no longer an excuse to not answer your calling. God has called you to reach the people your experience was designed to influence. Will you answer? There's hell to pay if you don't.

> For God's gifts and His call are irrevocable. [He never withdraws them when once they are given, and He does not change His mind about those to whom He gives His grace or to whom He sends His call.]
>
> Romans 11:29

The Bible was written to reveal the nature of God and prove we do not have, nor can we do in our own ability, what is necessary to ever be in right standing with God. Hence the account of man's redemption.

God's love for His creation is so complete it took the sacrifice of His deity through the person of Jesus Christ, who was crucified and suffered the penalty of sin to pay the price for what is valued most—you. The ultimate price of a holy and sinless life was paid so you and I would not have to. This is what most people in church and the masses of humanity do not realize. God's love demands justice.

> *He is the propitiation for our sins, and not for ours only but also for the sins of the whole world.*
>
> 1 John 2:2

> *While we were yet in weakness [powerless to help ourselves], at the fitting time Christ died for (in behalf of) the ungodly. But God shows and clearly proves His [own] love for us by the fact that while we were still sinners, Christ (the Messiah, the Anointed One) died for us.*
>
> Romans 5:6, 8

The preaching of God's wrath is a subject ministers of today's easy gospel avoid because of its offensiveness to the hearer. The one common thought among every class of people is that if God is a God of love, then why would He condemn people to such a terrible place as hell? The truth revealed in Scripture proves God doesn't: *you condemn yourself.*

There is a price to be paid for the sinfulness of your nature and the atrocities committed against God. This is why the Bible teaches Jesus became the atonement for sin and by doing so, the wrath of God has been turned away from the sinner who repents and cries out to Jesus for salvation. But for those of you who choose not to, the day is coming when you will stand alone before God to give an account for what you have done. As you find yourself on the other side of God's grace. There will be no compassion for your cries, no mercy or pity, but only the fierce execution of God's eternal wrath upon your rebellion of His Sovereignty.

> *"But when the Son of Man comes in his glory, and all the angels with him, then he will sit upon his glorious throne. All the nations will be gathered in his presence, and he will separate the people as a shepherd separates the sheep from the goats. He will place the sheep at his right hand and the goats at his left.*

*"Then the King will say to those on his right, 'Come, you who are blessed by my Father, inherit the Kingdom prepared for you from the creation of the world. For I was hungry, and you fed me. I was thirsty, and you gave me a drink. I was a stranger, and you invited me into your home. I was naked, and you gave me clothing. I was sick, and you cared for me. I was in prison, and you visited me.'*

*"Then these righteous ones will reply, 'Lord, when did we ever see you hungry and feed you? Or thirsty and give you something to drink? Or a stranger and show you hospitality? Or naked and give you clothing? When did we ever see you sick or in prison and visit you?' And the King will say, 'I tell you the truth, when you did it to one of the least of these my brothers and sisters you were doing it to me!'*

*"Then the King will turn to those on the left and say, 'Away with you, you cursed ones, into the eternal fire prepared for the devil and his demons. For I was hungry, and you didn't feed me. I was thirsty, and you didn't give me a drink. I was a stranger, and you didn't invite me into your home. I was naked, and you didn't give me clothing. I was sick and in prison, and you didn't visit me.'*

*"Then they will reply, 'Lord, when did we ever see you hungry or thirsty or a stranger or naked or sick or in prison, and not help you?' And he will answer, 'I tell you the truth, when you refused to help the least of these my brothers and sisters, you were refusing to help me.' And they will go away into eternal punishment, but the righteous will go into eternal life."*

Matthew 25:31-46

The Bible makes reference to God ordaining government for the good of people, and to bring punishment upon those who are lawless. If this is so in our natural world, what makes you think God is any different with mankind whom He created? God has complete control and governmental authority over our lives, and there's nothing you or I can do about it. As basic as I can describe it, this is my understanding of God's sovereignty. This being a natural attribute of God means what has been created, He rules over.

The biblical world-view of God's rule of law is a theocracy and not the democracy of man's rule. God is not concerned with nor persuaded by your perception of how things should be done. The rule of law we are to live by is spelled out in the Bible and to deviate from what Scripture teaches in any way, is to practice a false religion.

The churches, synagogues, temples and mosques encompassing all religious beliefs and meditations, consciences or practices are full of people who think they're safe, but are in danger of busting hell wide open. When, to their shock, as they stand before an angry God with no atonement for their sins, they realize the Bible has been correct all this time. The choice people have of trusting in the God of the Bible or in self-reliance and what they have or haven't done for other people, is the guideline God is bound by His Word to follow.

> Then Jesus said to his disciples, "If any of you wants to be my follower, you must turn from your selfish ways, take up your cross, and follow me. If you try to hang on to your life, you will lose it. But if you give up your life for my sake, you will save it. For the Son of Man will come with his angels in the glory of his Father and will judge all people according to their deeds.
>
> Matthew 16:24-25, 27

> "Work hard to enter the narrow door to God's kingdom, for many will try to enter, but will fail. When the master of the house has locked the door, it will be too late. You will stand outside knocking and pleading, 'Lord, open the door for us!' But he will reply, 'I don't know you or where you come from.' Then you will say, 'But we ate and drank with you, and you taught in our streets.' And he will reply, 'I tell you, I do not know you or where you come from. Get away from me, all you who do evil.' There will be weeping and gnashing of teeth, for you will see Abraham, Isaac, Jacob, and all the prophets in the Kingdom of God, but you will be thrown out.
>
> Luke 13:24-28

The Bible is clear in its description of a place of torment called hell; eternal separation from the presence of God created for Satan and fallen angels. According to Scripture, its capacity has been expanded for those of you who choose to live and do as you please with no consideration to the free gift of eternal salvation God is offering you. To reject this gift, is to spit in God's face. This is not something I recommend you do…

> *"Then He will also say to those on the left hand, 'Depart from Me, you cursed, into the everlasting fire prepared for the devil and his angels."*
>
> Matthew 25:41

> *For if God did not spare angels when they sinned, but sent them to hell, putting them into gloomy dungeons to be held for judgment; and to hold the unrighteous for the day of judgment, while continuing their punishment. This is especially true of those who follow the corrupt desire of the sinful nature and despise authority. Bold and arrogant, these men are not afraid to slander celestial beings.*
>
> 2 Peter 2:4, 9b-10

Christopher Hitchens is an example of a man who will be rudely awakened to reality upon the day of his death, when, to his shock, he finds himself standing before the God he so vehemently opposes. In his delusion he wrote a book that was released in 2007 titled, *God Is Not Great: How Religion Poisons Everything.* His book reached the #1 spot on the New York Times best sellers list three weeks after it was released.

Much like Bill Maher's documentary, *Religulous,* Mr. Hitchens' book focuses on world religions and the idiocy of what these followers believe to be God. In the book, he's pointedly critical of Christianity. This has earned him a platform on talk shows and lecture circuits, and he was recently listed by *Forbes Magazine* as one of the top twenty-five most influential liberals in media. I've listened to this man speak and I find nothing he says about Christianity to be in the least bit influential.

But true to the god he serves, Mr. Hitchens has nothing new to say. He is a confused and deceived man who cannot comprehend the simplicity of God's revelation of Himself. For a man with his life's experience, Christopher Hitchens' perceived enlightenment has in fact far removed "from his grasp" the ability to believe in what is so easily realized. I have no sympathy for a man like this and I believe his punishment will be far more agonizing when, upon the Day of Judgment, he realizes his fate. For an eternity, Mr. Hitchens, you will believe in God!

> For this reason also, God highly exalted Him, and bestowed on Him the name which is above every name, so that at the name of Jesus EVERY KNEE WILL BOW, of those who are in heaven and on earth and under the earth, and that every tongue will confess that Jesus Christ is Lord, to the glory of God the Father.
>
> Philippians 2:9-11

There is too much evidence in this world's art and historical writings, even apart from the Bible, that should convince people of the reality of hell. Jesus referred to this place of punishment more than any other topic He spoke about in the New Testament. You had better not make the mistake of finding out for yourself just how real hell is. I believe the greatest punishment endured in hell is the eternal accusing conscience of what you should have done, but chose not to.

> And he said to all, "If anyone would come after me, let him deny himself and take up his cross daily and follow me. For whoever would save his life will lose it, but whoever loses his life for my sake will save it."
>
> Luke 9:23-24

> "The time came when the beggar died and the angels carried him to Abraham's side. The rich man also died and was buried. In hell, where he was in torment, he looked up and saw Abraham far away, with Lazarus by his side. So he called

*to him, 'Father Abraham, have pity on me and send Lazarus*
*to dip the tip of his finger in water and cool my tongue,*
*because I am in agony in this fire.' "But Abraham replied,*
*'Son, remember that in your lifetime you received your good*
*things, while Lazarus received bad things, but now he is*
*comforted here and you are in agony."*

Luke 16:22-25

The immoral behavior that permeates American culture today is because preachers have compromised the message of this Biblical reality. In this day and time of political and cultural correctness and seeker-friendly emergent churches, self-expression is rampant while every lewd and vulgar lifestyle is paraded from the stages of entertainment and media, glorifying what this nation has become. It's nauseating.

Special interest groups are lobbying for equal rights and laws protecting their voice, while at the same time my right to speak truth is in jeopardy. This is the reason why the hate crimes bill has been signed into law and the fairness act has the backing to protect these special interest groups.

In reality, the government is in violation of our constitutional First Amendment, and is upheld by the liberal left's influence upon those who reside as judges of the Supreme Court. The arrogance of these people, who think they have the authority to police my thoughts, and even more my convictions? Who made them god?

I believe one of the reasons we are witnessing so much of the federal government's intrusion upon every aspect of our lives is because all consciousness of the Christian God has been removed from our schools curriculum and public perspective. Also removed is the education about ideals that became the conviction men had in the writing of our Charters of Freedom, and the founding of this nation.

One of the most debated documents in the issue of the separation of church and state is the letter Thomas Jefferson wrote to the Danbury Baptist Association in 1802. *"Believing with you that religion is a matter which lies solely between man and his God, that he owes account to none other for his faith or his worship, that the legitimate powers of government reach actions only, and not opinions, I contemplate with sovereign* reverence that act of the whole American people which declared that their legislature should "make no law respecting an establishment of religion, or prohibiting the free exercise thereof," thus building a wall of separation between Church and State." Why was "Church" mentioned first?

This letter was not written for the intent of removing Christian influence from the public sector, but was in fact introduced to legitimize the freedom of religious practice from federal interference. There has to be a moral guideline to rightly govern the decisions and behavior of a nation's leaders and its people. Those of you who insistently quote the term "separation of church and state" should read about the context and influence of world history that led to the writing of this document. Until then, you should keep your mouth shut. When you argue a topic like this from an uninformed perspective, you remove all doubt as to the depth of your stupidity.

An opinion made by Justice Rehnquist, presented the view that documents such as this were intended to protect religious liberty from federal interference. Justice Scalia has criticized the liberal left in their attempts to remove religion from American public life. I hold these just interpreters of law to be more credible than some clueless individual who screams that moral conscience has no right to criticize their lifestyle choice.

The platforms that are said to be the reason why we need these laws are nothing more than a smoke screen for the real issue at hand, which is to silence the Gospel of Jesus Christ. The only ideal that stands in the way of the United Nations controlling world government, economics and the New Age religion that will usher in the anti-Christ, is the conviction a person has in their belief of the sovereignty of the Bible.

Remember what happened to Europe, and thought crimes have recently become punishable by law in Canada. This is the intent for Mr. Obama signing into law the Matthew Shepard/James Byrd Jr Hate Crimes Prevention Act on October 28, 2009. They have painted the picture of equality and fairness for all people but the real purpose for this law is sinister. The ruling class are not far away from criminalizing thought here in America. With each new amendment and law they pass, eroding away the foundation of our constitution, is one step closer to socialism. When they take away our First Amendment, the class separations will fall. And when this happens, the proponents of hope and change will then understand the fool they were played to be. You better wake up!

Many of you reading this book will no doubt ask what gives me the authority to say what I do based upon my lack of education and having no experience in the government field. My answer to you is to remind you what God can do in a person's life who will give Him complete control. When that gentleman said to me, *"God doesn't call the qualified, He qualifies the called"* was God confirming His call upon my life to be a voice for Him in this day and time. If my life's transformation can attract the attention of the hearer, then just maybe they will listen to what God might have me say.

> *Because the foolishness of God is wiser than men, and the weakness of God is stronger than men. For consider your calling, brethren, that there were not many wise according to the flesh, not many mighty, not many noble; but God has chosen the foolish things of the world to shame the wise, and God has chosen the weak things of the world to shame the things which are strong, and the base things of the world and the despised God has chosen, the things that are not, so that He may nullify the things that are, so that no man may boast before God. But by His doing you are in Christ Jesus, who became to us wisdom from God, and righteousness and sanctification, and redemption, so that, just as it is written, "LET HIM WHO BOASTS, BOAST IN THE LORD."*
>
> 1 Corinthians 1:25-31

The only culture groups spoken of negatively and made fun of without the fear of an impending lawsuit or public criticism are those who believe the Bible is a true account of God, and its message means what it says. Well, not any more. I'm here to tell you that's about to change.

For the people involved in everything from politics to education, science to medicine, entertainment, media and the arts, to false world religions and those who just don't know, your time of accountability has come. The party is over.

Because of the moral state in the minds of people today, I believe God has ordained this time to call sin and immorality just what it is with no consideration to the ebb and flow of people's self-indulgence. Christian men and women, who are totally committed to the message of reconciliation, will boldly confront the sins of humanity, to reach people who are ready to hear the truth and to bring conviction upon those who oppose the Gospel of Jesus Christ. I believe this is what will usher in the great awakening in the last days to the truth of who Jesus really is.

> *Show yourself in all respects to be a model of good works, and in your teaching show integrity, dignity and sound speech that cannot be condemned, so that an opponent may be put to shame, having nothing evil to say about us.*
>
> Titus 2:7-8

> *'And it shall come to pass in the last days, says God, that I will pour out of My Spirit on all flesh; your sons and your daughters shall prophesy, your young men shall see visions, your old men shall dream dreams. And on My menservants and on My maidservants I will pour out My Spirit in those days; and they shall prophesy. I will show wonders in heaven above and signs in the earth beneath: blood and fire and vapor of smoke. The sun shall be turned into darkness, and the moon into blood, before the coming of the great and awesome day of the LORD. And it shall come to pass that whoever calls on the name of the LORD shall be saved.'*
>
> Acts 2:17-21

A man or a woman that has been to hell and come back will relate to people, because many will, for the first time in their lives, meet someone who's real and not afraid to say what needs to be said. I could care less what ignorance or unbelief has to say to try to justify why a person does what they do.

I lived a hard life of self-indulgence and it brought me nothing but emptiness, misery and pain. But God, by His mercy and grace, was patient during the process of my change and through this He has won a son who will live harder for Him than I ever did for me. I have come out on top knowing what God has done for me when everyone said I never would. If anyone should ever criticize my faith in Jesus Christ who saved me, I will be just as compelling in my witness as to the sovereignty of God, and His judgment of that person's sin. Bring it on baby! The time of biblical compromise and weak preaching is over. As Christians, we have to be bold in the preaching of the Gospel. This is what separates us from all other false religions proclaiming many different pathways ways to God, but in the end these ways are proven to be false.

What a terrible realization it must be for those who have lived thinking they were a good person and have walked closely with God, to then hear God call them wicked and lawless and be condemned to an eternity in hell because of their rejection of God's only gift of salvation. As a parent, how do you think it will make you feel to see your children in hell with you, and for an eternity hear their cries of anguish due to the lack of your guidance. *This is why I must tell you the truth.*

> *Beloved, my whole concern was to write to you in regard to our common salvation. [But] I found it necessary and was impelled to write you and urgently appeal to and exhort [you] to contend for the faith which was once for all handed down to the saints [the faith which is that sum of Christian belief which was delivered verbally to the holy people of God].*
>
> Jude 3

Being a Christian is not at all what these weak evangelical preachers teach as truth. They are liars and compromise the true Gospel that Jesus said would offend even those of your own family.

> *"Do not think that I have come to bring peace to the earth. I have not come to bring peace, but a sword. For I have come to set a man against his father, and a daughter against her mother, and a daughter-in-law against her mother-in-law.*

*And a person's enemies will be those of his own household.*
*Whoever loves father or mother more than me is not worthy*
*of me, and whoever loves son or daughter more than me is*
*not worthy of me. And whoever does not take his cross and*
*follow me is not worthy of me. Whoever finds his life will lose*
*it, and whoever loses his life for my sake will find it."*

Matthew 10:34-39

Jesus never wanted us to think His calling would be void of conflict or even persecution from those we are trying to reach. True Christianity is to reach a hopeless and dying people at any cost to your comfortable unreality of self-servitude. There is no more time for foolishness in the pulpits of Christian churches, and what these ministers claim to be the gospel. I believe Jesus' imminent return could be witnessed in my lifetime because world events written about in the Bible are happening right now, foretelling the end of time as we know it.

From the Garden of Eden to the twentieth century, people lived very similar lives. Since then there has been a knowledge implosion that was prophesied in the book of Daniel.

*"But as for you, Daniel, conceal these words and seal up the*
*book until the end of time; many will go back and forth, and*
*knowledge will increase."*

Daniel 12:4

At no other time in world history has there been so many advances in every aspect of life. The Bible also mentions the two witnesses killed by the anti-Christ. Their dead bodies will lay in the street three and a half days for the whole world to see. How else could this happen except through satellite television?

*When they finish their testimony, the beast that ascends out*
*of the bottomless pit will make war against them, overcome*
*them, and kill them. And their dead bodies will lie in the*
*street of the great city which spiritually is called Sodom and*

*Egypt, where also our Lord was crucified. Then those from the peoples, tribes, tongues, and nations will see their dead bodies three-and-a-half days, and not allow their dead bodies to be put into graves.*

Revelation 11:7-9

Next is the parable of the fig tree in Matthew 24:32, which is believed by many leading Bible scholars to have been the rebirth of the State of Israel in 1948. Jesus said this would be a sign of His return. And you wonder why the whole world follows Israel's example. The nation of Israel is God's chosen people of covenant, and regardless what Muslims or any other nation's people might believe, they are the world's timeline. According to what is revealed in Scripture, Israel's time of whoredom will soon come to an end.

*Then will appear in heaven the sign of the Son of Man, and then all the tribes of the earth will mourn, and they will see the Son of Man coming on the clouds of heaven with power and great glory. And he will send out his angels with a loud trumpet call, and they will gather his elect from the four winds, from one end of heaven to the other. "From the fig tree learn its lesson: as soon as its branch becomes tender and puts out its leaves, you know that summer is near. So also, when you see all these things, you know that he is near, at the very gates. Truly, I say to you, this generation will not pass away until all these things take place."*

Matthew 24:30-34

Jesus said before His return there would be great deception and many would be misled by false religion. I think this was proven in a previous chapter of this book.

*And He said, "See to it that you are not misled; for many will come in My name, saying, 'I am He,' and, 'The time is near' Do not go after them."*

Luke 21:8

This is now evidenced in everyone's inability to agree on any issue of what is right and what is wrong, the individual interpretation of what truth really is, and refusing to accept personal responsibility for their actions. In addition to these there are accounts of increased famine, disease, earthquakes and even the implication of impending nuclear war.

> *And this shall be the plague with which the LORD will strike all the people who fought against Jerusalem: Their flesh shall dissolve while they stand on their feet, Their eyes shall dissolve in their sockets, And their tongues shall dissolve in their mouths.*
>
> Zechariah 14:12

Both Hiroshima and Nagasaki are proof of what a nation's leaders are willing to inflict upon an enemy. And now the President of Iran, Mahmoud Ahmadinejad, has vowed to destroy Israel. Almost nightly the news channels are reporting on Iran's nuclear capabilities and what Israel's response will be. If military history is any indication, Iran's existence could be no more. Even though Israel has rejected their Messiah, God is still true to His covenant with Abraham.

In the thirteenth chapter of Revelation it is revealed that all people during the time of tribulation will be made to receive the mark of the beast in order to conduct any kind of commerce. The national identification card and the radio-frequency identification (RFID) verichip are irrefutable signs that the end of time is near. Advancements recently made with this technology will store all personal data of the person who has a tiny computer chip implanted beneath their skin. Do your research to find out what the government really wants to use this technology for. *They will know where you are at all times.* This is not something I will allow to be injected into my body.

> *And he causes all, the small and the great, and the rich and the poor, and the free men and the slaves, to be given a mark*

*on their right hand or on their forehead, and he provides
that no one will be able to buy or to sell, except the one who
has the mark, either the name of the beast or the number of
his name.*

Revelation 13:16-17

These events remove all doubt of the Bible being authentic, because it's the only book in world history to accurately foretell the future. All throughout history, people have attempted to discredit the authenticity of Scripture, but archeology and the recent findings of the Dead Sea scrolls prove the Bible's historical accuracy. Educated or ignorant, you cannot deny the validity of Scripture. Either you just don't know or you refuse to listen. You don't have time to be so crass about the only issue of importance. Reading this book may be the only opportunity you will ever be given to come to the saving knowledge of Jesus Christ. God may never draw you to Himself again...

*Jesus said to him, I am the Way the Truth and the Life; no
one comes to the Father except by (through) Me. If you had
known Me [had learned to recognized Me], you would also
have known My Father. From now on, you know Him and
have seen Him.*

John 14:6-7

Eternal salvation is not to be taken lightly or ignored. Its reality is more real than you are, and you will exist in one of only two eternal realms: in the presence of God to forever learn and discover the awesomeness of God but never to realize His fullness, or in eternal damnation with full knowledge of having no hope of salvation. I pity the fool who is so stupid.

Should you continue to live in rebellion to a Holy God, then by all means live hard and enjoy whatever it is you do. For in this life will be the only pleasures you ever enjoy. God loves you but He has no need of you, and if your lifestyle proves your contempt of God, He will honor your choice. All people who oppose the Gospel of Jesus Christ, though deceived, are the enemies of God. You and I both know nothing I say will reach you unless it's been ordained by

God. This is why it's so important for Christian leaders to return to the preaching of biblical doctrine, and forsake the lies being taught as truth to try to win those who really don't want to be won.

> *"Don't waste what is holy on people who are unholy. Don't throw your pearls to pigs! They will trample the pearls, then turn and attack you.*
>
> Matthew 7:6

I mentioned in an earlier chapter how the church has focused way too much on worldly issues, trying to be what the unsaved humanities deem relevant. This next passage of Scripture proves just how misled church people really are. I will never debate an unbeliever as to the validity of Scripture and give them an opportunity to try to solidify the lies that have deceived all of humanity.

> *O Timothy, guard and keep the deposit entrusted [to you]! Turn away from the irreverent babble and godless chatter, with the vain and empty and worldly phrases, and the subtleties and the contradictions in what is falsely called knowledge and spiritual illumination. [For] by making such profession some have erred (missed the mark) as regards the faith.*
>
> 1 Timothy 6:20-21a

In their delusion, unregenerate people think what they have to say is relevant when in reality; they have nothing to say worth listening to. The fairness act is a feeble attempt by these people to debate issues of moral relativity.

I have come to believe my responsibility as a Christian is to tell you the truth regardless of what you decide to do with it. God held Cain responsible for the blood of Abel and as Christians, we will be held accountable for the souls in our care that are eternally lost because of our negligence.

> *Then the LORD said to Cain, "Where is Abel your brother?" He said, "I do not know; am I my brother's keeper?" And the LORD said, "What have you done? The voice of your*

*brother's blood is crying to me from the ground. And now you are cursed from the ground, which has opened its mouth to receive your brother's blood from your hand."*

Genesis 4:9-11

Few people will respond to the message of the Gospel favorably, but I would rather have the whole world mad at me than for God to be angry with me. The only approval Christians should be concerned about are hearing the words *"Well Done"* as they stand before God and receive their reward for a life well lived.

God is deserving of respect and I'm going to do my part to make sure He is honored. If after reading this, you make the decision to answer God's call, use my example to believe in while becoming the person of your imagination. You are created by God to be the person He lives through.

Never settle for anything other than an expressive fullness of the person of Jesus Christ being demonstrated through the life you live. This is what people are waiting for.

*For [even the whole] creation (all nature) waits expectantly and longs earnestly for God's sons to be made known [waits for the revealing, the disclosing of their sonship].*

Romans 8:19

Live above that image of what is in your past and be the life and ministry of Jesus for people of this time to see. This is your new birth responsibility.

*And all of this is a gift from God, who brought us back to himself through Christ. And God has given us this task of reconciling people to him. For God was in Christ, reconciling the world to himself, no longer counting people's sins against them. And he gave us this wonderful message of reconciliation.*

2 Corinthians 5:18-19

The time I've given to learning about Jesus Christ and His nature has made me realize I can no longer justify my hate for people. I've come to the understanding of why God allowed what has happened in my life to reveal purpose and begin to walk out my calling.

> *Dear friends, let us continue to love one another, for love comes from God. Anyone who loves is a child of God and knows God. For God is love.*
>
> 1 John 4:7, 8b

I am not an English scholar, but the word "love" is probably the most misused word in the English language. I will be the first to admit I do not use this word to express my feelings about anything. I am just now at this time in my life beginning to associate with other people. This is not something I care to do.

I have come to understand love as a learned emotion that is expressed by giving of yourself, your time and what you have to someone, not for what you can get, but for who they are. Humanity is what God values most and at times, love is not what you would want it to be.

I am commanded by God to love and this is an emotion I do not have to give in my own ability. I have never in my lifetime experienced what this is like and it makes me cringe when I hear people us this word so frivolously. I do not like it when people I don't even know tell me they love me and then try to hug me, just because they think that's what should be done at church.

On many occasions, I have, as politely as I could, put my hand on someone's chest and asked them not to touch me. I would rather a person be brutally honest with me. I respect this more and it proves they really care!

This is why I made the statement that, because of what God has done in my life, I am now obligated to you. I have no desire to be intimately acquainted with other people and become one of the clique at church. But I do realize that I, as well as other people, see things and can say what should be done to correct what another person is doing wrong.

Sometimes love is tough. I am concerned with your eternal salvation, not about whether I've offended your ego because of what I have said. If you are among the masses of this nation's ill-informed and offended at the message of the Gospel, you are spiritually dead and in danger of eternal hell. The decision you are now faced with is, to whom will you trust your salvation? Get right with God or you will die a horrible death that will continue throughout all eternity.

> *"Truly, I say to you, all sins will be forgiven the children of man, and whatever blasphemies they utter, but whoever blasphemes against the Holy Spirit never has forgiveness, but is guilty of an eternal sin."*
>
> Mark 3:28-29

It took me a long time of study to understand what blaspheming the Holy Spirit meant. I have finally come to this resolve. When a person either ignorantly or deliberately and disrespectfully slanders the person of Jesus Christ through the ministry of revelation by the Spirit of God, denying Jesus' Lordship and that His death upon the cross is the basis of humanities redemption, they are condemning themselves to an eternity in hell. This is the only sin that a person's natural death will never allow them the opportunity to be forgiven of. Only on this side of eternity is God offering this free gift.

Being a committed Christian is not easy, and for those who say it's a crutch and only the weak in mind succumb to religion, try to understand how I feel having written this book. During an interview with Playboy Magazine, the former Governor of Minnesota Jesse Ventura made this statement: *"Organized religion is a sham and a crutch for weak-minded people who need strength in numbers. It tells people to go out and stick their noses in other people's business."* True to the mentality of people today, his statement was applauded by the masses.

How ignorant can a person be who thinks they have within themselves what it takes to make right the injustices done to not only other people, but to God? This is why so many people in this "enlightened culture" are opposed to the true Christian witness. The Bible makes one thing very clear in Scripture to not mislead the reader as to how the unsaved humanity of this world will look upon those who answer God's call.

> *If the world hates you, know that it hated Me before it hated you. If you belonged to the world, the world would treat you with affection and would love you as its own. But because you are not of the world [no longer one with it], but I have chosen (selected) you out of the world, the world hates (detests) you.*
>
> John 15:18-19

I've had to ask myself this question, "Am I prepared for this journey?" I don't know, but upon the publishing of this book, I will soon find out. The one hope I do have is knowing what God has delivered me from and after coming this far, I have no choice but to tell you the one decision you had better make.

Can we even begin to imagine just how frustrated with humanity God must be? The arrogance of people and the flaunting of their sin in the face of God is leading up to that terrible day of reckoning. Like God has done in times past before His judgment comes, He is warning people of the consequences of their behavior. So to answer Mr. Ventura's statement and to confront those of you who are of the opinion, "What right do you have to try to tell me what some obscure book says is the way I should live?", this is my response to you...

Weak people are the ones who succumb to the lies of deception and then live their lives controlled by the dictates of a sinful nature, always seeking temporary pleasures and the pursuit of financial security. They never realize that the giving away of everything they hold dear is what obligates God to get involved in the fulfillment of His plan and purpose for their life. If anyone wants to be fulfilled in what they do, become a Christian. It is the greatest struggle a person will ever face.

Only those who are willing to stand up against the flow of humanity and stay true to their conviction and the hope they proclaim, are worthy to be called Christians. All others are cowards who fear the unknown and are not willing to look beyond their natural reasoning to believe in what they cannot understand. It takes integrity and complete trust in a God we cannot see with our natural understanding to live an effective Christian witness.

God has given the example we are to strive for in how Jesus lived while He was here on the earth. Imagine having to put up with what He did, knowing who He was. Anyone who accepts the call to live the Christian witness has a moral obligation to educate, provide for and protect not only their family, but also those in their sphere of influence. You are an Ambassador for God. You represent His Law, you represent His Authority, you represent His Judgment and you represent His Sovereignty. Truth spoken is love uncompromised.

> *I CHARGE [you] in the presence of God and of Christ Jesus, Who is to judge the living and the dead, and by (in the light of) His coming and His kingdom: Herald and preach the Word! Keep your sense of urgency [stand by, be at hand and ready], whether the opportunity seems to be favorable or unfavorable. [Whether it is convenient or inconvenient, whether it is welcome or unwelcome, you as preacher of the Word are to show people in what way their lives are wrong.] And convince them, rebuking and correcting, warning and urging and encouraging them, being unflagging and inexhaustible in patience and teaching. For the time is coming when [people] will not tolerate (endure) sound and wholesome instruction, but, having ears itching [for something pleasing and gratifying], they will gather to themselves one teacher after another to a considerable number, chosen to satisfy their own liking and to foster the errors they hold, And will turn aside from hearing the truth and wander off into myths and man-made fictions. As for you, be calm and cool and steady, accept and suffer unflinchingly every hardship, do the work of an evangelist, fully perform all the duties of your ministry.*
> 2 Timothy 4:1-5

Where in this exhortation does the reader assume that Christianity is to be the weak, tiptoe-through-the-tulips, God-loves everybody watered-down gospel we hear every Sunday? I don't read this, and it's quite evident to me by this passage of Scripture that a Christian's calling is to be a voice advocating the moral standard of behavior every person will be held accountable to by a Sovereign Judge.

When your life has been truly transformed, you are the most influential person among any group of people. Of all the culture groups promoting their agenda, you speak the only words of importance. For only the Gospel of Jesus Christ has the power to transform a life. This is why you must study the Bible to be ready to give an account to anyone who might question the faith you proclaim.

> But in your hearts set Christ apart as holy [and acknowledge Him] as Lord. Always be ready to give a logical defense to anyone who asks you to account for the hope that is in you, but do it courteously and respectfully.
>
> 1 Peter 3:15

So many times confidence is confused with arrogance, but when you know who you are and the mandate God has given you to be a witness of His Gospel, you have no choice but to defy any government, law or false religion that attempts to deny or discredit the Gospel of Christ.

This is why the hate crimes legislation was hidden within a military defense bill and pushed through Congress to be signed into law so forcefully. There is but little time before God's judgment, and demonic oppression is doing all it can to deceive humanity. The men and women making up the body of the United States government who claim to be Christian, Catholic, Muslim or whatever religion they might practice, are in fact servants of Satan and are used at this corrupted spirit's will. I'm sure there are a few people whom God has placed in positions of influence to try to reach the lost, but few is a word I've chosen carefully. Once you have truly studied the Bible, it's very easy to know a person's spiritual foundation by their actions and what they believe. Knowing or ignorant, if a person does not adhere to Biblical teachings, they are an unregenerate, eternally lost servant of Satan. There is no middle ground.

The powers that be are doing everything possible to silence Bible-believing Christians, for we are the only voices that can expose people to the truths of Scripture, to then give them a chance of choosing their eternal home. Now that the hate crimes bill has become law, it could soon be a crime to preach biblical doctrine because it exposes the sin in each and every person's life. Not exactly what most people would consider being culturally correct.

These are truths the enemies of God do not want to have to face, but as you understand what is taught in Scripture, you realize just how deceived people really are. It makes no difference how far God is removed from a society's conscience. God will judge all of humanity anyway. And these are the people you have trusted with your hope of change...

If your hope is in another person who is damned to an eternal hell, I don't care how much education you have; you are not a very smart person. You just might want to take some time away from the influence you are so familiar with to learn the truth. It's the only hope you have.

This is why I had to ask myself, "Am I prepared for this?" Am I willing to go to jail for preaching the Gospel? Are you? I think my book answers this question for me, but what about you? Will you suffer? Will you bleed? I would hope this is a decision you have already made because as a Christian, you really don't have a choice.

> *"Now if you are ready, at the moment you hear the sound of the horn, flute, lyre, trigon, psaltery and bagpipe and all kinds of music, to fall down and worship the image that I have made, very well. But if you do not worship, you will immediately be cast into the midst of a furnace of blazing fire; and what god is there who can deliver you out of my hands?" Shadrach, Meshach and Abed-nego replied to the king, "O Nebuchadnezzar, we do not need to give you an answer concerning this matter. "If it be so, our God whom we serve is able to deliver us from the furnace of blazing fire; and He will deliver us out of your hand, O king."*
>
> Daniel 3:15-17

I am not in the least bit concerned about what this nation's government or a culture group is doing to keep me from proclaiming God's law. God has my back, and whatever He will have me say or any place I am to go is not for me to concern myself with. God will make a way, and He will also deliver me.

One more issue of importance that needs to be dealt with is the cleansing of the temple. Discipline must be swift but accurate in the removal from positions of leadership the people proven to be false teachers within the Christian faith. There is a host of well-known televangelists and mega-church pastors who are really enemies of the cross of Christ. I don't have to name them individually, but it's quite evident by their stand on doctrinal issues as to whom they really serve.

If a pastor or a ministry leader supports any issues that are in contradiction to Scripture, they are false teachers and leading you to an eternal damnation. You need to ask questions of these people that can only be answered by biblical doctrine, and their answers will be a witness of their honesty or dishonesty by the Holy Spirit.

> *For such men are false apostles, deceitful workmen, disguising themselves as apostles of Christ. And no wonder, for even Satan disguises himself as an angel of light. So it is no surprise if his servants, also, disguise themselves as servants of righteousness. Their end will correspond to their deeds.*
> 2 Corinthians 11:13-15

There is no mainstream denomination or independent movement this does not apply to. In the attempt to be more inclusive, the Evangelical Lutheran Church now embraces openly gay people and has voted overwhelmingly to ordain sexually active homosexual and lesbian clergy to lead Christian congregations. Show me in Scripture, Old Testament or New, where God approves of this. It's not found nor is God anywhere near a church where people are in blatant violation of Scripture. When I hear someone try to justify their behavior by saying God made them like this, I have to disagree. God cannot make you what He is not. God is not confused with His identity, you are.

*But understand this, that in the last days there will come
times of difficulty. For people will be lovers of self, lovers of
money, proud, arrogant, abusive, disobedient to their parents,
ungrateful, unholy, heartless, unappeasable, slanderous,
without self-control, brutal, not loving good, treacherous,
reckless, swollen with conceit, lovers of pleasure rather than
lovers of God, having the appearance of godliness, but denying
its power. Avoid such people.*

2 Timothy 3:1-5

It frustrates me to no end when I hear people on the Larry
King Show who profess to be Christian leaders avoid taking a hard
stand on an issue like the homosexual agenda or one of the many
culturally correct hot topics of our time. This is why in an earlier
chapter I referred to people like this as "spineless wimps." How can
a Christian ever influence their culture by saying what will only
appease the hearer?

The Gospel is offensive and intended by God to provoke emotions
that would lead a person to a decision of either accepting or rejecting
Jesus as their Savior. Jesus spoke the truth and the impact has been
global, and is still changing lives today. Who are we in this day and
time to do anything less?

*"You are the salt of the earth; but if the salt loses its flavor,
how shall it be seasoned? It is then good for nothing but to
be thrown out and trampled underfoot by men. You are the
light of the world. A city that is set on a hill cannot be hidden.
Nor do they light a lamp and put it under a basket, but on a
lampstand, and it gives light to all who are in the house. Let
your light so shine before men, that they may see your good
works and glorify your Father in heaven."*

Matthew 5:13-16

It's not wrong for people to want to worship God or feel accepted,
because this is something innate within each of us. But what needs to
be said is that God does require a lifestyle change. There is nothing
inclusive about the Gospel of Jesus Christ. It is God's way or no way.

This other gospel of compromise has crippled Christian influence and drastic action must be taken. You who are truly born again and Spirit-filled and leaders already, must begin to pray for the judgment of God to begin at the house of God. Accountability begins with true repentance. For we will never save the world with our own house in disarray.

Repentance is the work of the Holy Spirit, and it's your willingness to do for another person with an expectation of the same being required of you that becomes the seed of compassion to ignite in people a desire to change. You cannot teach what you have never done. Everything you have experienced was to prepare you for a lifestyle of expressing God's love by serving people in compassion, while leading them to a fullness of both their soul's transformation and their spiritual salvation.

> *Love does no wrong to others, so love fulfills the requirements of God's law.*
>
> Romans 13:10

> *Now we who are strong ought to bear the weaknesses of those without strength and not just please ourselves. Each of us is to please our neighbor for his good, to his edification. For even Christ did not please Himself.*
>
> Romans 15:1-3a

Everything with God will be in His time. God was compassionate to me when I was in sin and He proved His love by leading me to the man I have become. Because of this, I now have compassion and the confidence to challenge the inappropriate conduct of your life's expression. I really do encourage the experience of God's fullness in everyday life. God did this for me and in time, He will do the same for you.

> *For God does not show favoritism.*
>
> Romans 2:11

# GOD'S SIGNATURE
଼ ଼

After coming through all of this, I understand why God brought me back home to transform my life and prepare me for what I'm called to do. I've written this chapter to honor the one person who has been truly kind to me. I honestly believe this message, "Living in the Hope of My Imagination" as timely as it is would be incomplete if I did not briefly describe events and mention the person God ordained to bring what was once just hope to the reality of my here and now.

There has never been a person in my life that has done for me what Shannon has and because of her willingness to give with no other motivation than wanting the same in return, a faith in the goodness of people has been reborn in me.

Through each page of this book was a description of my lack of confidence in people. In my lifetime there have been few people I have had a reason to like or respect and I expected them to respond to me in the same way. Even when I was not prepared, God proved His willingness to give me what I have always dreamed about.

> *Take delight in the Lord, and he will give you your heart's desires.*
>
> Psalms 37:4

I have met a woman who completes me. It's not what I have or what I can give but the hope that was done to another person will one day be done for me. This has captured my emotions and stripped away all excuses to not be what she unselfishly gives to me. For being this example and giving me time to write about what has now become an expectation of what our future will be like, I have dedicated this book to Shannon.

I had no faith in people and thought trust was something I would never experience. It just goes to prove how God knows what each person needs and is willing to set things in motion to reveal His handiwork through whatever it is you hope for becoming reality.

> *Trust in the Lord with all your heart; do not depend on your own understanding. Seek his will in all you do, and he will show you which path to take.*
>
> Proverbs 3:5-6

On December 15, 2006, life as I knew it forever changed. I am amazed at how God uses people and circumstances that have no relevance to orchestrate a plan of events and set up what He intends to accomplish. Shannon and I have talked about what occurred to bring us together, and we know it was through nothing other than the Hand of God. Too many unanswered question's can have you scratching your head when an awareness comes, and it's only as the pieces of a puzzle come together can the magnitude of what happened really be understood.

> *For just as the heavens are higher than the earth, so my ways are higher than your ways and my thoughts higher than your thoughts.*
>
> Isaiah 55:9

The restaurant where I met Shannon was a part-time job I had for several years. It's recognized as the oldest restaurant in the city and employs the longest term wait staff compared to any restaurant in this nation. Its Italian fare is consistently good and voted the most romantic dinner date in the region. The ambiance of the dining room is Olde World style and dimly lit, and a fireplace burns during cold months with blown glass candle lampshades and white linens on each table. Italian Opera or jazz music is played throughout its rooms and during weekend evenings live classical guitar is featured. Waiters dress formally and give the attention to anticipate most any need, so if you are ever in the area I highly recommend having dinner at Ristorante Renato in Olde Town Fredericksburg, Virginia. Thank you, Teresa, for the time you allowed me to work for you.

I had been gone from Fredericksburg for eight months when Teresa called one evening and asked if I was available to work for lunch the next day. Just an hour before, I had quit my job and was in need of money, and at that time I had no clue as to what was about to happen.

The next morning, after getting up and driving an hour to the restaurant, I was told by Teresa I would be working a private party by myself. I went to the room reserved for this group and made sure everything was set up. As the guests began to arrive it was my responsibility to have water and bread on the tables and make any drinks they ordered. I didn't give much attention to anyone other than asking what each person needed. The guests arrived separately, so I went up front to greet people as they came in. I will never forget the emotion of what I felt as Shannon walked in the door.

She was an attractive woman and I took notice. Her slacks were black with a moderate flare to the cuff and her shoulderless top was white with a black lace design on the front. Her shoes were black toeless flats and jet black hair flowed down over her shoulders. I was worthless. As she walked by, she never even looked in my direction but that was alright with me—I was enjoying the view. Following her to the back room, I waited until she sat down and then I asked what she would like to drink. I couldn't put my finger on it, but something about this young woman struck me as different and I made a decision to introduce myself.

About forty-five minutes into the event, Shannon came to the head of her party's table and was talking to several physicians whom she worked for. With no thought of what to say I walked over and asked, "Can I pick on you?"

Her response was, *"Yes."* with an inquisitive expression on her face.

I asked, "Are you married?"

*"No."*

I then asked, "Do you have a significant other?"

Again she said, *"No"* and my thoughts were, "Yes!" thinking I was getting somewhere.

Now the bombshell! I asked, "Would you be willing to have dinner with me?"

She said, *"Yes, and your name is?"* By this time there was an audience of the entire table of thirty people hanging on every word we said.

Over the next couple of hours her eyes never left me. I know this, because mine never left her except when I had to leave the room. After lunch was over, we went to a local bar and talked for several hours. I asked if she would be willing to attend a church service with me and the next Sunday became our first official date.

At that time I had no desire to date anyone because I was unsure of where life was taking me. I had no goals or direction, just today and what money I could make. I thought this job would be only for the day because it had been eight months since I'd worked there last.

I left on good terms and told the owner if she needed help just call and depending on my availability, I would make the drive up. Little did I know that would be the day I would meet my future wife.

I didn't see Shannon for three days after the lunch party and from that time until now only two days have seen us apart. It has been a whirlwind of emotion and amazement at how God can manipulate the powers that be to accomplish what He wants done.

Our story is still in the making and only God knows what is in the future, but I do want to describe what recently happened to us. It removes all doubt and proves that when you put God first, He will move heaven and hell for you.

When Shannon and I met, we were both angry and confused, and doing our best to escape what we thought would be all we would ever know. I had been doing my study for about a year and this book was in its infancy. When I told Shannon what I was doing, she became intrigued, and told me about her past and being angry with God because of how her life had turned out, including her father dying at the young age of forty-nine.

She was bitter and acted out in anger towards everyone and everything, and she got drunk every evening. As we talked, she asked a lot of questions I was able to give her some answers to, but I encouraged her to read the Bible to have God answer what I couldn't.

During the transition of leaving Richmond and coming back to Fredericksburg, I was homeless again and living out of my car. Shannon had lost her privilege to drive as the result of a DUI, and she asked me to consider moving into the house where she lived because it was winter time and I could give her a ride to and from work. It was a good trade off because her job was thirty minutes away from where she lived. The house she lived in was about six thousand square feet and it sat on five acres of wooded land. There was a family of four who lived upstairs and we had the entire basement. Ever since that time, I have been "Driving Mrs. Shannon."

I will not argue the right or wrong of this decision with those who say it's wrong for a man and a woman to live together and not be married. Unless you have lived here, you have probably never been exposed to the cost of living in and around the Washington, DC corridor, or the traffic congestion we had to deal with every day of the week. And honestly, when we met neither of us were living right and in spite of being in the same house together and drinking every night, God moved anyway. God knows your intentions and if truth be told, that's all He really needs.

I was reading and writing every moment I wasn't working and Shannon watched me do this. The restaurant was slow and I had a part time job supplementing my income by working for two women who owned an interior decorating business. The jobs were inconsistent and money was tight for a reason I hadn't yet figured out. Shannon then asked me to consider only working as the restaurant needed me, and to devote the rest of my time to writing my book. She was willing to take care of the finances. This is when everything began to change for us.

As Shannon watched me study and write, cry, edit and rewrite she would often comment on the subtle changes that could be seen in me. My scowl began to go away and I'd smile more often. It soon became a twelve to fifteen, sometimes twenty hours a day project, leaving me mentally exhausted, but emotionally exhilarated. When I asked, Shannon would read what I had written and her response often humbled me. How could I write the things I was describing? Where was it coming from?

Seeing this change in me is what led Shannon to repentance. She began reading the Bible and would write out the Scriptures that influenced her most. Her journal now fills several note pads and I had the opportunity to watch her change.

Shannon had been married twice before to abusive men who had scarred her both emotionally and physically. She did not trust men and when we first met, she had no desire to be with anyone either. It blew her away to know I had lived such a violent and hate-filled life, and yet I treated her the way she had always hoped a man would. I told her I had always wanted to be in a relationship with someone who would accept me for the person I was, and I was now ready to be the man she needed me to be. Her defenses crumbled when I told her she had captured my emotions. I knew she was the one for me.

This was new for us and it was exciting. By this time I discovered a talent I had with words and how to use them in a way to paint a picture in your imagination that made it seem real. Shannon has often asked me to tell a story about something we are going to do together in the near future. She now believes the things she had always wished about in her past will one day soon become reality. I say this to encourage you to always believe in the power of a dream.

Shannon and I are discovering just how involved God will become in our day-to-day activities as we give our time to what really matters most. People began to comment on the changes they could see in our behavior, and we would both say what God was doing and how we had helped each other.

Everything began to come together. We thought alike or we'd say the same thing usually at the same time. We were becoming one and shared the same desire to reach out in any way we could to help people who were in life where we had come from.

Neither of us wanted to be in Virginia any longer and I began to post my resume online to resorts and high-end restaurants across the nation. It seemed to end the same way my previous local job search had ended. No restaurant would hire me nor would any other job I applied to. This went on for almost a year. I would work once, maybe twice a week at Renato's but nothing else came along.

Shannon believes the time I've had to study the Bible and write my book was ordained by God, and He wasn't going to allow anything to pull me away from what I needed to do. It was hard for me to not go to work and even though I got frustrated, Shannon would remind me why I was writing my book. This helped me to stay focused.

So one evening when I was mad about my work situation, I suggested that Shannon post her resume online. The next day she received a phone call from a nurse manager attempting to hire qualified registered nurses to fill vacancies at a Psychiatric Hospital in Reno, Nevada. As they talked, he told Shannon he was a Christian also.

They talked for forty-five minutes on the phone and even though Shannon is a licensed practical nurse, he offered to double what she was making and pay for the relocation expenses. Arrangements were then made for accommodations and flying her there for the official interview. Money was still tight and to our shock, Shannon's mother and grandmother paid the $600 for my ticket so she wouldn't have to go by herself.

After coming back home, I told my employer I would be moving in three weeks and I was never asked to work another shift. I even went to the day labor agencies. There were no jobs available, anywhere! I was beginning to stress and Shannon said if God wanted us in Nevada, He would make a way.

For those three weeks I didn't work, and the day before we moved, there was $193 in our bank account. That night, Shannon's direct deposit would post. She received the paycheck at work and to her surprise, a garnishment from the court handling her DUI case two years before had taken a large portion of her check. This happened on the evening before we planned to move across country.

When she called to tell me this, I could have bitten a nail in half. We had $900 in the account and the rental car was priced at $697. The drive was 2,700 miles and the cheapest gas we paid for was $3.24 per gallon. Needless to say, I was not feeling confident about the move. My car was old and dependable around town, but it would never have made a drive that far, so I gave it to a friend of mine so he could part it out and maybe make some money with it. That's why we had to rent a car.

As Shannon was getting off from work, she called and said to come and pick her up. When I arrived she was as cool as a cube of ice. I was angry as she made her rounds to say goodbye to all of her coworkers and when we walked outside, she handed me an envelope and said everything was going to be okay.

The doctor Shannon worked for was upset because she was leaving and had once before offered money from her own paycheck to keep Shannon from leaving. After being told what the other hospital had offered, she admitted her practice couldn't come close to that dollar amount and she encouraged Shannon to pursue the opportunity.

She then told Shannon the partners of this clinic had decided against a bonus severance as a goodbye gift and instead they gave her a cake. But as I opened the envelope, I discovered that the doctor Shannon worked for had given her a personal check for a $1,000. I had nothing to say as Shannon looked at me while tears ran down my face.

The check was deposited and we now had $1,900 in the account. Shannon had the job offer but we still had no place to live once we arrived in Reno. I spent a lot of time online looking at the apartments and efficiency hotels, and even posted our profile on a roommate website. There were a couple of emails and phone calls from people on this site, but nothing I was really interested in. We picked up the rental car and packed it with our clothes and what paperwork we wanted to keep. Everything else had been given away, so we were traveling light.

The next morning we woke up early and hit the road about 7:30 AM. We drove to Somerset, Kentucky where Shannon's mother now lives. After greeting everyone, Shannon's grandmother gave her an Easter bunny and basket as a gift because it was Good Friday.

Shannon had never been really close to her mother and grandmother and it was just in the time I had known her, that she and her mother began to get close again. So what happened next came as a complete shock to both of us.

When Shannon sat down on the couch with her gifts, I could see a puzzled look on her face. There were several paper tissues placed in different pockets, a pant leg and under the hat of this big bunny. Wrapped in these four bundles were $250 each. Another $1,000 in cash! We looked at each other and once again the tears flowed. We now had $2,900 but still no place to live nor a car to drive once we got to Reno. I was still stressed…

We stayed the night and then drove to Evergreen, Colorado to visit Shannon's uncle and his wife, who were very nice and even took a day off work to show us the beauty of the area. We stayed for two days and then drove nonstop to Elko, Nevada.

The next day we drove into Reno and upon arrival God provided us a place to live, a vehicle to drive and the time we needed to stand on our own. We were both in awe at how God worked through this entire situation. This whole move, in spite of my kicking and screaming all the way across country for not being the one in control, was effortless. What a lesson I have learned. This is what can happen when God is allowed to do what He does best.

It wasn't long after our arrival when Shannon and I began to understand this move was for a reason much bigger than us. Even in Reno I was not able to find a job, so my days were given to more study and reading. The manuscript was, for the most part, finished and I had never in my lifetime read any literature on the subjects I'd written about. I had written from memory the things I heard people talk about or from my own experience. I haven't owned a television in five years and it wasn't until we moved to Nevada that I became exposed to information confirming my thoughts.

This information came from books I've had the opportunity to read and websites inundated with factual documents, to videos I've watched on YouTube and SermonIndex. During the time I'd attended evangelical charismatic churches, never once did I hear the name Charles Spurgeon, one of the greatest preachers of modern church history. This man who lived in the nineteenth century, more than a hundred years ago, spoke of what the church as we know it would become because of the compromise of biblical doctrine.

A more recent evangelist by the name of Leonard Ravenhill, spoke convincingly about why the modern-day church would not see revival unless there was true repentance and the return to holiness by the conduct of our lives. The messages these men preached are at the core of what God revealed to me in Scripture, and this helped me to understand where I needed to focus my studies.

I was amazed at just how far away the well-known mega-church pastors of today, and all of those who try to emulate their example, are from what the Bible actually teaches.

What I have learned explains why America is now under the judgment of God. His presence has departed due to immorality in the lives of Christians, and its effect upon this culture. This is why it's necessary for preachers to return to a fire and brimstone message to bring the fear of God's sovereignty and His judgment upon the church first, before we will ever be effective in reaching the unsaved. This is when I truly understood my calling in life, and the answer to why so many bad things had happened to me.

After we moved, we had the opportunity to attend Calvary Chapel of Reno, whose pastor taught on relevant issues for the day and time we live. This was the first time ever in my adult life I heard a minister do so.

God brought me nearly 3,000 miles away from what I was familiar with to then point me in the direction I needed to go. At the same time, He provided proof of what was revealed in Scripture through the mouths of other people. This gave me an opportunity to read over my manuscript and make the necessary changes that were needed to complete the book you are now reading.

Some of these people were Christians, but quite a few worked for the news media or wrote from a secular viewpoint. It just goes to prove we are all in the hands of God and He uses us to accomplish His will. God is so much bigger than we could ever imagine. He is concerned with the smallest of situations you will ever face and when you ask for help or the opportunity to help someone else, get ready for God to move.

There is no time or distance God cannot bridge to close the gap between someone's hopelessness and a firm hand help them stand on their own. God has brought Shannon and me out of everything in today's culture believed to be normal, to prepare us to go back to where He delivered us from as an example of what only God is capable of doing.

On July 24, 2008, Shannon and I were married. Through most of the first year in Reno, we were put into situations that really tried our patience. We were more than willing to get involved in any way we could to help someone, but I found out the hard way how easily people will try to take advantage of you.

The first place we moved into the day we arrived was, in the beginning, a blessing. Just before we left Virginia, a lady had contacted us through an online roommate website. We talked briefly, but Shannon had no interest to live with another couple. The night we stayed in Elko, this lady called again, so we agreed to meet upon arriving in Reno. As we pulled up to the house, sitting there in the driveway, was a car that had "4 sale" written across the back windshield. This was never mentioned during our brief conversations on the phone. That evening, after talking with this couple and seeing the house, we agreed upon a monthly rent amount of $500 and moved in. We didn't buy the car, but offered to make the payments for both it and insurance. And for a few weeks, we were happy. But it soon became a nightmare. You know how roommates can be. We soon saw past their facade. In six months of living with this couple we gave away $14,000 to help them try to get on their feet.

They were having marital and financial problems and the husband eventually moved out. They claimed to be Christians and I spoke with the husband several times about his relationship with God and with his wife. He did not respond to my encouragement of reading the Bible and praying with his wife and as he worsened, I confronted him on his behavior. This was not something he was used to and our contention became very sharp. I did not respect him for how he treated his wife, and I told him as much.

He did everything he could to try to get me to respond in a way that would give him a legal right to have a restraining order filed against me, so that his wife would have no other option but to depend upon him to provide for her and their son. Shannon, though very upset at his actions, helped me immensely and by her intervention, I didn't do anything I would have regretted.

After he moved out, the wife was very happy that we had helped her to stand on her own, but it soon became a situation of entitlement and we were expected to continue giving. Yet nothing was ever given in return. None of the things we asked for were honored and her family soon ran the house Shannon was paying for. After numerous pleas to respect our privacy and to clean up the mess they made, Shannon and I moved out. All of the money we had given and everything else we had done meant nothing to these people. In their minds, we were now horrible people and a bad Christian witness. She even threatened to have my book and name defamed... I still have the email.

It wasn't that we were bad people, but rather she was required to be an adult and accept responsibility for her actions, which at the time of our leaving, she had yet to do. Remember, people don't like to change when it's not easy.

I agonized over the decision of moving out, because I knew our roommate could not afford the rent on her own. But everyone was telling us to get out before the situation got even worse. Shannon had been offended and this began to have an impact on how she viewed the whole situation. That's when I made the decision to move. Our relationship was more important. Just as God will remove His hand, there comes a time when a person needs to be left alone to do some soul searching and make the decision of laying down their pride. Only then will God get involved to make things right.

While all of this was happening, I had become active in one of Reno's largest outreach ministries feeding the homeless. Hundreds of people came to be fed after listening to someone speak. Things were done that I did not agree with but I just watched what was happening. People were talked to but I didn't see any real evangelism and the first time Shannon came with me, we witnessed an event that infuriated both of us.

There was a young woman speaking and to my shock, she took an offering from the homeless people, stating God needed someone to give in order to move Him to give something in return. I could not believe what I was witnessing and Shannon was just as offended as I was. I went to the person in charge of this ministry and asked if he was going to stop what was happening and he didn't. He said he did not feel as though it was an inappropriate thing to do. It angered me at the insensitivity of these people for not sensing God's Spirit had been grieved. That was the last time I went. I would have nothing to do with a ministry being run by people like this.

The second place we moved into was with an older couple. I had been doing a Bible study with the husband for about two months. This man was a friend of Shannon's uncle in Colorado. He knew about the stress in our living situation and he and his wife said we could stay with them for a few months to save money and then get place of our own. We were there about two months and did our best to be as unobtrusive as possible. I cooked for them occasionally and we did whatever we could to be helpful.

At the end of the second month I thought everything was fine and then twice without any warning, this man cussed me out and threatened to put us on the street. The first time I let it go, but the second time it crawled all over me. To my knowledge we hadn't done anything wrong and I had Shannon to be concerned about. So I got in his face and asked what his problem was. Over his shoulder I could see Shannon at the end of the hallway drawing a finger across her neck, telling me to shut up. So I did.

I was cooking dinner at this time and as I walked into the kitchen, a heavy conviction came upon me. I began to weep when I realized how wrong my actions had been, and knowing God's Spirit had been grieved. It was sobering to realize the closeness of God and He was not pleased with my behavior. I calmed down and a few minutes later I apologized to this man, and he responded in like manner. He was upset about some things in his personal life and I just happened to bear the brunt of his frustration.

Just a few days later, we were introduced to someone he knew renting properties in Reno and we settled on an apartment. We were in the process of buying a used car from this renter and the car had some mechanical problems that were supposed to have been fixed. They weren't and I had to spend $600 of our money on this car to try to find out what was wrong with it. That's when the deal went bad.

This man was a Christian also and he wanted us to make payments on the vehicle in addition to the $3,000 the dealership said it would cost to fix these problems. I told him I was not about to do this and to be fair, I wanted half of the money I put into the car given back to me, which he did. I then gave him the car back and told him I didn't want it. He called me an idiot, and I would have been if I had done what he wanted!

Why do things like this happen? Christians are supposed to be different than everyone else, but true to my life's experience, this is seldom the case. There's not a person who isn't susceptible to the influence of this world and the only way out is by the influence of God's Word. The more I studied and edited my book, the more I realized this is how people will, with their preconceived notions, look at me. I've written a book that challenges every culture and class of people to come up to a higher standard of living and if this book is to be successful in reaching these people, its author must first be this example.

Did I do what was right in these situations? I want to think I did and based on what other people have said to me, I did. It bothered me that I had to be so firm in what I thought was the right thing to do, because people were offended. But this is when I realized people will respond to the Gospel in the same way, and all of this was a part of my training.

I am amazed at how God uses everyday circumstances and people to show us what He requires of us. I am not angry at these people. I just hope they will, like I have, see the errors in what they've done and the influence they have upon other people.

The one good thing that has happened is the opportunity Shannon and I have been given to help a family. During the winter season of 2008/2009, our neighbor's electricity was turned off and soon after they were evicted. The mother has an alcohol and drug addiction and both her eleven and fifteen-year-old daughters were the victims of her neglect. We became involved when the mother left her daughters alone with no electricity or food for the weekend when she flew to another state to attend an Eagles concert. We moved the girl's beds into a spare bedroom and they stayed with us for about three months.

We tried to help the mother to get on her feet again, but we were unsuccessful. She would stay gone for days at a time with no contact. After being confronted and given the choice of signing over custody of her children or having Child Protective Services becoming involved, she left with her children. For several months there was no contact. Then one evening as Shannon and I were eating dinner, there was a knock on the door.

The sister of the woman whom we had tried to help told us a very sad story of the situation she and her three-year-old and her two nieces were in. Once again, this woman was gone and the sister was left alone to provide for these children. She was only twenty and was seven months pregnant, and the father of her child-to-be was in jail. She had no money and no job, and they hadn't eaten for two days. She told us they needed help and because of what we had done back in the winter, she knocked on our door.

Shannon left with her to go buy some food and when she came home, in walked the whole family with their clothes and personal belongings. They too had been evicted, and had no place to go. Shannon looked at me and said, *"What else could I do?"* Since then, we have become legal guardians of the two young girls. The mother is a fugitive and at the time of me writing this book, she is running from the law. We do not understand why God brought this upon us, but the destination will have taught us much.

This is why I made the statement about Christians having few choices when it comes to how our lifestyle is perceived by other people. What we say and the things we do will determine whether the people God has placed around us will experience the hope of what they want to believe is real or see another liar just like them. As I began to understand this, it made me want to be a better person in my representation of God, for my wife and anyone I might have the opportunity to help.

Through all of this, Shannon helped me keep my cool and not do anything wrong. I am so thankful for God bringing her into my life. She is my balance and the realization of an emotion I have always hoped to experience.

I wanted to write about what has just happened to us as a final thought in the message I have presented to you. It is an exclamation mark on what we believe God is leading us into and just as He has brought us this far, Shannon and I are both convinced God will continue to show off. We are not sure how or with whom, but the one thing we are sure of is this, *God is definitely in control.*

The only way to describe what has happened in the two and a half years we have known each other is a modern day journey into the unknown. *Wow,* dreams do come true! I have watched Shannon blossom from a bruised and angry woman, to having hope and an expectation of experiencing a fairytale she says every young girl dreams about. She now jokingly calls me her "Knight in Dented and Tarnished Armor."

The way she looks at me and what I hear her say have melted the years of hardness keeping people at bay, and freed me to enjoy the experience of doing for someone else just because I can. Being another person's desire has brought closure to what had been, "*If only my life was like*" when waking up to the, "*So this is what it's like*" reality of each day. I don't ever want to lose this. I look forward to what God has in store for us to experience as we paint a picture of accomplishment together.

*And I am certain that God, who began the good work within you, will continue his work until it is finished on the day when Christ Jesus returns.*

Philippians 1:6

Writing my book has helped me understand the reality of this passage of Scripture, and its application to our lives today. What an awesome responsibility Christians have been given to try to help people realize just how important it is to make the decision to seek out their own salvation. God will use your life's witness, but only if you let Him.

As I was challenged to my face by God Himself in the environment I had allowed to influence what I thought of me, I am now challenging you to come to God just as you are. You do not have to quit doing anything or change in any way to be not only accepted, but welcome in the presence of God, whose love for you is unconditional.

Through the developing of a relationship learning about Jesus Christ and the purity of who He is, whatever it is you do that's not pleasing to Him loses its appeal and you turn away. Little by little, God will bring you to maturity to one day stand upright and unashamed, knowing your life's experience was for a purpose He called you to influence. As you make time to study the Bible and learn the truth about the person of Jesus Christ and what He has done, you'll realize He is "I Am", the only True and Living God. Jesus is everything you will ever need Him to be.

> Jesus answered, "I tell you the truth, before Abraham was even born, I Am!"
>
> John 8:58

This is the foundation Scripture for learning about who we are as Christians.

> "Truly, truly, I say to you, he who believes in Me, the works that I do he will do also; and greater works than these he will do; because I go to the Father. Whatever you ask in My name, that will I do, so that the Father may be glorified in the Son. If you ask Me anything in My name, I will do it. If you love Me, you will keep My commandments. I will ask the Father, and He will give you another Helper, that He may be with you forever; that is the Spirit of truth, whom the world cannot receive, because it does not see Him or

*know Him, but you know Him because He abides with you and will be in you."*

John 14:12-17

What God revealed to me in the Bible has created an expectation of these truths, so I now believe that He will bring it to pass in my lifetime.

*Faith is the confidence that what we hope for will actually happen; it gives us assurance about things we cannot see.*

Hebrews 11:1

There is nothing of greater value than realizing God's desire for every human being is a place of oneness with Him in spirit. This is where heirs of salvation take possession of everything made available to those who, with an expectation, submit their will to a higher purpose. Sons and daughters of God are revealed to the world, living above the natural plane of sense knowledge while actively fulfilling the great commission every Christian is called to. As living epistles seen and read, we are the expressive demonstration of Jesus' life and ministry to all people.

I know what I've written is strong and those who read this will be either challenged or offended, but it needs to be said. Now that I have, my purpose is to encourage you to do what I've done to secure the hope of your salvation and be this example for others.

I hope these words will encourage you through a discovery of truth while learning about the person God created you to be. Enjoy the journey. It's worth the wait!

*But with God all things are possible.*

Matthew 19:26b

LaVergne, TN USA
18 February 2010
173570LV00002B/8/P